WILEY PLUS
for *Introduction to Inclusive Education*

Study More Effectively with a Multimedia Text

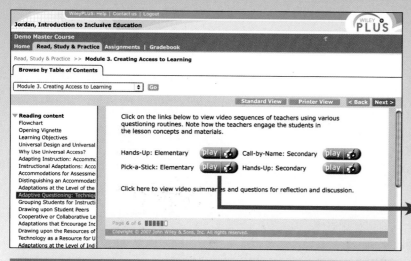

This multimedia version of your text brings your readings to life by integrating video clips, self-assessment quizzes, interactive exercises, and hyperlinks throughout. *WileyPLUS* gives you control over how you learn.

Click on e-book hyperlinks and video play buttons to instantly access extra resources.

Interactive Exercise 3-4

Grasp key concepts by exploring the various interactive tools in Read, Study & Practice.

Preparing for a test has never been easier! *WileyPLUS* brings all of your course materials together and takes the stress out of organizing your study aids. A streamlined study routine saves you time and lets you focus on learning.

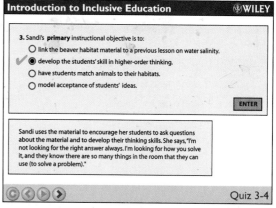

Quiz 3-4

John Wiley & Sons Canada, Ltd.

WILEY PLUS

for *Introduction to Inclusive Education*

Complete and Submit Assignments On-line Efficiently

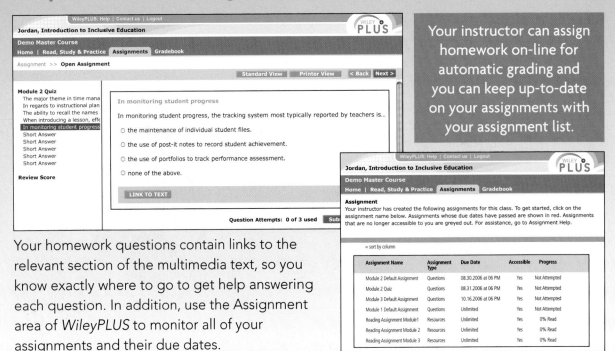

Your instructor can assign homework on-line for automatic grading and you can keep up-to-date on your assignments with your assignment list.

Your homework questions contain links to the relevant section of the multimedia text, so you know exactly where to go to get help answering each question. In addition, use the Assignment area of *WileyPLUS* to monitor all of your assignments and their due dates.

Keep Track of Your Progress

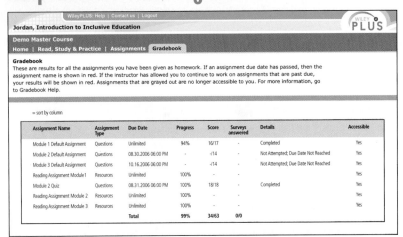

Your personal Gradebook lets you review your answers and results from past assignments as well as any feedback your instructor may have for you.

Keep track of your progress and review your completed questions at any time.

introduction to
INCLUSIVE EDUCATION

introduction to INCLUSIVE EDUCATION

Anne Jordan, PhD

Ontario Institute for Studies in Education
of the University of Toronto

BICENTENNIAL
1807
WILEY
2007
BICENTENNIAL

John Wiley & Sons Canada, Ltd.

Library and Archives Canada Cataloguing in Publication

Jordan, Anne, 1944-
    Introduction to inclusive education / Anne Jordan.

Includes bibliographical references and index.
Also available in electronic format.
ISBN-13: 978-0-470-83788-7
ISBN-10: 0-470-83788-8

    1. Inclusive education--Textbooks. I. Title.

LC1200.J67 2006   371.9'046   C2006-904566-6

Production Credits

Editorial Manager: Karen Staudinger
Acquisitions Editor: Michael Valerio
Publishing Services Director: Karen Bryan
Media & Developmental Editor: Elsa Passera Berardi
Editorial Assistants: Sara Dam and Sheri Coombs
Marketing Manager: Joan Lewis-Milne
Design: Interrobang Graphic Design Inc.
Cover Photo: Jim Cummins/Taxi/Getty Images
Anniversary Logo Design: Richard Pacifico

Printed and bound in Canada
1 2 3 4 5 TRI 11 10 09 08 07

John Wiley and Sons Canada Ltd.
6045 Freemont Blvd.
Mississauga, Ontario L5R 4J3
Visit our website at www.wiley.ca

To Warren, Allison and David

About the Author

Anne Jordan taught in an inner city school in the UK before arriving in Canada to pursue her master's and doctoral degrees in Education at the University of Toronto. She then held a teaching position at Queen's University and, since 1974, has taught at the Ontario Institute for Studies in Education, now part of the University of Toronto, in the graduate and teacher preparation programs. Formerly Chair of the Department of Special Education and Adaptive Instruction, she is currently a member of the Department of Curriculum Teaching and Learning. Anne's research examines the relationships between knowledge, beliefs and practices of general education classroom teachers who include students with special education needs in their classrooms. She also analyses the impact of special education legislation and policy on school and classroom trends. Anne has published over 50 scholarly papers and is the author of four books.

Preface

Goal of This Text

Teachers face increasingly diverse classes of students. The heterogeneity of the student population is the result of numerous influences: changes in immigration patterns and population demographics; advances in medicine that increase the survival rates of children; social programs that are no longer delivered in segregated locations but are integrated into the community; an increase in the numbers and types of disabilities being diagnosed and numbers of students identified as having a disability; and changes to legislation that recognize the rights of people to access educational resources and services in the mainstream of society.

With these trends come policies and requirements, research, teaching methods, and resource and support services aimed at assisting teachers to meet the demands of this diverse classroom community. Students with learning difficulties, including those with disabilities and those who are underachieving or at risk of failure in our schools, are represented in the range of students in a typical classroom.

In the past 30 years I have observed teaching in over 100 classrooms, in a variety of schools and school systems. I have also discussed with many teachers the challenges of working in modern classrooms, and the pressures they face from both their students and the changing demands of a large and complex school system. I wrote this book because I have become increasingly convinced that teaching that is effective for all students, and that is personally and professionally gratifying for teachers, is an achievable objective.

Effective inclusive teaching is the ability to recognize the range of learning needs of one's students and to be able to draw upon a multitude of instructional alternatives that can be geared to that range. Effective inclusive teaching depends on preparing teachers to adapt instruction, both at the pre-service level of teacher training, and at the in-service level of professional growth. It also requires that they are supported in meeting the diverse needs of their students.

This text addresses effective adaptive instruction in elementary and secondary classrooms in the context of inclusive schools. The material is written for and about Canadian teachers and classrooms. Therefore, whenever possible, I have drawn on Canadian research and used terminology and examples typical of Canadian school systems. The principles and techniques presented here are equally important for teaching students who excel, those who barely understand the language of instruction, and those who struggle with issues of cultural, racial, and gender identity. However, the focus will be on learners who are underachieving, including those who have difficulty with various components of the curriculum (curriculum-related disabilities), and those who have more serious disabilities that are compounded by physical, psychological, neurological, and/or sensory impairments (complex disabilities).

The book sits at the interface of good classroom practice and special education. In this context, special education is not a place or a program. It is a process whereby teachers provide the best possible learning opportunities adapted to the needs of their students. In this process there are more than instructional techniques at work; inclusion involves teacher confidence that they can make a difference and teachers' understanding of, and attitudes toward, students' differences. I adopt the definition of inclusive education used by the Roeher Institute, with its emphasis on affect. Inclusive education is defined here as "arrangements where all learners:

- are welcome and included, in all their diversity and exceptionalities, in the regular classroom in the neighbourhood school with their age peers,

- participate and develop to the fullest of their potential, and

- are involved in social valued relationships with diverse peers and adults."[1]

My intention in this project is to show teacher candidates and teaching professionals how to broaden their repertoire of skills to address a range of learning needs and, in doing so, improve their overall effectiveness to the benefit of all their students. The reader will be encouraged to learn, explore, and reflect upon effective teaching practices and practices they currently employ.

This text, although primarily designed for teaching in the classroom, will also be of interest to special education and resource teachers, administrators, and those preparing for special education qualifications. It details the reciprocal role of the special education and resource teacher with the general education/subject teacher in supporting the inclusion mandate. The skills described here will be useful not only in special education and withdrawal/resource settings, but will also enable classroom teachers to collaborate with special education personnel to implement the

[1]Crawford, C. (2005) *Supporting teachers: A foundation for advancing inclusive education.* Toronto: Roeher Institute.

adaptive methods described in Individual Education Plans (IEPs). The material is therefore an essential guide to practice in the collaborative framework of inclusive schools.

Interactive nature of the text

An exciting and unique feature of *Introduction to Inclusive Education* is that it was conceived, written, and designed primarily as an interactive e-text. Using the *WileyPLUS* platform, the electronic version of this text is a first in education texts. It is designed to take advantage of electronic possibilities, such as interactive case studies and exercises; the use of video clips and television programs to illustrate concepts; on-line tracking of progress; and instant links to sources on the World Wide Web. The shift from linear text to electronic interactivity opens up multiple opportunities for the author and publisher to present material in new ways. For example, a particularly innovative feature of this e-text is the integration of video sequences that illustrate the concepts discussed in text. Filmed expressly for this book in Canadian classrooms, examples of both elementary and secondary classroom techniques are used. By showing segments of a lesson, the reader sees the steps as they appear in practice and is then led to interact with the video-sequence material to identify key components and their results.

Through *WileyPLUS*, instructors are also supported and assisted by the electronic format of the book. Instructors are able to customize the e-text material to reflect their content and evaluation preferences. Instructors may choose which exercises are formative and which are summative. They can add their preferred readings, generate on-line exercises and essay questions, insert their own evaluation requirements, and view student grades in the on-line gradebook. Thus, much of the task of monitoring student performance can be accomplished on-line.

Organization and Features

This text has been designed as a series of modules in order to offer maximum flexibility for the instructor and student. The electronic format allows the opportunity to move in any direction through the modules and in any sequence. The challenge of producing a printed version of an e-text is its inherent linearity. While the printed text does not also allow for viewing animations, film clips, or for clicking out to extra references, every effort has been made to incorporate within it many of the interactive features. Features of *Introduction to Inclusive Education* include:

Opening Vignettes

Each module begins with a video clip and discussion questions to engage learners and introduce module topics.

"In the Classroom" Video Clips

A variety of brief film sequences have been developed to bring the text material to life. These video clips highlight authentic classroom situations and demonstrate good teaching practices, essential to effective learning. One-on-one interviews are also included.

CBC Videos

Relevant CBC programs have been integrated within the multimedia text. Accompanying video summaries and discussion questions are also provided.

Interactive Exercises

Animated case studies help illustrate various classroom issues and situations and provide interactive tasks for learners to complete. These sequences are followed by a quiz to encourage critical thinking and analysis.

Think it Over

A series of thought-provoking activities and questions have been integrated throughout the modules. Think it Over boxes are designed to encourage personal reflection and/or group discussion.

Pre-Tests and Post-Tests

Self-study practice questions located throughout the multimedia text help students gauge their level of understanding as they prepare for class time or a test. Immediate feedback is then provided for this self-paced learning component.

Student Polls

These surveys are integrated throughout the c-book, providing students with the opportunity to register their opinion on a variety of special education topics and issues. After they have voted, students can compare their vote with those of other students taking this course across Canada.

Research Boxes

These link-out pages provide students with in-depth research information that support the content and the context of the e-text. The Research Boxes have been appropriately integrated into the printed version.

Case Studies

Based upon real-life research, these case studies have been specifically written to demonstrate how theories can be applied to practical classroom situations.

Links to Glossary Terms

The **highlighted terms** throughout the multimedia text are linked to the corresponding definition for quick and easy access.

Acknowledgements

Introduction to Inclusive Education has been a long time in the making. First and foremost I want to thank the reviewers who generously read and gave their feedback to the initial proposal for this project.

Sally E. Brenton-Haden, *University of Alberta*

David Buhler, *Ontario Institute for Studies in Education of the University of Toronto*

Lily L. Dyson, *University of Victoria*

Alan Edmunds, *University of Western Ontario*

Elizabeth Jordan, *University of British Columbia*

Cathy Koolen, *University of Western Ontario*

Hazel McBride, *Ontario Institute for Studies in Education of the University of Toronto*

Michelann Parr, *Nipissing University*

I would especially like to thank those colleagues who reviewed the modules. Their insights were invaluable, constructive and helped to shape what you have before you.

David Buhler, *Ontario Institute for Studies in Education of the University of Toronto*

Jack Goldberg, *University of Alberta*

Joan Jeary, University of Calgary

Elizabeth Jordan, *University of British Columbia*

Hazel McBride, *Ontario Institute for Studies in Education of the University of Toronto*

Donna McGhie-Richmond, *University of Alberta*

Mike Parr, *Nipissing University*

Gary Smith, *University of British Columbia*

Paula J. Stanovich, *Portland State University*

Marilyn Thain, *University of Western Ontario*

David Young, *University of Western Ontario*

Special thanks go to David Buhler, Elizabeth Jordan, Hazel McBride, and David Young who reviewed and assisted in the different stages of this project's development.

I would like to especially thank the principals, teachers, and students in the many schools who have welcomed me to observe, chronicle, and question their work. Public, private, and Catholic school systems have all contributed in demonstrating for me what works and explaining why. The case studies and vignettes in the book are based on exemplary teachers who have generously welcomed me into their classrooms, and to whom I am deeply grateful. In particular, I thank the Durham Catholic District School Board for its long-standing commitment to my research program, and its generous support of it. The support of the administrators included access to their schools to videotape their teachers as they conducted their lessons. A special thanks is given to those teachers and students who appear in the video sequences.

Teachers in the schools in which I worked taught me so much about good teaching, and allowed me to draw on their time and energies to translate their teaching into the material of this project: Martha Barrett, Eva Black, Kevin Deuchars, Carolyn Graham, Sandi Hopkins, Wilma Lehman, Bonnie Roynon, Tanya Sweeney, among others.

Thanks also to Jon and Maureen VanLoon and Fran and Ashif Jaffer for agreeing to the videotaped interviews that appear in the e-text. Their open and forthright telling of their stories were both eloquent and brave.

My thanks to many people who have supported the content of this project, through challenging and amplifying my thinking and reasoning and contributing their expertise, especially Jennifer LeClerc, Kristin MacIsaac, Kathryn Marcus, Joseph Morin, Eileen Schwartz, and Kathryn Underwood. A special thanks to my long-time colleague and friend, Paula Stanovich, and to Keith Stanovich, for mentoring both of us.

The people at Wiley have been magnificent in supporting this project. I have worked closely with them, especially Elsa Passera Berardi, Developmental & Media Editor and Michael Valerio, Acquisitions Editor. My sincere gratitude also goes to Joan Lewis-Milne, Marketing Manager; Luke Curtin, On-line Marketing Manager; Alexandar Bondar and the dedicated TES team; and to the sales representatives for bringing this project to your attention and promoting its efforts.

I welcome your comments and suggestions.

Anne Jordan
ajordan@oise.utoronto.ca
Toronto, Ontario
August 2006

Brief Table of Contents

Table of Contents

Case Studies, Interactive Exercises, Think it Over and Research Boxes

MODULE TWO

MODULE THREE

All Modules also feature **Student Polls** on a variety of special education topics and issues. These surveys are available in the hardcopy text, as well as on-line. The on-line versions provide students with the opportunity to register their opinion and compare their vote with those of other students taking this course across Canada.

Disability, Ability, and Responsibility

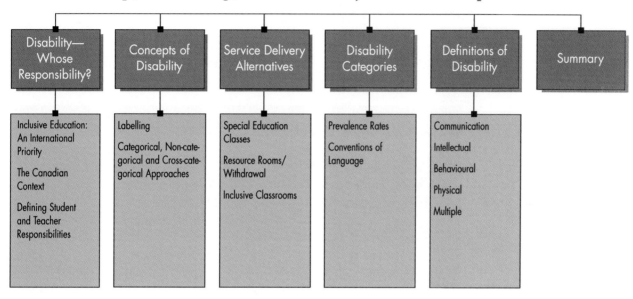

Disability—Whose Responsibility?	Concepts of Disability	Service Delivery Alternatives	Disability Categories	Definitions of Disability	Summary
Inclusive Education: An International Priority The Canadian Context Defining Student and Teacher Responsibilities	Labelling Categorical, Non-categorical and Cross-categorical Approaches	Special Education Classes Resource Rooms/Withdrawal Inclusive Classrooms	Prevalence Rates Conventions of Language	Communication Intellectual Behavioural Physical Multiple	

Learning Objectives

In this module, teachers will learn:

1. to use the concept of inclusive education to adapt instruction to the needs of a wide range of students

2. how the variety of understandings about special education may contribute to variations in practice, as seen in the current educational context in Canadian schools

3. to distinguish between differences in the personal theories, beliefs, and assumptions that teachers hold about the nature of disability and ability, and how these differences impact their understanding of teaching roles and responsibilities

4. a framework for understanding how differences in beliefs may be linked to differences in teachers' instructional practices and, as a result, the opportunities that they provide for students to achieve

In the second part of the module, teachers will learn concepts of disability, including:

5. the pros and cons of **labelling** someone as having a disability

6. **categorical**, **non-categorical**, and **cross-categorical** approaches to the delivery of special education, and how these are related to labelling

7. definitions of major categories of disability in light of the preceding framework, and the strengths and shortcomings of each definition

Opening Vignette

"We want a Canada in which citizens with disabilities have the opportunity to contribute to and benefit from Canada's prosperity—as learners, workers, volunteers, and family members."
                                     —Speech from the Throne, February 2, 2004

Ashif Jaffer will be starting his university studies in the fall. Watch the video to see Ashif describe his school experiences. Then watch Mrs. Jaffer, his mother, describe Ashif's school and family experiences, his struggles to learn, and his membership in the family. To date, Ashif is not aware that he has **Down syndrome**.

After viewing the video, consider the following questions:

1. What factors have contributed to Ashif's current achievements?

2. Describe Mrs. Jaffer's perspective of disability.

3. Mrs. Jaffer offers five pieces of advice to mothers of children with Down syndrome. What are they?

Gerber and Semmel (1984) suggest that "teachers aim their 'instruction plans' at…relatively homogeneous groups in an apparent attempt to reduce the sheer cognitive complexity of planning and instruction associated with broad ranges of student characteristics and ability. Classroom teachers naturally orient, both in terms of effort and positive affect, toward students whom they consider teachable and away from students [who] are…difficult to teach"(p.141).

The purpose of this module is to present a research-based conceptual framework for guiding teaching practice. The premise of this framework seems simple: teachers are responsible for meeting the needs of the wide variety of students in their classrooms. This premise requires that teachers reflect about their current teaching style, skills, and beliefs about practice, and how they work with other educators in their schools. Some already teach in just the ways discussed, and the module will therefore serve to affirm beliefs and practices. But teaching is a complex process, and there will almost certainly be unfamiliar techniques that teachers may want to try.

Teachers encounter situations weekly, if not daily, that challenge their assumptions about their roles and their responsibility for students in their care. Often they may question themselves about how they are currently teaching, and why they teach this way. They may seek ways to change their current practices through formal coursework and reading, and through daily reflection about and self-analysis of the decisions they made during a school day. These modules demonstrate how teachers can extend their range of instructional effectiveness by adapting the repertoire of skills they use throughout the day.

The conceptual framework presented in this module does not require that teachers radically change their skills. It also does not require that they learn specialized, individual instructional techniques specific to the needs of students with disabilities in their classes. Rather, the framework asks teachers to examine how they can develop, adapt, and perhaps fine tune their existing skills and techniques for instruction. By developing a conceptual

framework, teachers will be able to increase their effectiveness and add a set of instructional skills to their teaching repertoires. These skills will assist **all** students to access the curriculum, whether students are identified as exceptional; are struggling with acquiring, understanding, or expressing knowledge for any number of reasons; are achieving at grade-level expectation; or are excelling and wanting to zoom ahead of their classmates.

The approach taken, therefore, is that working with students with special education needs requires extending and refining the best practices of regular teaching. Working with these students, particularly in an inclusive classroom setting, can be a powerful form of professional development that equips teachers to be more skilled with all students (Stanovich & Jordan, 2004). This is not to deny that there are some specific instructional techniques that will be needed for individual students; for example, using a Phonic Ear® to amplify speech for a student with a hearing impairment, or understanding how a piece of assistive technology will help a student to learn. But these specialized skills are not the main substance of these modules for two reasons: first, the teacher in an inclusive classroom needs to develop and draw upon a variety of skills that can be accessed by all students and that will encompass those with special needs (**universal access**); and second, the specialized techniques needed for any given student with a disability must be tailored to the characteristics of that student and are therefore best understood when the student arrives in the class (just-in-time delivery).

The term "**just-in-time delivery**" is used in business and industry to indicate that, rather than stockpiling quantities of spare parts (in this case, highly specialized knowledge about the many disabling conditions that exist and how to treat them), a supplier is asked to deliver the part just before it is needed for use. This and later modules address how technical expertise can be delivered through a collaborative process in a school's delivery system, enabling teachers to receive the specialized information and support they need on a just-in-time basis. Specialized techniques will also be discussed in later modules, particularly as they pertain to teaching core skills such as literacy and numeracy, and behaviours needed in a community-centred classroom.

The initial modules, however, focus on universal access, or how teachers can adapt their instructional repertoires to influence the widest possible range of student needs at any given time. Meeting the needs of individual students will also be considered, but not in terms of how students may first be categorized under a disability label in order to access the services needed to meet those needs. These modules are not about how to "match, batch, and dispatch" students with learning difficulties; that is, they will not address how to identify disabilities in order to match students with a category or label to justify grouping them with a batch of similarly labelled students, and then dispatch them to a location outside the regular classroom.

As we will see, diagnostic skills for identifying disabilities are not the domain of the classroom teacher. Rather, learning to teach—both at the pre-service level of teacher preparation and at the in-service level of professional growth—depends on developing skills to meet the diverse needs of students in any class. The heart of excellent teaching is the ability to recognize the range of learning needs of students and to be able to draw upon a multitude of instructional alternatives that can be geared to that range, within the ongoing flow of instruction.

Teaching in a modern classroom is highly complex, and takes several years to master. Skills that enable teachers to recognize diverse learning needs, adapt their instruction to meet those needs, and tailor the classroom community to maximize each student's engagement in learning take practice, intensive reflection about what works and what doesn't, trial and error, and a good deal of personal commitment. Special education in this context, therefore, addresses how teachers can adapt their instructional skills to teach students whose language, literacy, and numeracy skills, thinking strategies, behaviours, and social and self-identity characteristics create barriers for them to learn.

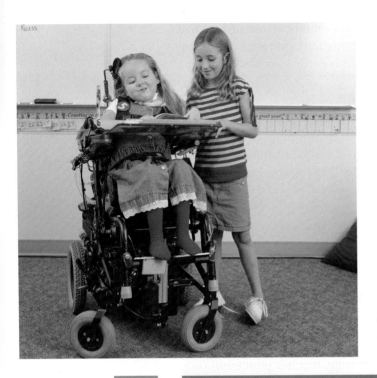

Effective special and inclusive education is considered in the context of regular classrooms in inclusive schools. The principles and techniques presented here are as important for teaching students who excel as for those who barely understand the language of instruction, and those who struggle with issues of cultural, racial, and gender identity. However, the emphasis will initially be on learners who are underachieving, including those who have difficulty with various components of the curriculum (**curriculum-related disabilities**) and those who have more serious disabilities compounded by physical, psychological, neurological, and/or sensory impairments (**complex disabilities**).

learning objective
1-1

Disability—Whose Responsibility?

Inclusive Education: An International Priority

The pragmatic reason for adapting instruction is that it is a required educational policy. The more philosophical reasons include the universally accepted view that all students have a right to learn in the regular classroom. Despite the professional, legal, and political debates and arguments throughout North America that surround the principle of including students with special needs in the regular classroom, it appears, as Florian (1998) noted, that "The concept of inclusive education enjoys a high profile around the world by virtue of its incorporation into the policy documents of numerous international organizations" (p.13).

One of the most significant and powerful documents is the Salamanca Statement and Framework for Action on Special Needs Education (the Salamanca Statement, UNESCO, 1994), which resulted from a meeting of over 300 participants representing 92 governments and 25 international organizations. The meeting was jointly sponsored by the government of Spain and UNESCO in 1994. The statement was adopted by acclamation and thus can be seen as representing a worldwide consensus in favour of inclusive education. Among other things, the proclamation states that:

- Regular schools with this inclusive orientation are the most effective means of combating discriminatory attitudes, creating welcoming communities, building an inclusive society, and achieving education for all; moreover, they provide an effective education to the majority of children and improve the efficiency and ultimately the cost-effectiveness of the entire educational system.

The Salamanca Statement also calls upon all governments to:

- adopt as a matter of law or policy the principle of inclusive education by enrolling all children in regular schools, unless there are compelling reasons for doing otherwise

- develop demonstration projects and encourage exchanges with countries having experience with inclusive schools

- invest greater effort in early identification and intervention strategies, as well as in vocational aspects of inclusive education

- ensure that, in the context of systemic change, teacher education programs, both pre-service and in-service, address the provision of special needs education in inclusive schools (pp. vii-ix)

Inclusion is a phenomenon that is here to stay. Florian (1998) says, in reference to the Salamanca Statement, "Although this [inclusion] means different things in different places, there is a universality to the underlying human rights philosophy of inclusion which suggests that the concept is destined to persist rather than represent the latest educational fad or bandwagon" (p. 13).

The Canadian Context

learning
objective

1-2

In Canada, the belief that every student has the right to an education that fulfils his or her potential to grow is central to the federal Charter of Rights and Freedoms and to the human rights legislation in each province and territory. It is understood that not only is education a right rather than a privilege, but also that no child should be the victim of discrimination as a result of race, national or ethnic origin, colour, religion, sex, age, or mental or physical disability (Canadian Charter of Rights and Freedoms, section 15, 1985).

According to a 2004 Government of Canada report,

> "one in eight Canadians has a disability, a total of 3.6 million people. For Canada's Aboriginal population, the rate of disability is particularly high; more than one and a half times the rate for the non-Aboriginal population. Women are more likely than men to have a disability, regardless of age. Women on average also live longer, which makes them more likely to develop an age-related chronic condition that leads to disability. Over 2 million Canadian adults with disabilities need assistive aids and devices. About 67% of these adults have all their needs met. Roughly half of children with disabilities have all the assistive aids and devices they need. More than 80% of Canadians believe there has been some progress in including people with disabilities in Canadian society over the past decade. Yet only one in ten believes these individuals are fully included today. Canadians feel that people with disabilities should have the opportunity to participate in life to their fullest potential—that this is part of the "Canadian way" of doing things. Most feel that while the solutions might be expensive, they are necessary and the social benefit is worth it."

(Advancing the inclusion of persons with disabilities; available at www.sdc.gc.ca/en/gateways/topics/pyp-pup.shtml).

The national picture: underachievement and possible causes

Despite the international recognition that inclusive education is the standard for educational delivery for people with disabilities, legislators and school systems in Canada still have a way to go before they meet the inclusion mandate. Indeed, there is some scepticism about the concept of inclusion. There is considerable diversity from one province to another, from school system to school system, and indeed from school to school in how special education programs and services are delivered. This is in part caused by differing, and sometimes opposing, political and ideological positions taken by policy makers about the nature and purpose of special education. As will be seen in this module, it is also exacerbated by a lack of consensus among educators about their responsibilities for students whose achievement does not meet the expectations for admission to post-secondary education.

Refer to Case Study 1-1: Should the Number of Students with Disabilities in Regular Classrooms Be Limited?

case study

1-1

Should the Number of Students with Disabilities in Regular Classrooms Be Limited?

The following article appeared in the Tri-City News, serving Port Moody and Coquitlam, British Columbia, on May 10, 2006. Read it, then consider the questions that follow.

CONCERNS ABOUT KIDS DUE TO CLASS SIZE LIMITS

By Diane Strandberg The Tri-City News

May 10, 2006

A bill to limit numbers of students with special needs in B.C. public school classrooms could push kids out of their neighbourhood schools and make it tougher for them to get courses they need, says a family and support liaison for the Simon Fraser Society for Community Living.

"Rather than firefighting, we need to get back to the core issues," Rachel le Nobel said in response to the provincial government's proposed Bill 33, which would ensure that no more than three special needs children with individual education plans (IEPs) are allowed in a class unless the superintendent and principal approve and the teacher is consulted.

The bill, which was introduced in the legislature two weeks ago, was drafted after consultation with a Learning Roundtable of parents, trustees and educators in response to teachers' concerns about class sizes and composition. Bill 33 would also cap at 30 Grade 4 to 12 classes, except with the consent of teachers for the younger grades and consultation with teachers for Grades 8 to 12.

But according to le Nobel, whose group belongs to the B.C. Association for Community Living, which this week came out against the legislation, Bill 33's focus is too narrow. Classroom teachers would be better off with more resources and training, and possibly smaller classes, when special needs students are factored in.

Instead, the legislation marginalizes students with IEP—numbering in the hundreds in School District 43—and puts up barriers to their education, le Nobel said.

"I don't think it solves the problem to single out one group of kids," she said.

Le Nobel said students with IEPs are just one group that needs extra support in today's complex classrooms, and many of them come with support workers and extra funding.

"The message it sends out is that these kids are the big problem," she said.

Le Nobel, whose agency supports families with children with special needs, said parents have been contacting radio stations and MLAs with concerns that the caps will force educators to make tough decisions that could result in elementary students leaving their neighbourhood schools and deny access to academic classes or electives to older students.

"If there are four Grade 9 classes and 15 students [with IEPs], what happens to the other three [students]?" le Nobel said, adding, "Is the administrator going to have the power to make a fifth classroom?"

One of the big questions is whether school districts will get any extra funding to cover the extra costs of the legislation. Coquitlam Teachers' Association, which gave a cautious support to the legislation, said it hopes schools will be able to keep funding that would ordinarily be lost due to declining enrolment, worth more than $1.4 million in School District 43.

According to preliminary school district figures last fall, there were 539 students in special funded categories enrolled in local schools, and 1,340 students with learning disabilities, though not all have IEPs.

Questions:
1. What are the positions taken on capping the number of students with disabilities by the following groups?
   - Rachel le Nobel and the Simon Fraser Society for Community Living
   - The Learning Roundtable of parents, trustees, and educators
   - The Coquitlam Teachers' Association

2. What are the issues in this debate?

3. What are the pros and cons of the proposed legislation?

4. In the last line, we are told that not all students with learning disabilities have IEPs. What might the implication of this be for the proposed capping policy?

Let's examine the outlook for students with disabilities and their under-achieving peers. Starting at the end of schooling—i.e., what befalls students who are below the achievement criteria for secondary school graduation?—the outlook for their adult lives is not good. Here are some documented sources of conflict.

Graduation rates and aspirations of students

One potential risk for students with disabilities is dropping out of school before finishing. Vulnerable students who are at risk of failing to complete high school make up about 29% of Canadian children (Willms, 2002). According to Bowlby and McMullen, (2002), half of students who dropped out of school were making reasonable academic progress and left because of personal difficulties or were asked to leave. The outlook for success in adult life for students who drop out and do not drop back to complete their high school graduation is particularly grim.

Those who stay in school face the prospect of low rates of graduation in all provinces, varying from 70% in Ontario and 72% in British Columbia to 83% in New Brunswick.[1] National newspapers in October 2005 reported that rates of failure to graduate were actually increasing in several provinces. Keeping in mind that graduation rates are set by provincial authorities, and are linked to the outcomes of annual province-wide testing, one wonders about the impact of a 30% failure-to-graduate rate on students' motivation and willingness to continue to learn, and, for those who have dropped out, to return for further education.

The potential for school failure also challenges the motivation and achievement aspirations of those who stay to complete their secondary school education. Eighty percent of students in the middle grades of their high school years in provinces other than Quebec expect to do well in university and a further 10% to do well in college (Looker & Thiessen, 2004). This represents a total of 90% of students who, in their middle grades, anticipate graduating and continuing on to postsecondary education. Yet this stands in contrast with the approximately 70% of students in the final grade of secondary school who will actually

---

[1] These rates reflect students who were enrolled in Grade 9 four years before, and excludes students who are returning or retrying grade 12 completion (King et al. 2005).

graduate. A further obstacle is that universities have the capacity to take only 50% of students graduating from high school, although King et al. (2005) indicate that the capacity may be closer to 33% in Ontario. These statistics suggest that less than 30% of the students in the middle grades in high school (outside Quebec) will eventually enter university, not the 80% who expect to do well there. (Quebec statistics differ in part because of the CEJEP system). King (2005) indicates that of all the students who reach the end of high school without dropping out, 33% will go to university, 19% will go to college, and 18% will enter the workforce.

One can see that a large proportion of students leaving secondary schools will have their achievement aspirations dashed. Consider then what the outlook is for students with disabilities. These students tend to be most frequently represented in the lower achievement tracks and as a result, the outlook for their graduation and subsequent post secondary education is lower than for their non-disabled peers. Ashif Jaffer, featured in the opening video vignette, is the exception rather than the rule. So the task of the teacher is to motivate and challenge these students in the face of poor odds for later success, and limited post-secondary opportunities—a tall order.

Alternatives to post-secondary education

Secondary schools are, in general, heavily focused on post-secondary education (King et al., 2005; Looker & Thiessen, 2004). With the advent of provincial testing and curriculum standards in most provinces, students receive time-limited opportunities to succeed, and school staffs may give less attention to those who are not likely to pass critical tests within those time limits and therefore to graduate (Fenstermacher & Richardson, 2005). These modules also discuss the "triage" dilemma faced by teachers who see themselves as having to select the students whom they will teach on the basis of who is most likely to succeed.

There is also a lack of desirable, prestigious routes to the professions and trades (Bowlby & McMullen, 2002; Rae, 2005; Scofield, 2004). Colleges, designed to provide a range of programs from basic skills training to applied degrees, are increasingly filled by students who already hold university or college credentials. In Ontario, 20% of college students hold such credentials (Rae, 2005). Rae also notes there is an urgent need for colleges "to recognize apprenticeships as a post-secondary destination and to treat them as a core business" (Rae, 2005, p.48).

In secondary schools where alternatives to entering postsecondary education are offered, such as cooperative and job-training programs, these programs are often unpopular and enrolments are frequently low. As a result, college-preparation courses may be withdrawn in some schools. Sometimes, students themselves see these programs as undesirable and stigmatizing (King et al., 2005). Some schools may have a peer culture that values post-secondary program eligibility and denigrates work-study and cooperative work programs. Other settings may also have a stigma attached to alternative schools and vocational training (King et al., 2005). There is also evidence from studies in Alberta that the education–work relationship in apprenticeship programs tends to benefit the employer and conforms to the workplace rather than providing a meaningful, progressive bridge between academic and vocational goals (Lehmann & Taylor, 2003; Taylor, 2003; 2005).

Refer to Interactive Exercise 1-1: Rainman: Pervasive Developmental Disability.

interactive
exercise

1-1

---

interactive
exercise

1-1

Rainman: Pervasive Developmental Disability

Watch the movie *Rainman* in which Dustin Hoffman plays Raymond (seen on the left side of the picture), a man with a Pervasive Developmental Disability—known widely as autism. Hoffman does a fine job in portraying features of this disability. He interprets symbols literally, stopping midway across a cross walk when the pedestrian light switches to "stop." He "perseverates" or fixates for long periods on objects, such as a deck of cards. He expects and is controlled by routine (e.g., he is upset by the lack of toothpicks to eat his food in a restaurant because he has not been allowed to use cutlery in the institution). Raymond also has an enormous store of knowledge about very specific topics: his father's car and baseball. Consider the following study questions related to this movie and how disability is perceived in the larger community.

1. What are the reactions of different members of society toward Raymond? Do their reactions differ?

2. How do Charlie's notions of Raymond's motives and abilities change throughout the movie?

3. Think of other movies that portray people with complex disabilities, such as *Forrest Gump* and *Radio*. How does society respond to each of these characters in these movies?

4. Compare the clinical treatment that was provided to the characters in these movies in terms of the era in which the films were set.

5. What were society's expectations about the standard way to treat these individuals (e.g., Gump's schooling, Raymond's special home)?

6. How did their families' attitudes about their disabilities influence what happened to these characters (e.g., Forrest's mother, Raymond's father and brother)?

7. Did the opinions of people in the society surrounding these characters change as a result of how the characters developed?

Streaming

In secondary schools, the specific stream and school program in which students are placed is highly influential on the success of students (Looker & Thiessen, 2004). The largest drop out rate is from the second track, the applied or general stream (King et al., 2005). This stream should in principle lead to apprenticeships, trades, and vocational education. However, the high dropout rate shows that the second track does not result in success for many students. Students in this stream accumulate only about half the number of course credits as those in the top-track academic stream, even though the courses are supposedly designed to meet their needs (King et al, 2005). Those designated as exceptional or working from an IEP (Individual Education Plan) and provided with special education support tend to complete alternative programs and courses, but also have similarly low rates of course completion and graduation.

The dilemma of streaming at the secondary level is that it is not clear whether streaming expands or narrows students' access to learning. Supporters of streaming believe that low-track placements help struggling learners and that grouping students heterogeneously diminishes the achievement of high-track learners (Loveless, 1998). Opponents of streaming believe that streaming itself, if not low-track placement, is the cause of and not the solution to low achievement (Heubert & Hauser, 1999; Oakes, Ormseth, Bell, & Camp, 1990). They draw on evidence that an enriched curriculum with high expectations is more effective than a remedial curriculum in raising the achievement levels of low-achieving students. Burris, Heubert, and Levin (2006) note that, in a period in which the school system is held accountable for ensuring that all students meet high academic standards, it is ironic that the solution has been to offer low-track classes with a slower-paced curriculum for low achievers and high-track classes with enriched and accelerated instruction for high achievers.

In the United States, the *No Child Left Behind* (NCLB) legislation has spurred a great deal of research in this issue. Darling-Hammond (2006) reports that poverty accounts for the majority of variance in students who do not succeed in school. But the quality of instruction also explains almost as much of the variance in achievement as poverty does. In studies comparing the eventual achievement outcome of two groups of elementary students with similar academic learning potential, one given a high quality of instruction (curriculum at a high level with a focus on higher-order thinking and high achievement expectations) and the other given a low quality of instruction (an emphasis on rote and factual learning and low expectations), the former group achieved significantly higher by the end of high school (Darling-Hammond, 2006).

The impact of standardized curriculum and provincial assessments

At both the secondary and elementary levels, a further source of conflict is provincial testing. These tests are typically administered at grades 3, 6, and 9, in math and language arts in Alberta, British Columbia, Ontario, Manitoba, Newfoundland and Labrador, the Yukon, and in French in Quebec. In some jurisdictions, examinations are high stakes graduation requirements (e.g., the OSSLT in Ontario; provincial certification examinations in Newfoundland and Labrador). In Nova Scotia, literacy testing occurs at grades 6 and 12. The government of the Northwest Territories is currently planning to adopt Alberta's grade 12 provincial tests. New Brunswick sets achievement standards. Saskatchewan tests only students who work with non-accredited teachers. There is currently no provincial testing in Nunavut. Further information is available at **http://www.edu.gov.on.ca/eng/relsites/oth_prov.html**.

Provincial testing has been criticized for giving conflicting messages to educators about priorities for teaching. One result is a trend for teachers to channel their priorities into covering the curriculum, compelling them to engage in triage-like teaching, resembling emergency room doctors who select those on whom to focus their time and effort, and those whom they must abandon (McLaughlin & Jordan, 2004; Fenstermacher & Richardson, 2005; OSSTF, 2001). In Canada, this interpretation is fortified by policies in those provinces that conduct wide-scale testing that exempt students designated as "disabled" from participating. This contrasts with the legislative requirement in the United States that all students must participate in state-wide testing, with appropriate accommodations.

THINK IT OVER 1-1: High-stakes Assessment

What do you think are the pros and cons of including or exempting students with disabilities from participating in **high-stakes assessment**?

- Should students with disabilities be included in order to be part of the accountability criteria that such testing places on schools?

- Should students with disabilities be exempted where their participation in the tests would yield questionable results?

Teachers' beliefs and instructional quality

Some teachers believe they cannot counteract the influences of family/society to which students return each day. They see the school as having little impact (Kagan, 1992; Boykin, 2005). "At-riskness" is located in students themselves, their families, and cultures, not in their educational history and current learning environment (Howard, Dryden, & Johnson, 1999). Yet teachers can make all the difference for youth (Crespo & Carignan, 2001). "There must be at least one educator in a student's life who is totally committed to the success of that student" (Montecel, 2004). There is ample evidence that students who succeed, often despite the worst odds, had caring teachers and safe classroom experiences. They appear to develop **resilience**, in part as a result of the role teachers played in providing such experiences. When teachers focus on *what needs to be* (the student's strengths and needs) rather than on *what is* (a preoccupation with psychopathology, family disorder, and personal weakness), they move away from identifying risk to assessing and building on capabilities (Artz et al., 2001; Wotherspoon & Schissel, 2003).

There is also a consensus in the literature about the characteristics of schools that are effective in promoting the achievement of at-risk students, preventing school failure, and reaching out to cultural and linguistic minorities (Boykin 2004; King, 2005; Levin, 2004; Montecel et al. 2004). These include:

- staff and student stability

- multidimensional leadership (school administrators are leaders, educators, and communicators)

- continuous commitment to improvement, including job-embedded training and professional development for teachers; school staff, especially teachers, are equipped with tools to ensure their students' success, including the use of supports, technology, and mentoring programs

- multiple stakeholder involvement (including parents, students, custodians, crossing guards, lunchroom staff, etc.)

- families are valued as partners with the school, and are part of the team that is committed to ensuring that equity and excellence are present in a student's life

- all students are valued; the focus is on educating the whole student, including affective and social development

- students are able to see that what they learn in school is applicable to life outside of school; courses are closely tailored to students' abilities and aspirations

At both secondary and elementary levels, students with learning disabilities and other learning difficulties cannot participate to the fullest without the mediation of teachers and parents. Both groups need to understand that each person is in some way unique, and that such uniqueness comes from the combination of past and current experiences and personal and interpersonal characteristics.

Irrespective of individual uniqueness, each person has the right to fulfil his or her potential to learn and grow in society. However, this is where the water gets muddy. While everyone agrees with this statement, people—including parents and teachers—differ widely in what they implicitly understand to be the essential characteristics of a successful person. Why do some people fail to achieve while others excel? Individual attributions of what and who is responsible for achievement also vary widely. The following sections explore these differences in personal theories, the beliefs that underlie people's explanations for success and failure.

For an in-depth look at some of the international research that identifies these differences in understanding, read Research Box 1-1: Attitudes and Beliefs about Disability.

research box

1-1

---

research
box

1-1

Attitudes and Beliefs
about Disability

Research indicates that effective instructional practices in inclusive classrooms are related to classroom teachers' beliefs about the nature of learning and learning disability (Pajares, 1992; Jordan & Stanovich, 2001, 2003; Stanovich & Jordan, 1998). Teachers' beliefs have a major influence on shaping what they perceive and notice about their students, and this in turn has a profound influence on how they teach. For example, teachers' beliefs about their roles and responsibilities in inclusive classrooms influence both the quantity and the quality of their instructional interactions with students both with and without disabilities (Jordan, Lindsay & Stanovich, 1997) (see Research Box 1.4).

Until recently, teachers' beliefs about working with students with disabilities have been characterized as lying along a bipolar continuum. At one end are teachers with interventionist beliefs, who see themselves as responsible for removing barriers to students' access to learning (Booth, 2000). Teachers with interventionist beliefs:

- interact more and at deeper levels of cognitive engagement
- have higher levels of efficacy about their teaching
- achieve higher scores on measures of overall classroom effectiveness
- interact with students both with and without disabilities at higher levels of cognitive engagement (Jordan & Stanovich, 2003)

Teachers whose beliefs are located at the other end of the continuum hold pathognomonic beliefs (derived from path = disease, gnomon = naming, or naming the pathology). They view disability as a stable, internal condition of the student, characterized by a medical–pathological condition, and generally not amenable to instructional intervention. They expect diagnosticians to label the disability and they believe that students with confirmed disabilities are the responsibility of specialists outside of their classroom. Teachers who hold pathognomonic beliefs therefore tend to interact little with students with disabilities who are included in their general education classrooms. Interactions tend to be managerial rather than instructional, and of limited cognitive engagement with the student. In effect, students both with and without disabilities in the classrooms of interventionist teachers experience qualitatively and quantitatively superior instructional interactions with their teachers (Jordan, Lindsay, & Stanovich, 1997; Stanovich, & Jordan, 1998). Since academic engagement is significantly related to achievement, researchers speculate that students both with and without disabilities in the classrooms of interventionist teachers have a better opportunity to learn (Jordan & Stanovich, 2001).

Recently, Underwood (2002) has expanded the pathognomonic–interventionist construct and renamed the dimensions to align with distinctions made by Finkelstein (1980), Oliver (1990), Rioux, (1998), and Tregaskis (2002). The pathognomonic or **individual perspective** continues to be characterized by an emphasis on the internal medical–pathological condition of the individual. One consequence of this perspective is that the locus of responsibility is placed on the child and his or her family for meeting the gate-keeping criteria for furnishing evidence of the existence of the pathological conditions that will lead to access to specialized services.

The **situational perspective** is aligned with the interventionist belief structures previously described, but with an additional distinction from the **socio-political perspective** of understanding disability. The situational model is expressed by Leicester & Lovell (1997):

> "Disability is not conceived as a condition of the individual person. The experiences of disabled people are of social restrictions in the world around them; the individual experience of disability is created in interaction with a physical and social world designed for non-disabled living."

One important difference between this and the individual perspective is that it locates responsibility for action to the society at large, and in the case of schooling, to the teachers and support staff surrounding the child. Appropriate actions include reducing the barriers to the child's participation in the classroom. This perspective underlies the policy of providing accommodations to students with disabilities.

Neither perspective, however, deals with the systemic problem of equity or discrimination in the educational system and workplace. Tregaskis (2002) claims that "cultural images have been used to socially construct disabled people as an unwelcome 'other' whose subjugation is necessary to the continuation or restoration of mainstream society." Kalyanpur & Harry (1999) distinguish between holding the disabled person responsible for meeting the criteria to qualify for compensatory resources, as in the individual perspective, and holding the whole family responsible, by implicating them as causal in the disability. Both of these discriminatory perspectives go beyond the situational model to give rise to active alienation and exclusion. This third group of beliefs characterizes Underwood's term, **socio-political** perspectives. People who focus on the system as implicated in defining disability either support this discrimination by subscribing to the exclusion of people with disabilities, or they tackle the discrimination by actively seeking to reduce it through political and legal forms of recourse. In the latter case, their focus is on the rights of the individual with a disability to compensatory services and resources to remedy the biases and injustices caused by the system.

How special education evolved in Canada

The current status of special education has evolved over many decades. Indeed, it continues to evolve, and as experienced teachers know, the techniques that are in vogue one day may have changed the next. It is therefore helpful to have a historical overview from which to evaluate each new trend. A brief history of the development of provincial and federal policies and legislation for inclusive special education is the topic of Research Box 1-2. Refer to Research Box 1-2: A Recent History of the Development of Inclusive Special Education in Canada below.

research box

1-2

A Recent History of the Development of Inclusive Special Education in Canada

Special education emerged as a discipline under the newly minted public school systems in Canada in the 1920s (see Research Box 1-4). It was in part influenced by the expectation of the times that society had an obligation to undertake care and support for children and adults with disabilities, and this was understood to mean care in a separate, segregated, or institutionalized setting. At the time, people with disabilities comprised only a small proportion of the population, since disability was defined in terms of the conditions that are now viewed as severe or complex.

In 1974, the author experienced the environment of a closed institution for people with profound intellectual disabilities on a visit to a regional centre that was typical of the institutional facilities of the time. While the visitors sat as a group, medical staff wheeled in one after another "case" to view, in the manner of a string of exhibits. The doctors talked about each person openly in front of them, describing their physical features, their histories, and secondary characteristics. It was assumed that none of these patients could understand anything that was said. This institution still exists today, although with a much smaller client group.

Fortunately, times have changed. There is no longer the disregard for the dignity of each person that was witnessed in the past. We now expect people with disabilities to be cared for within the larger society wherever possible, in settings that range from supported care in their own homes to small group homes. Children with disabilities are educated in classes that are as close to a regular education setting as possible. Indeed, most school systems offer a range of special educational settings for students with disabilities, so that each child can be served according to his or her needs. In some school systems, all segregated classes and separate settings outside the regular classroom have been eliminated, and staff are assisted to include all students within regular education settings.

One impetus for this change in attitude toward people with disabilities was the human rights movement in the United States. Although the movement began as a reaction to racial discrimination, it evoked a broader set of sensibilities in the general public that has had a lasting impact. Today this movement continues to evolve, taking place over racial, cultural, and religious differences and against the stereotypes and labels that human beings are so apt to apply to each other. The rights of people with disabilities are still not fully valued, however. Governments, special interest and social groups, and organizations continue to press for equity and equality on behalf of people with disabilities.

In special education, the first groundbreaking piece of legislation appeared in1974 in the United States, with the enactment of Public Law 94-142, The Education of all Handicapped Children Act. This legislation explicitly required that all students be served in the Least Restrictive Environment (LRE), meaning an educational setting as close to the general education classroom as possible for each student with a disability. Since then, this legislation, known as the Regular Education Initiative, has evolved through several revisions: The Individuals with Disabilities Act (IDEA) and recently the *No Child Left Behind* (NCLB) initiative that requires that all students who are encountering difficulty learning must be given intensive support, especially in the early years, and that schools and teachers be held accountable for the growth of learning that results. The main provisions in IDEA are that each state and locality in the United States must have a plan to ensure:

- identification of students with disabilities

- Free Appropriate Public Education (FAPE)—public education at no cost to the parent

- due process—students' and parents' rights to information, informed consent, and an impartial appeal process

- Parent/guardian/surrogate consultation on matters pertaining to the student's evaluation, placement, and IEP

- Least Restrictive Environment (LRE)

- Individualized Education Program (IEP)

- non-discriminatory evaluation of the areas in which a student has a suspected disability, without bias due to language, culture, or disability

- confidentiality—records are to be kept confidential, but can be accessed by the parent or guardian

- professional development—in-service training for all personnel including regular classroom teachers to assist them to meet the needs of students with disabilities

Spurred on by the legislation and policies that were evolving in the United States in the 1970s, Canadian provinces began to establish policies in the early 1980s, first for the right of students with disabilities to receive an appropriate education—which surprisingly had not been previously required—and then to ensure a setting that contained elements of the Regular Education Initiative. In 1980, Ontario introduced a bill to amend the Ontario Education Act, known as Bill 82. This bill became law in 1985, coinciding with the signing of the repatriated Canadian Charter of Rights and Freedoms. Bill 82 was a landmark piece of legislation that, for the first time, gave parents or guardians the right to represent their children's interest in decisions made about the identification of their disability and their educational placement. Bill 82 also enshrined the rights of parents to appeal decisions about identification or placement of their children with which they disagreed.

Even today, parents of children without disabilities do not enjoy the same rights to consultation and participation in decision making for their children as do parents or guardians of children with disabilities. Although Bill 82 was a complex piece of legislation, it contained many of the features that were introduced in US legislation a decade before (Keeton Wilson, 1984):

- Identification—school boards are required to implement procedures for the early and ongoing identification of the learning abilities and needs of students. The Minister also defined categories of disability and required their use when school systems reported.

- Free appropriate education—school boards are responsible for providing appropriate special education programs and for students with disabilities without payment of fees.

- Parent/guardian consultation—parents have the right to give or withhold informed consent for assessment, identification, and placement decisions.

- A "due process" provision—parents or guardians have the right to appeal the decisions made by the school board about their child's identification and/or placement. (Note that the term "due process" is used in American rather than Canadian and Quebec law).

- Continuous assessment—special education programs are based on and modified by the results of continuous assessment that meets the needs of the child. This later became formalized as a series of standards for the design and implementation of IEPs in 2000.

All provinces and territories in Canada now subscribe to some degree to these five principles: freedom from discrimination, access to schooling at public expense, assessment of educational needs and appropriate placement, appropriate services, and provision for self advocacy ("due process") by or on behalf of students with disabilities (Andrews & Lupart, 2000). The policies vary from province to province in terms of the status of their legal mandate, from guideline to legal requirement, but all provinces have provisions for a child with a disability to be given an Individual Education Plan, and for parents to be invited to be part of the decision making process for placement. Each province in Canada currently has either a policy or legislation in place that guarantees the rights of students to a placement in a school that meets his or her educational needs in a setting that is as close to a regular classroom as is possible for that student. In other words, all provinces now have some form of provision for inclusion, although they differ (Hutchinson, 2006). The right to a placement of the parent's choosing is not provided in any province, although parents in Quebec are offered a choice of public schools. Identification of students as exceptional is required in all provinces, and entails designating the student within a category of disability. In three provinces—Quebec, Ontario, and Saskatchewan—the categories are governed by binding definitions.

For a synopsis of the people who have contributed to the evolution of special education beliefs and practices in Canada, read Research Box 1-3: People Who Influenced the History of Special Education.

research
box

1-3

People Who Influenced the History of Special Education

The history of special education is not heroic. Prior to the Middle Ages, children born with disabilities were outcasts, often regarded as an indication that a person or family had displeased a higher being and that the family was cursed. These children were left to die, or even killed. Mental disabilities were regarded as possession by demons or spirits, and children with these disabilities and their families were punished or rejected. In the Middle Ages, people with disabilities were often the objects of amusement (Reynolds & Fletcher-Janzen, 2000). They were used for entertainment, as portrayed by the character of the fool in Shakespeare's plays. Around this time, the church began to provide humane care for people with more severe disabilities in the form of asylums, as much to protect such people from the public as to protect the public from them. During the Renaissance, a new interest in the dignity and worth of human beings began to emerge, which in turn contributed to a developing interest in education for people with certain types of disabilities. People with sensory disabilities such as blindness and deafness were the first to be regarded as able to benefit from education, largely at the instigation of churches. However, the sequence of these events was by no means linear. Until very recently, in some societies children with disabilities have been assigned to menial jobs in the fields or factories, without the possibility of an education.

In 1555, a Spanish monk named Pedro Ponce de Leon (1520–1584), taught a small group of children who were deaf to read, write, and speak. The first book on teaching people who were deaf was written in 1620 by another Spaniard, Juan Pablo Bonet (1579–1629). This was followed by a book in England on the same subject in 1680 by John Bulwer (1614–1684). The first school for the deaf, however, was not founded for another hundred years, in 1767 in Edinburgh, Scotland by Thomas Braidwood (1715–1806). Apparently the enrolment in the school was not large, so Braidwood moved it to London in 1783 to draw more students. Braidwood's assistant, Joseph Watson (1765–1829) later founded the first school in Great Britain for students who were both poor and deaf.

In the new wave of immigrants to North America in the 19th century, three individuals stand out as founding schools for children with disabilities. Samuel Gridley Howe (1801–1876) was the superintendent of the first school for the Blind in the United States: the Perkins School in Watertown, Massachusetts (**http://www.spartacus.schoolnet.co.uk/USAShoweG.htm**). He influenced his friend, Horace Mann (1796–1859), who founded the training of teachers for the "common schools" in Massachusetts (**http://www.cals.ncsu.edu/agexed/aee501/mann.html**). Mann and Howe saw the progress of Laura Bridgeman, a young woman who was deaf and blind, to be a powerful example of their pedagogical ideas. John Hopkins Gallaudet (1787–1851) founded a special education institution that became the first university in North America for students who are deaf. Gallaudet lived next to Alice Cogswell, a deaf woman whose father promoted Gallaudet's work.

Anne Sullivan Macy (1866–1936) had a serious vision disability until her late teens. She attended the Perkins School for the Blind, and then became the beloved teacher of the famous Helen Keller. Anne was recommended for the position by none other than the Canadian forefather of special education, Alexander Graham Bell, who is pictured on the right. Several books have been written about the relationship between Anne and Helen, such as Joseph Lash's (1980) *Helen and Teacher*. For further information and books about these teachers, visit **http://college.hmco.com/education/hunt_marshall/ except_child/4e/students/great_teachers/**.

In Canada, Bell (1847–1922) developed many inventions, some of which were intended to assist his mother—who was profoundly deaf—to communicate. Thus was born the telephone. In 1884, Bell used the term "special education" at a National Education Association meeting in Wisconsin (Winzer, 1998). From this first record, the field of special education was launched as a discipline in Canada.

Until the middle of the 19th century, special education was designed only for those children with complex disabilities: severe deafness and/or blindness or mental retardation. However, as the public school system grew and established itself as a primary provider of education, special education also increased to encompass a larger proportion of children, and segregated classes became a feature of public schools as the 20th century began.

Why did the interest in education for people with disabilities begin with people with sensory impairments? Winzer (1998) explains that in many ways, special education has preceded and indeed enlightened general education. In the middle of the 17th century, philosophers speculated about the nature of knowledge and thought, and how these were associated with the development of language. These epistemological questions propelled deafness into prominence as deaf people were recruited for the scientific and philosophical exploration of the relationship of logic, thought, and reasoning to language.

Winzer notes that William Holder, John Bulwer, and other British members of the Royal Society in London probed the thinking of deaf people in a somewhat misguided attempt to discover the secret of what people were like before language shaped their cognition. One important strand of these studies was to see if alternatives to spoken language were appropriate for learning, thus challenging the prevailing belief that inability to speak was akin to inability to think. The notion that people with prelingual deafness were unable to communicate and hence were "dumb" remained for many years, evolving into its subsequent connotations of lack of intelligence. However, the investigations into the relationship between cognitive and linguistic development, started during this 18th and the following 19th century, gave rise to a gradual shift in understanding about disability and the place of individuals with disabilities in society. With this shift came a range of alternative methods for communication, and the expectation that people with disabilities could develop their own languages, cultures, and skills. This understanding is still evolving, although we now understand that a disability does not define the person, but is one of many individual attributes that contribute to each person's uniqueness.

Defining Student and Teacher Responsibilities

The spectrum of beliefs about the nature of disability gives rise to considerable confusion when professionals and parents plan how best to meet the needs of each student. The very range of differences in these beliefs creates a barrier to communication. At committee meetings, where students may be recommended for special education, some of the people present may speak from a perspective that others fail to understand. For example, the purpose of one particular meeting was to plan the programs and services to be made available to the student. Yet some members of the committee saw the task as using test data to confirm that the student indeed qualified to be labelled as disabled (confirmatory assessment), while others saw their role as developing the instructional conditions that would assist the student to achieve (instructional assessment).

Those who focused on confirming the deficits in the student's profile tended to attribute her lack of achievement to the nature of her disability. For example, she was struggling to learn *because* of dyslexia, or ADD, etc. On the other hand, those who saw the purpose of the meeting as designing the instructional programs and services to address this student's learning profile had little interest in the designation of the student's disability. They were interested in:

- what instruction worked and what didn't in assisting the student to learn

- her strengths as a learner

- the ways in which a teacher would be able to get through to her in the classroom

For example, was she struggling *because* she had missed crucial concepts in earlier grades that needed to be re-taught, or *because* her hearing problems during early development might have resulted in a keener set of visual observation skills that needed to be the focus of her instruction?

This contrast in understanding the mission of the meeting stems in part from deep differences in the assumptions and beliefs that people hold about the nature of disability. At one end is a traditional perspective that emphasizes the pathological nature of the disability. People who hold such beliefs assume that a disability is an internal, biological, or organic attribute or trait of a person. They further accept that, since this trait is a stable and long-term characteristic of the person, it can be reliably measured by standardized tests and/or clinical procedures. Thus, a teacher may pinpoint the disability as the reason why the student is not learning easily: "It's because his scores on IQ tests are pretty low," or "It's because she has a learning disability." Attributions are the reasons that people give as the causes for the events they observe and experience. Differences in people's attributions tell tales of their beliefs about who or what is responsible for events and outcomes, such as the success or failure of a student.

Before examining how attributions are related to larger belief systems, review Research Box 1-4: A Brief Explanation of Attribution Theory.

---

research box 1-4

A Brief Explanation of Attribution Theory

People generate explanations for why events happen in the real world that reflect their own feelings of being able to influence the event. This is called attribution. The theory of attribution holds that there are two factors that influence the attributions people make: whether they feel able to control or influence the event, and whether the event arose from sources that were internal or external to them. Together, these two dimensions give rise to four sets of explanations (see chart below). Teachers' explanations for students' learning are one set of events that teachers explain by attribution. Teachers can use any of four groups of reasons to explain an event, such as a student's learning or failure to learn. By attributing learning outcomes to causes, the teacher "explains" why the event occurred. On the two-by-two dimensional attribution chart, one dimension is whether the effect is caused by factors internal or external to the learner. The other dimension is whether the learner has any control over the effect.

TABLE 1-1: Attribution Theory

	Where is the source?	
Can the person control it?	**Internal**	**External**
Yes	Effort	Support
No	Ability	Luck

So a teacher might attribute a student's success to any of the following: effort ("He really tried hard"), ability ("She is so talented"), support ("I was able to give him the guidance he needed" or "His mom must have helped him!"), or luck ("It must be beginner's luck" or "He lucked out this time!").

There are many more reasons that can be used as attributions, of course, and each of them can have either positive or negative connotations. Believing in the ability of a student to learn and in one's own skill in fostering learning are only two of many possible types of attributions that teachers make about why students learn. The general tendency of a teacher to favour one type of attribution is reflective of his or her implicit theories about learning. It also reflects the teacher's sense of personal efficacy, the sense that he or she is able to have an impact on even the most difficult students. Both the teacher's attribution and sense of efficacy are linked to his or her teaching practices and effort in promoting student achievement. Teachers with a strong sense that they are responsible for how students progress (internal and under one's control), and a strong sense of confidence or efficacy in their ability to promote achievement, give rise to attribution statements that reflect positive views of students' effort and ability and their own support (e.g., "He succeeded because he really worked at it" or "because I found a way to help him understand"). Conversely, teachers with doubts about their efficacy and who hold beliefs about learning being the students' responsibility tend to make external attributions about student failure due to lack of effort or ability (e.g., "She's just lazy"; "He just doesn't get it").

Referring a student to special education can be couched in terms of "confirming" that a student has a deficit, or in terms of what learning, knowledge, and skills the student has acquired and how instruction can best help him or her to learn. A discussion of teacher efficacy, and what teachers can do to promote it, is considered in Interactive Exercise 1-3.

Pathognomonic and interventionist perspectives

The term **pathognomonic** is derived from the Greek "pathos" or suffering, and "gnomon" or naming; hence, "naming the pathology." By attributing the disability to the internal state of a student, a teacher is using a pathognomonic explanation that absolves him or her of the responsibility for the learning of that student (e.g., "Students with disabilities like his/hers don't belong in my class"; "I'm not trained to teach kids with these kinds of difficulties"). To be fair, these beliefs are not necessarily a result of negative attitudes that have been carefully formulated against people with disabilities. The beliefs are more like a set of unexplored assumptions than a theory that consists of carefully thought-through propositions. As a result, the term "personal theory" is used to indicate this set of working assumptions used by people in everyday practices, and the term pathognomonic is used to describe this personal theory or set of beliefs that emphasizes the internal attributes of a person as an explanation for how they learn and behave.

Pathognomonic personal beliefs arise in part because teachers do not feel trained or competent to address the learning needs of students with disabilities and learning difficulties. Fear leads to attributions that leave responsibility with the other; that is, disability or underachievement is something that resides in the student, and for which the teacher therefore cannot be responsible.

Such a pathognomonic perspective also seems to be related to a similar set of beliefs or assumptions about the nature of ability and intelligence. That is, the personal theory might hold that ability is an internal and stable trait or characteristic of an individual that is not very responsive to change. As a result, it is largely immune to influences from the learning environment. Again, teachers who carry such a belief claim to have, by implication, little or no responsibility for a student's academic outcomes, since the problem resides in the student and is therefore beyond their realm of influence.

An example of pathognomonic thinking might be as follows:

Mrs. Smart, a secondary English teacher, speaks to the head of the Student Services unit, Mr. Brooks: "Four of my students in the grade 11 Applied English program are receiving extra help in your unit. They claim they already know the material that I am currently teaching to that class. That's impossible. They aren't as smart as the other students, yet they think they know as much as the others. I think you should take a look at how your remedial teaching is being conducted, because those students shouldn't be able to keep up with mine since they have such deficits."

On the other end of the spectrum of beliefs is a differing perspective about both disability and ability. These are termed **interventionist** beliefs because people who express them also believe that they are responsible for intervening on behalf of students with disabilities. People who hold interventionist beliefs see disability as created in part by social conditions. They hold that society creates barriers that prevent people who are outside the mainstream of society from enjoying society's privileges. This view emphasizes the social factors that discriminate between subgroups in society by setting conditions that prohibit some of them from participating. By extension, society is therefore responsible for creating the discrimination that gives rise to the labelling of people with disabilities. As a result, the larger society is also responsible for re-establishing equity for everyone by removing these socially created barriers that limit access for people with disabilities.

An example of interventionist thinking might be:

Mrs. Smart, a secondary English teacher, speaks to the head of the Student Services unit, Mr. Brooks: "Four of my students in the grade 11 Applied English program are receiving extra help in your unit. I'd really like to know what they are being taught so that I can reinforce those skills when they are with me. You know, this could be a two-way street. I would like to let their resource teacher know what I am teaching, because it would make sense if the extra help that these students are getting with her could prepare them to tackle the grade 11 English curriculum when they are in the regular stream with me."

The impact of the interventionist perspective is evident when considering the adaptations made in our environment, such as the construction of wheelchair ramps, accessible washrooms, and door opening devices to create access to public buildings. In addition, visual fire alarms allow people with hearing impairments to respond, and tactile strips along the edges of subway platforms can be felt by people with visual impairments. These adaptations are the result of the work of people who view access for everyone as a social rather than an individual responsibility.

Recent research suggests that teachers and other educators who hold an interventionist perspective or personal theory have often themselves experienced disability first hand, with a sibling or parent or as a result of working closely with people with disabilities. Such people do not express fear of disabilities, even though they may be apprehensive about their skills to interact with people with different disabilities. But they do believe they have a responsibility to advocate for people with disabilities, and that they are capable of making a difference in the daily lives of such people.

Refer to Interactive Exercise 1-2 on the following page to compose your own definition of disability.

interactive exercise

1-2

Disability

Compose a short definition of the term "disability."

You may want to include some of the following:

- Fixed? or responsive to factors of environment?
- An attribute of a person? of how we communicate? of how we interact?
- Barriers to access created for the convenience of the mainstream society?
- A pathology, a part of human variation, an alternative culture?
- Where and with whom does responsibility lie?

When extending the different notions of disability to that of ability, the same debate exists between those who hold a "nurture" compared to a "nature" view of intellect. For example, there continues to be a controversial debate about the nature of intelligence as measured by IQ tests. At its root, the proponents of a **nativist** view of ability—the view that intellectual capability is largely genetically predetermined and an internal, stable characteristic—face off against those who hold to a view that IQ scores are heavily influenced by the opportunity to learn that is provided to each individual through his or her environment. In a strict nativist view, the genetic potential of an individual is provided at birth and the environment has only a limited effect on how that potential plays out during development. People who hold the **nurturist** view consider environmental factors such as nutrition, lack of stimulation, economic deprivation, and emotional traumas to be important in accelerating or inhibiting the development of intellectual potential.

Of course, as with most theories, the eventual explanation may rest between these extremes; the potential to learn that is present at birth needs to be activated by environmental triggers during development to fully develop. Yet universally, people carry assumptions about the nature of ability and disability that have not always been thought through in a

logical way. For example, the wide use of epithets such as "retard," "idiot," and "stupid" imply there is a nativistic hopelessness to the state of a human being. Intelligence testing, too, has given rise to societal norms about ability and lack of it, centred around a limited set of intellectual traits associated with verbal ability and reasoning skills, and that exclude skills such as creativity, physical prowess, social skills, motivation, maturity, and emotional stability. Yet such skills are often essential for success in adult life.

A framework for understanding difference

The distinction between different beliefs and assumptions about the nature of disability, and by extension, ability, is important in these modules. It underpins differences in the attributions that teachers and parents make about children's learning. When working with a student who makes progress, teachers are willing to take the credit—the teaching was responsible. Conversely, when a student struggles and teachers seem unable to find a way to assist him or her to learn, they may blame the student for lacking effort or ability. Even more important, beliefs seem to have a powerful influence on the instructional practices that teachers select.

learning
objective

1-4

The distinction between pathognomonic and interventionist beliefs is not a simple one, however. People do not subscribe exclusively to one or another point of view. They tend to fluctuate between explanations of student achievement based on pathology-based and environmentally influenced factors, sometimes as a result of how confident they feel about being able to change a student's learning, or how successful they have been in assisting the student to achieve. There are two effects at work here: **personal efficacy** and **teacher efficacy**. They are complex characteristics that can influence the personal theories and beliefs teachers hold. Personal efficacy, or the extent to which teachers are confident in their ability to make a difference in the learning of their students, has frequently been linked to good teaching practices. Teacher efficacy is a related effect; it is the beliefs teachers hold about the influence that their teaching can have, despite the influence of student, family, and community characteristics.

Read Interactive Exercise 1-3: Rate Your Personal and Teacher Efficacy for a review of these concepts, and complete an activity that allows you to rate your own levels of personal and teaching efficacy.

interactive
exercise

1-3

Rate Your Personal and Teacher Efficacy

Excerpted from: DiBella-McCarthy, H., McDaniel, E.A., & Miller, R. (1995). How efficacious are you? *TEACHING Exceptional Children*, 27(3), 68–72.

Self Efficacy Quiz

Consider each statement below and indicate the extent to which you agree or disagree with it. In the box next to the statement, please write the number that best indicates your opinion or your self perception. There are five possible ratings:

(1) Strongly disagree
(2) Disagree
(3) Neutral
(4) Agree
(5) Strongly agree

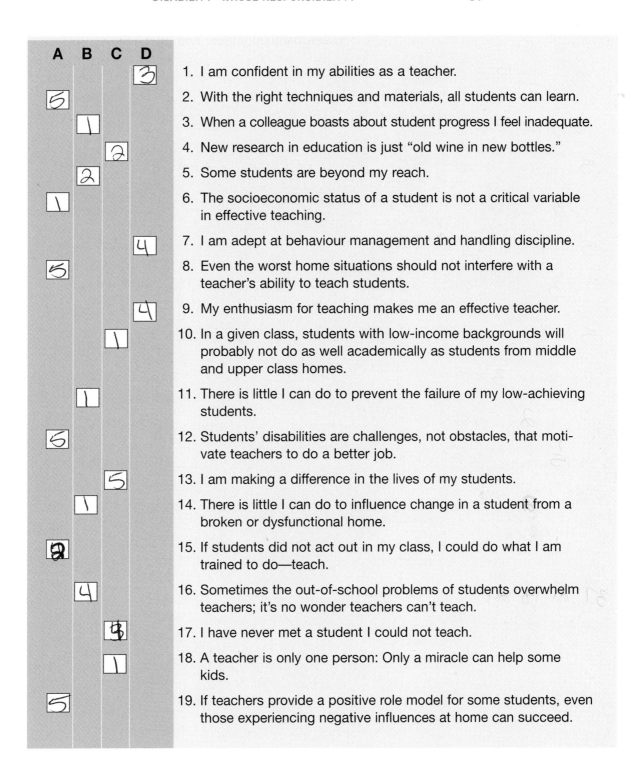

A	B	C	D
			3

1. I am confident in my abilities as a teacher.

A	B	C	D
5			

2. With the right techniques and materials, all students can learn.

A	B	C	D
	1		

3. When a colleague boasts about student progress I feel inadequate.

A	B	C	D
		2	

4. New research in education is just "old wine in new bottles."

A	B	C	D
	2		

5. Some students are beyond my reach.

A	B	C	D
1			

6. The socioeconomic status of a student is not a critical variable in effective teaching.

A	B	C	D
			4

7. I am adept at behaviour management and handling discipline.

A	B	C	D
5			

8. Even the worst home situations should not interfere with a teacher's ability to teach students.

A	B	C	D
			4

9. My enthusiasm for teaching makes me an effective teacher.

A	B	C	D
		1	

10. In a given class, students with low-income backgrounds will probably not do as well academically as students from middle and upper class homes.

A	B	C	D
	1		

11. There is little I can do to prevent the failure of my low-achieving students.

A	B	C	D
5			

12. Students' disabilities are challenges, not obstacles, that motivate teachers to do a better job.

A	B	C	D
		5	

13. I am making a difference in the lives of my students.

A	B	C	D
	1		

14. There is little I can do to influence change in a student from a broken or dysfunctional home.

A	B	C	D
2			

15. If students did not act out in my class, I could do what I am trained to do—teach.

A	B	C	D
	4		

16. Sometimes the out-of-school problems of students overwhelm teachers; it's no wonder teachers can't teach.

A	B	C	D
		4	

17. I have never met a student I could not teach.

A	B	C	D
		1	

18. A teacher is only one person: Only a miracle can help some kids.

A	B	C	D
5			

19. If teachers provide a positive role model for some students, even those experiencing negative influences at home can succeed.

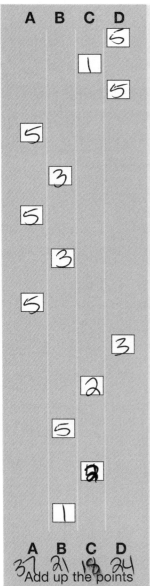

A	B	C	D	
			5	20. My students' progress is a reflection of my teaching.
		1		21. Teachers have little effect on student motivation to learn.
			5	22. My students know that I care about them, and they try hard to meet my expectations.
5				23. Effective teachers are powerful influences in the lives of their students.
	3			24. Most of my colleagues seem to be more innovative and resourceful than I am.
5				25. Powerful teaching can overcome many negative home environmental factors.
	3			26. There is little I can do to help a student who just doesn't care about learning.
5				27. Good teachers continually search for new ideas from research and inservice training to enhance teaching.
			3	28. I am confident in my subject matter and can answer students' questions in depth.
		2		29. A teacher's influence on student achievement is limited compared to the influence of the home environment.
	5			30. In some subjects, I feel I am just a page or two ahead of my students.
		2		31. Certain disabilities of my students interfere with my ability to teach them.
		1		32. When my students fail to make the expected progress, I get discouraged and begin to doubt my skills as a teacher.

A B C D
37 21 18 24
Add up the points
in each column.

Interpreting your scores:

Teaching efficacy: Expecting that teaching will have an impact on student learning despite ability and family background.

Personal efficacy: Belief in one's teaching capabilities and confidence that one can get through to students

Column A: (High teaching efficacy). If you scored 25 or more, you have a healthy sense of teaching efficacy. You believe in your students and their ability to learn. You look for evidence in their performance that enhances your belief.

Column B: (Low personal efficacy). If you scored 20 or more, you are having self doubts about your competence as a teacher. You lack confidence in being able to overcome student difficulties or home or community disadvantages.

Column C: (Low teaching efficacy). If you scored 20 or more, you probably believe that your ability to affect change in your students is limited by external factors, These factors may decrease your motivation to look for effective teaching techniques for certain students. If your students achieve success, you may attribute it to something other than your teaching.

Column D: (High personal efficacy). If you scored 25 or more, you feel confident in your teaching and in your ability to make a difference with your students. You put forth effort to overcome negative, home, community and student factors because you feel that you make a difference in the lives of your students.

The students in a university class on special education in the teacher preparation program took up the issue of how to maintain interventionist beliefs in the face of evidence or opinions in the field that this is not realistic. How does someone maintain a belief in his or her own **efficacy** in the face of others' disbelief? Read Case Study 1-2: Beliefs in Your Role as a Teacher for a synopsis of this discussion.

case study
1-2

Beliefs in Your Role as a Teacher: Idealistic or Possible?

In a university class on special education in the teacher preparation program, Carrie ventured:

"You said that the majority of us—the research says at least 50% of us—will vacillate between pathognomonic and interventionist beliefs. In our early years as teachers, this will be even higher. I want to ask you and the rest of the class: How do you keep your faith in yourself as a teacher when others don't support you? For example, in my teaching placement, a teacher in the staff room told me that thinking I could make a difference to the learning of one student with a disability was 'idealistic—straight out of the Ivory Tower.' She said that reality in schools wasn't like the textbooks. There are too many kids with too many problems and too much history for teachers to be able to tackle them."

Other students concurred—they too had experienced comments about the idealism of teacher preparation and how it differs from the reality of schools and classrooms. While such comments had been made by a very few teachers, they were enough to cause the young trainees to doubt their aspirations. The class discussed keeping faith with yourself (see Interactive Exercise 1-3 in this Module for a self-rating scale of teaching efficacy). They discussed the "staff room Mafia": the small minority of nay-sayers who can leave teachers doubting themselves. Inevitably, in a profession as large and complex as teaching, there will be differences of perspective.

The class talked about Serena, Emma, Keith, Maria, Keiko, Ben, and Jill and other teachers who will be encountered in this series. These are real teachers; people whom the author has met, observed, and documented, who have much to give to students, to teachers in training, and to novice teachers. These people are the true foundation of these modules, and it is their beliefs, knowledge, and practices that have inspired such notions as the difference between pathognomonic and interventionist beliefs, the practices that make inclusion possible, and how to pursue a vision of one's role that guides one's development as a teacher.

Here are some of the ways to maintain or repair teacher- and self-efficacy when they seem to be flagging:

1. Maintain a record of student assessments. Collect data on how students progress toward instructional goals. Let the students be part of this monitoring so they can show their achievements to you and their classmates. Review it frequently to remind you of the gains you are fostering.

2. Ask for and respond to student feedback. By adjusting your teaching to student needs and performance, you can provide feedback to students about their progress, and they in turn can provide you with explicit examples of their growth.

3. Foster a friendship with a colleague whom you admire. Develop a mentor relationship with people who will guide you when you feel defeated or stuck.

4. Establish realistic expectations for yourself. Focus on your areas of strength and celebrate your successes. Identify one or two professional learning priorities and set aside the time to pursue them.

5. Rate yourself on the teaching checklists in Module 2. Keep notes of the gains you are making.

6. Seek support from family and friends. Support systems and a life outside school help to keep the daily challenges that occur in school in perspective.

Personal theories, beliefs, and instructional practices

Teachers (and perhaps everybody) carry personal theories and assumptions that give rise to different attributions about their own and others' learning—indeed, about many things they experience. Differences in these beliefs and assumptions influence the decisions they make and how they therefore respond. Read and reflect upon Research Box 1-5 that contains a summary of a research study conducted in Canadian classrooms in the mid 1990s by Jordan, Lindsay, & Stanovich (1997).

This study demonstrates how differences in teachers' personal theories about disability are linked to how responsible they see themselves for working with students who are under-achieving, how much instructional time they generate, and how they use it.

research box	How Teacher Beliefs
1-5	**May Influence their Teaching**

In nine grade 3 classrooms visited in the early 1990s, a striking example of the results of tradeoffs of teachers' managerial, organizational, and instructional time was evident (Jordan, Lindsay, & Stanovich, 1997; Jordan & Stanovich, 2001). The researchers had intended to record the teachers' talk with their students who were designated as at-risk and exceptional, so they asked the teachers to wear a radio-frequency mini-microphone which recorded their talk to one channel of a dual-channel tape-recorder located in the corner of the classroom. On the other channel of the tape recorder, the researchers made field notes: with whom the teacher was talking, the activity in which they were engaged. The researchers watched the teachers conduct short expository language arts or mathematics lessons with the whole class, followed by individual seatwork tasks designed to reinforce the lesson concepts. They later analyzed the number, length, and complexity of those teacher–student interactions. They also asked the students to complete the Piers-Harris Self Concept Scale (Piers Harris, 1984) as an indication of the outcome that teachers' different styles of interaction might have on the students themselves.

In six classes, to greater or lesser degrees, teachers spent a good deal of their lesson time talking to students about how to set up their tasks, where to find resources, and what to do. They were frequently interrupted by students who wanted to have directions repeated or details checked. There was a sense of organizational downtime while everyone figured out what materials they needed and how to start. In the remaining three classes, the teacher talk was usually about academic content. Overall, almost twice as much time was used for instruction. Teachers seemed to have the time to linger with individual and groups of two or three students, conducting interactive question-and-answer sessions. These interactions elaborated students' thinking about the concepts and skills of the lesson, and explored misunderstandings. Teachers lingered to develop ideas, correct misconceptions, and stimulate higher-order thinking such as predicting, evaluating, and estimating. The researchers termed this "cognitive extension" and recorded it at two levels: **partial cognitive extension**, with short teacher–student interactions, and **full extension**, with lengthy dialogue between the teacher and student.

When the researchers analyzed the transcripts of the teacher–student interaction during the seatwork segment of each class, they discovered that the three high-academic-talk teachers spent almost 50% more time in dialogues with individual students and small groups than in the other classrooms. Further, during this time, they interacted with their low-achieving at-risk and exceptional students for approximately twice as long as with their other students. The researchers wondered at first whether this confirmed the often-heard claim that such teachers give disproportionate amounts of their time to low-achieving students at the expense of their other students. But when they compared the interactions in these three classes between teachers and students who were not low-achieving, with that of the other six low interaction classes, the researchers found an interesting pattern. In the low-interaction classes, the teacher talk to the low-achieving students was generally sparse and largely on non-academic topics such as clarifying routines or dealing with misbehaviours. The teacher talk to the other students was, however, also seldom related to the lesson content, and while the interactions tended to be longer with more interchanges, the total length and complexity of academic talk was less than that in the three comparison classrooms.

In other words, in six low teacher–student interaction classes, the low-achieving students received the least instructional assistance, while those in the three high-interaction classrooms received the most. But the typically achieving students in the six low-interaction rooms were still receiving less academic talk and instructional interactions with their teacher than the typically achieving students in the three high-interaction classes. It was not the case that the number or severity of the needs of low-achieving students was diverting the teacher from instructing the rest of the class. Rather, some teachers chose largely to ignore the low achieving students, but then tended to take up large chunks of their instructional time with managing and organizing rather than with lesson-related or academic talk. When they were able to teach, they only had time for brief questions or encouragement about a student's work, or transmissive statements that told a student what to correct. The three teachers who were able to provide a large amount of instructional talk to their low-achieving students also found more academic talk time overall, working with both low and typically achieving students in extended dialogues that prompted student responses, connected ideas, and chal-

lenged students to think about their seatwork. The most obvious difference between the two groups was that the three high-interacting teachers had "all the time in the world" to concentrate on individual student performance, to prompt and coach, correct and amplify students' understanding. Teachers in the six other classrooms had placed themselves at the centre of all activity and were therefore constantly in demand to deal with student behaviour and needs.

The results of this study show the importance of considering adaptive instruction at the level of teacher–student interaction. Englert, Tarrant, and Mariage (1992) claim that effective teachers are able to maximize their instructional time by minimizing time spent on organizational and managerial tasks. They do so by establishing well-understood routines and expectations for behaviour and achievement. Instructional time is then used, in part, to address the learning needs of the class and of individuals and small groups by calibrating instruction to current levels of students' understanding through questioning and probing each student's knowledge. In this study, teachers demonstrated such characteristics of effective instruction. Indeed every teacher demonstrated interactions that extended student thinking. No teacher could be characterized as using an exclusively transmissive style of teaching. What was remarkable was the difference in the extent to which they were able to find the time to engage in cognitively extending interactions.

Surprisingly, there were differences between these two groups of teachers in their personal theories and beliefs about teaching and learning. The three teachers with high proportions of instructional time that was used to engage students in high level thinking also had the highest Interventionist scores on a measure of pathognomic–interventionist beliefs. The six teachers with more pathognomonic scores tended to ignore their low-achieving students and to spend comparatively little time engaging their typically achieving students in learning.

The results of this study are available on the next page in Table 1-2.

TABLE 1-2: Pathognomonic–interventionist scores of teacher groups, and frequency and type of interaction by student groups

Group	N	Mean PATH/INT score	Student Group	Non-academic Interact	Number of Academic Interactions	Comprehension Monitoring[1]	Partial Extensions[2]	Full Extensions[3]
PATH	3	2.34	EX/AR[4]	50	8	6	1	1
			TA[5]	23	6	0	4	2
MID	3	3.53	EX/AR	55	15	2	11	2
			TA	25	7	2	4	2
INT	3	4.39	EX/AR	13	31	1	3	26
			TA	17	14	1	0	13

[1] Comprehension monitoring—the teacher monitors the student's work but does not interact beyond checking it as correct or wrong

[2] Partial cognitive extensions—the teacher interacts briefly with the student about the student's work, but does not push the student to develop his/her thinking

[3] Full cognitive extension—the teacher engages the student in a discussion about the student's work, and pushes the student to extend his/her thinking

[4] Exceptional and at-risk students

[5] Typically achieving students

This study was later extended by linking the differences in teachers' beliefs about their roles and responsibilities, and the amount and use of instructional time, to measures of students' academic self concept (Jordan & Stanovich, 2001). The findings indicated that differences in teachers' styles of using instructional time and their beliefs about disability affected how students saw themselves as competent learners. Overall, typically achieving students reported higher self-concept scores than those designated exceptional and at-risk. This finding is similar to previously reported differences (Chapman, 1988; Gresham, 1984, 1986; Hattie, 1992; Stanovich, Jordan, & Perot, 1998; Swanson & Malone, 1992). However, the more provocative finding was that, in the classrooms of the teachers expressing pathognomonic beliefs, the self-concept Total Scale scores of both groups of students were significantly lower than those of students in the class of interventionist teachers. Even students who were not disabled in the classes of the teachers with pathognomonic beliefs felt less sure about themselves than the students who were exceptional and low achieving in the classrooms of the teachers expressing interventionist beliefs.

There seems to be considerable evidence that teachers make a difference not only to how students learn (Blackorby, 2003; Rice, 2003; Wayne & Youngs, 2003; Wilson, Floden, Ferrini-Mundy, 2001) but also to how students feel about their ability to learn (Jordan & Stanovich, 2001). Furthermore, there is mounting evidence that teachers' beliefs as well as their practices have a significant impact on student achievement (Ashton & Webb, 1986; Rosenholtz, 1989; Muijs & Reynolds, 2002). Recent work shows how characteristics of special education teachers also impact the learning of students with special needs (Nougaret, Scruggs, & Mastropieri, 2005). Only a few years ago, people believed that the five hours students spend in the classroom could have hardly any effect on the students' achievement compared to influences from the other 19 hours of their day. Researchers have known for some time that this is not the case (Rosenshine & Stevens, 1986; Bickel & Bickel, 1990).

One factor that therefore seems to make a big difference to students' success is the subtle communication of a teacher's beliefs about the student's potential to be successful, which in turn stems from the teacher's underlying personal theories and assumptions about the fixed or malleable nature of ability and disability. This may be communicated through the teacher's instructional practices, although there is only speculation about how this occurs. But students do get a sense of how important their learning is to their teachers, how high the expectations are set that the student will achieve, and how much personal responsibility the teacher takes to ensure that the student will succeed.

Concepts of Disability

Labelling

learning
objective

1-5

A debate has existed for years (Hobbs, 1976; Weisel & Tur-Kaspa, 2002) about the benefits or dangers of labelling people's disabilities. On the one hand, designating people as belonging to one or another group with a given label allows those people to receive the benefits available to the group (e.g., being unemployed can make someone eligible for employment insurance payments). Being designated as having a disability might allow someone to have special arrangements for taking examinations, such as extra time to complete it, or a scribe to write to his or her dictation.

There are many documented accounts of how people who had suffered from a disability were relieved when it was finally correctly diagnosed, since they had suffered from self-doubt, prejudice, and feelings of helplessness before they were finally able to understand their own condition and take charge of coping with it. Jon Van Loon in the opening vignette in Module 2 is an example of this. Another example is Liane Holliday Willey's book *Pretending to Be Normal* (1999), the autobiography of a woman who learned only in adulthood that she had Asperger Syndrome. This disability is related to autism spectrum disorder, and occurs in people with high verbal skills. This discovery served to relieve many painful challenges in her life, and enabled her to assist her daughter to avoid similar challenges.

On the other hand, labelling someone tends to have the effect of the label taking over the entire person. Sarason and Doris (1979) noted that when resources and benefits are dispensed based on people's eligibility for membership in a group, the focus becomes "a search for pathology" in that person in order to qualify them to draw upon the resources intended for the group. As Sarason and Doris wrote about the designation of someone as "mentally retarded," labels allow people to focus on deficits as if they were "it," and "when 'it' becomes focal, all else fades into the background." In this respect, labelling someone can lead to pathognomonic attributions on the part of others, and to assumptions about the individual that are overwhelming. It is interesting that George
Bernard Shaw took up this theme in *The Doctor's Dilemma*, his play about the pretensions of a doctor who viewed his patients from the perspective of their medical characteristics alone. A scene from the play is shown here.

A further effect is that the responsibility for finding the evidence that a person meets the eligibility criteria shifts to that individual and his or her family, and away from the broader society. For example, in Ontario between 1997 and 2005, the provincial government funded several millions of dollars

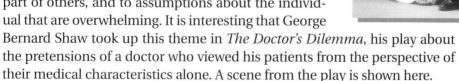

to school boards who could prove they had students who required intensive supports for special education programs and services. The Intensive Support Amounts (ISA) were allocated on a case-by-case basis. Responsibility fell upon the school system for collecting the educational and psycho-educational evidence to show that each student merited the disability label that made them eligible for the funding. Often this required that the school system pass on to the child's family the responsibility for securing medical assessments, records, and evidence of pathology required to support the funding application. The parent organizations for students with curriculum-related disabilities, with assistance from cash-strapped school boards, were thus motivated to maximize resources for their children, despite the overriding focus on verifying pathological characteristics. Parents of students with complex disabilities, however, sometimes were shocked by the requirement to "prove" that their children needed intensive support. Their preference would be to focus on what would create opportunities for their children to develop. This funding system is therefore an example of a policy based on categorical, and therefore pathognomonic, assumptions about the students.

Categorical labels may not in and of themselves be bad; how these labels are used can have negative effects on the students whom they are intended to assist. Labels can create a "slippery slope" in school systems. Special education is delivered only to students who have been designated as belonging in one of the disability categories because they have passed the pathology criteria for that category. As a result, teachers and others in the school system focus on finding the evidence to confirm that the student meets those pathology criteria in order to get help for the student. The message gets around that only students who qualify can receive specialized help. Finding eligible students then takes precedence over taking the time to find out whether the student can be accommodated within the available resources of the regular classroom. The focus shifts from early prevention of possible difficulties to confirming the severity of difficulties to qualify for resources. The result is a press to segregate instead of to integrate such students.

In some schools where categorical special education is delivered, teachers nominate new students for special education as early as the previous school year so as not to have their students miss out when the special education resources run dry. The mindset for teaching staff is to jockey to have their students removed for special education; if teachers succeed in getting the lowest performing student removed from their class and sent for special education, they will tend to nominate the next lowest for removal, and so on, while the door to special education is still open.

Another message implicit in this kind of service delivery system is that homogeneous classes are better, and therefore the teacher's job is to reduce the diversity of students in them. For an alternative way of identifying those who need specialized services, see the **three tier intervention system** in the next section on developmental disability.

Research Box 1-6 considers studies that have attempted to measure the relative effective of placement on student achievement. Attempting to find definitive evidence about the effects of placement is no easy matter, and may even be a lost cause. To find out why, review Research Box 1-6: The Effectiveness of Inclusion.

research
box

1-6

The Effectiveness of Inclusion

The debate about whether students with disabilities should be educated alongside their same-aged peers without disabilities in regular classrooms is complex and has many facets. One way to address the question might be to measure the relative effectiveness of students' achievement following placement in a regular classroom compared to following placement in a withdrawal (pull out) or segregated (contained) setting. On the face of it, this is a simple research question. However, conducting such a study is fraught with problems.

Before we examine why, think about how such a study might be conducted.
Assume you have unlimited resources.

- What would you need to do?

- What are the difficulties you would face in designing such a study?

Consider a study with the characteristics of a quantitative, quasi-experimental design. It would take a large number of students with disabilities and assign them randomly to each of the settings to be compared: the regular classroom, a resource or withdrawal setting, a contained class, and perhaps another setting such as "reverse integration" where non-disabled students are brought into the special education class for periods of the school day. Outcome measures would be required, perhaps in the form of gains in achievement, social skills, behaviours, and self-esteem. These would be collected at the beginning of the study and again at the end. In the intervening time, the amount of instruction would be held relatively constant for all groups.

Such a study has a number of pitfalls that make its results suspect and its conclusions questionable.

At the practical level:

Because students with disabilities have such varying ranges of educational strengths and needs, it isn't possible to group them to compare the relative influence of settings on outcomes. To group students with disabilities would be to make the unwarranted assumption that they were similar. As we have seen, this would not be justified.

At the pedagogical level:

The effectiveness of a student's placement has a great deal to do with the characteristics of the teaching in a given placement. Schools differ considerably on the prevailing understanding of the school community or school norm. In schools with an inclusionary norm, the principal's belief that students should be included has a dramatic effect on how teachers teach (Stanovich & Jordan, 1998). Collectively, the teaching staff at these schools see their roles and responsibilities as working with students with disabilities. They carry similar expectations about how they work together and supply support and expertise to one another to include all students.

Teachers in schools with principals who do not make inclusion a priority and who subscribe to a more traditional delivery model for special education spend less time with students with disabilities and believe that the responsibility for their education rests with the staff trained in special education. Stanovich and Jordan (1998) measured the teaching skills of teachers through extensive observation in schools both with and without an inclusive norm. In a similar study (Jordan & Stanovich, 2001), they also watched the instruction that students at risk of failure and students formally designated as exceptional individually received. Teachers who worked in schools where there was a strong inclusionary school norm provided more and better instruction and at a higher level of student engagement than did teachers in schools without this understanding or norm. The superior instruction was exhibited with students both with and without disabilities.

At the ethical level:

In a well-designed experimental study, students with disabilities are randomly assigned to groups; in this case, to a placement in a regular classroom, a resource withdrawal, or a segregated class setting. In reality, this cannot be done. Not only do the real life dynamics of families, students, and schools play a part in where and how students are placed, but there would be major ethical problems with placing students randomly without taking into account their needs and the resources available locally.

At the moral level:

Many proponents of inclusion for people with disabilities would say that the whole notion of comparing placement effectiveness is flawed. They might argue that inclusion is not about placement but about removing the barriers that society creates for people with disabilities to participate. Hence it is a social problem, not one of location. Testing the relative effects of a placement therefore misses the main point in the debate about human rights.

Researchers have attempted to address the question of the efficacy of inclusion in ways other than through empirical research. There are many qualitative analyses, including case studies of effective teachers in both the special education setting (Stough & Palmer, 2003; Nougaret, Scruggs, & Mastropieri, 2005), and in general education (Jordan, Lindsay, & Stanovich; 1996; Jordan & Stanovich, 2000). There are also meta-analyses that attempt to draw together the findings of many empirical studies to identify statistically significant trends in the collective results (Swanson & Hoskyn, 1999). Although these meta-analyses will be examined in subsequent modules, the findings on the

efficacy of alternative placements can be summarized: the jury is still out. Researchers have more recently turned their attention to studies that look at the impact of teaching quality on student outcomes (Rice, 2003; Wayne & Youngs, 2003) to capture what effective literacy and mathematics teachers do with students both with and without learning difficulties (Foorman & Schatschneider, 2003; Haager, Gersten, Baker, & Graves, 2003; Pressley et al., 2001; Reynolds & Muis, 2003; Roehrig et al., 2003).

Dyson, Farrell, Gallannaugh, Hutcheson, and Polat, (2004), and Dyson, Polat, and Gallannaugh (2005), writing from the perspective of researchers in Britain, note that despite the multitude of studies conducted, the knowledge base about the effectiveness of placements is not robust. They identified 14,000 reports that addressed the question of the effectiveness of school-level actions that promoted student participation. Of these, only 41 addressed issues of inclusion, and of the 41 studies, only 6 were deemed to be highly relevant and trustworthy in terms of their research and reporting standards.

Dyson, et al. (2005) summarize these six studies.

"The findings suggest that inclusive schools are, in reality, somewhat different from the stereotype that emerges from the bulk of the research literature. They are, for instance, much less unequivocally committed to explicit principles of inclusion, much less consensual in their approach and much more willing to group pupils on a pragmatic basis than the literature sometimes suggests. It may therefore to be helpful to think of inclusive schools as operating in the context of an 'ecology of inclusion' within which schools seek to maintain a fragile balance between competing demands and imperatives—within which any commitment to inclusive values is only one factor amongst many."

Categorical, Non-categorical, and Cross-categorical Approaches

learning objective

1-6

Providing educational resources on the basis of the numbers of students allocated to specific categories is termed a categorical approach. Categorical approaches to delivering special education depend on identifying students as belonging to a category, grouping students by a categorical label, and delivering instruction to the groups. Often, these groupings have been associated with **withdrawal** or "**pull-out**" programs such as instruction in a special education resource room, or in segregated special education classrooms.

The alternatives, which focus on the learning characteristics and needs of students and the allocation of resources to address them, are termed **non-categorical** and **cross-categorical**. Non-categorical approaches to delivering appropriate instruction focus on the specific learning needs of each student, and on providing the instruction to meet these needs. These approaches are often associated with differentiated instruction in regular classroom settings, sometimes with additional resource people to support the classroom teacher. Cross-categorical approaches also focus on the specific learning characteristics of students, but students with similar learning needs may be grouped for instruction for some activities on a temporary or short-term basis. A special education teacher may then work with the group on these learning needs. This might take place in the classroom as a small group activity, or in a withdrawal setting such as a resource room.

In contrast to the categorical approach, the message to school staffs who subscribe to a non- or cross-categorical model of delivery of resources tends to be to look for the learning strengths and needs of students so that resources can be supplied that will support the teacher's job of providing effective instruction. Schools using a non-categorical approach deliver special education on the basis of individual learning needs without reference to a student's category of disability. This is frequently the case in independently funded (private) schools. Funding in a non-categorical school system would be given for the programs and personnel that support regular classroom teachers delivering services to students, based not on the number of students who qualify but on the priorities for program delivery set by the teachers, school, and board. This is hard for funding agencies such as governments to monitor and regulate, however, and leaves publicly-funded school boards to compete for and manage their revenues for special education with less accountability than in a categorical model.

As seen in Research Box 1-2: A Recent History of the Development of Inclusive Special Education in Canada, the public, through its prevailing government, sometimes requires that school boards account for how their revenues are spent. This has in part shaped special education policy both at home and abroad. In schools using a cross-categorical approach, the learning objectives and instructional levels of students form the basis for instructional groupings. Information from assessments of categorical features, as well as functional and instructional levels, determines the starting point for instructional delivery. Teachers then provide instruction to students with learning difficulties on the basis of their learning characteristics and instructional needs rather than on the basis of their categorical designation. Some ways in which students can be assigned to groups both within and outside the regular classroom are explored in Module 3.

While the cross-categorical approach to service delivery is more complex than the categorical one, it lends itself better to an interventionist perspective about teachers' roles and responsibilities. As examined previously, there is some evidence that teachers who hold interventionist perspectives also conduct instruction in ways that benefit more students. It is easy to allocate students to categories and then prescribe solutions for the entire group. It is far harder to consider each student's needs individually, to examine individual profiles of strengths and needs, identify which resources will assist them to succeed, and then make the case for receiving those resources and for using them effectively. However, this process—assess needs, intervene with programs and services, assess outcomes, and plan next steps—is precisely the **instructional cycle** that effective teachers use all the time with all their students in their everyday teaching.

Working with students with disabilities and learning difficulties is in many ways no different from working with other students. It requires a resource base, materials, and supports that extend beyond grade level norms, and knowledge that is wider than grade level curriculum. It also requires a high degree of collaboration with other personnel who can deliver instructional and support services, and some early and ongoing curriculum-linked assessment of each student's learning needs and potential to learn. Every class has students who achieve below and beyond the grade limits. Diversity, not homogeneity, is the norm in classrooms, and indeed, diversity in the modern classroom, as argued in the introduction to this module, is here to stay. Since all students are part of a classroom teacher's responsibility, modern teachers can expect to work with students with wide ranges of skills and backgrounds.

Service Delivery Alternatives

School boards and the schools in them have a great deal of latitude about how they offer services to students with disabilities. These alternative models of delivery, or **service delivery models**, are often dictated by how the school system allocates money and resources to schools, and are also influenced by the preferences of the leaders of the school and by the prevailing norm or collective understanding of the staff of a school, as seen in Research Box 1-6.

Many school boards subscribe to a range of settings for students with disabilities. This is known as the "Cascade Model" of service delivery, because it contains a pyramid of alternative placements ranging from highly segregated to fully included in the regular setting. The cascade model includes delivering special education:

- in a specialized residential setting in which students both live and go to school, including hospitals in which students receive education while undergoing treatment, developmental daycare facilities, and youth

detention centres that may be managed by a social services agency, and in which the school board supplies the teacher

- in a **special education class**, also called a **segregated or contained class**, usually located in either a special school designated for students with specific disabilities, such as Schools for the Deaf or the Blind, or in a community school

- through a **resource room** to which students with learning difficulties are withdrawn for extra help, which is perhaps the most popular; students are listed on the class register of a regular class or grade and are withdrawn from the class or grade for specific subjects or for designated periods to receive help from a resource teacher in a separate room

- in the regular classroom, either with or without extra help from a special education teacher, a Teaching Assistant or E.A., or other specialized support

There are several variants of these models. Special education may be offered in a special education class for a part of the school day, and in regular classes for the remainder of the day. Sometimes, students without disabilities join students with disabilities in special education classes in a system known as **reverse integration**.

Each form of special education delivery is more than an issue of placement, however. Each one has implications for the roles of both regular and special education personnel and how they work together, as well as for how material resources and equipment are allocated.

think it over

1-2

THINK IT OVER 1-2:

Delivery Model Alternatives

What are the positive and negative effects of each of the primary types of models of delivery?

Special Education Classes

The theory behind special education contained classes is that students may receive intensive specialized instruction, either to help them close the gap in performance between them and their regular class peers or to equip them with skills that are not explicitly taught in the general education curriculum, such as communication and job preparation skills.

Advantages:

Fuchs and Fuchs (1994) note the advantages of such classes:

- Teachers are trained in special education

- Teachers can draw on a variety of instructional methods, curricula, and motivational strategies

- Individual progress can be monitored

There is mixed opinion about whether students in contained classrooms experience stigma by being isolated from the general school community. Some students report feeling safer and more comfortable in a contained setting, while others report feeling socially neglected and stigmatized by their non-disabled peers.

In a deep and powerful description of a teacher who works with six students with complex physical and communication disabilities, Donna McGhie-Richmond (2001; McGhie-Richmond, Jordan, & Underwood, 2002) described how a talented teacher works in a segregated class setting. This account emphasizes that the skills, confidence, and esteem of students could only be developed by a teacher working in this intensive, segregated instructional setting.

Disadvantages:

At the student's level:

- Students in these classes are isolated from their non-disabled peers

- Depending on the composition of the class, students may not have access to spoken language and social models other than those provided by a single person—the teacher

- The students lack role models, for example other students who model appropriate behaviour and social interaction

- Students often do not have a sense of "belonging" in the school community; they may be unable to participate in extracurricular activities, and may not even share recesses and assemblies with their non-disabled peers; social interactions with peers may further be restricted by different lunchroom times or facilities, and early or late arrival and departure times

At the teacher's level:

- Teachers in contained classes need to be able to deliver curriculum across all subjects and grade levels, which becomes increasingly difficult as students move through the grade levels

- Special education teachers in contained settings have limited or no opportunity to work with the general education staff to increase the participation of their students in regular classrooms and to find inclusive solutions

- Similarly, the availability of a contained setting provides little incentive for teachers in the regular stream to work with special education teachers to re-integrate students with disabilities

At the school level:

- Non-disabled students do not have the opportunity to experience students with disabilities and to form friendships with and understanding of them

- The school community may be split along disability lines, sometimes with separate physical facilities such as a "special education wing" and separate timetables for transportation and extracurricular events

Resource Room or Withdrawal Models

The resource room, withdrawal or pull-out, model of service delivery has been the most popular model since the 1980s. Students are often registered in a regular class or grade, with the advantage that they have a home room and peers with whom to relate. They are then removed from the regular class for specific subjects, or for varying portions of the school day, to receive their instruction in a resource room or specialized setting.

Advantages:

- Students with disabilities have a greater chance of interacting with their non-disabled peers

- The instructional program for each student can be more individualized since students receive their instruction from different teachers according to their strengths and needs

- Teachers in both the **special education resource** and the **regular education programs** have more opportunity to interact and collaborate in designing and implementing programs and monitoring progress

In their **meta-analysis**, Swanson et al (1990a; 1999b) aggregated the findings of 180 studies that had attempted to measure the effects of differing instructional and placement characteristics on students with learning disabilities. There are many aspects to their findings, but one that emerged was that the resource room model had a slight advantage over other delivery models in raising student outcomes. However, it should be noted that the number of studies on which this finding was based was small, and the researchers warn that it would be unwise to generalize from it.

Disadvantages:

- Resource room programs can be disruptive to the routine of the regular classroom; withdrawn students are often removed during an ongoing class (thereby missing the entire lesson), or returned during the class (having missed the beginning of the lesson)

- While co-planning and monitoring students between the regular and special education teachers is facilitated in theory, in practice the time to collaborate is often minimal or non-existent

- The program that students receive in the resource room may not be aligned with or complement the program in the regular setting; as a result, students with disabilities may actually be penalized for missing important classroom content while being withdrawn to receive instruction that is supposed to help them

- **Resource teachers** often have a considerable student case list, requiring them to group students and to apply "formula remediation," which is not necessarily in each student's best interest

- Withdrawal can be stigmatizing for the student

Vaughn, Moody, and Schumm (1998) investigated what took place in 14 resource room withdrawal programs designed to assist students who were lagging in reading and literacy development. Their examination revealed that teachers typically provided whole-group instruction to relatively large groups of students with little differentiation of instruction or materials, despite the wide range of reading abilities (between three and five grade levels in a group). Most of the teachers identified "whole language" as their primary method of instruction, with little emphasis on strategies for word recognition and decoding or comprehension. The authors claim the study reveals a series of broken promises. The most obvious is that students and parents understood that an individualized reading program would meet the specific needs of the students. A second is that teachers felt overwhelmed by the sheer size of their caseloads, and by the lack of resources and time to fulfil their role. Finally, the reform initiatives, designed to provide "specifically designed instruction at no cost to the parent, to meet the unique needs of the child with a disability" (IDEA, 20 USC 1401 et seq.) were clearly not being met.

Inclusive Classrooms

Inclusive models have had a chequered history, as noted in Research Box 1-2. One factor involved in the current controversies about inclusion and its merits has been the focus on placement rather than on the instruction, services, and resources available within each placement. As the Supreme Court of Canada noted in its decision concerning the child Emily Eaton, the emphasis on placement may have been as misleading as the emphasis on identifying students with disabilities according to a category or label.

Examine Research Box 1-7: The Supreme Court of Canada and the Eaton Decision.

research box

1-7

think it over

1-3

THINK IT OVER 1-3:

Including Students for Non-academic Subjects

Students who receive their education in contained special education classes are often integrated with their non-disabled peers into music, physical education, and art classes.

What do you think are the advantages and disadvantages of this practice?

The Supreme Court of Canada
and the Eaton Decision

Since the 1990s, the implementation of special education legislation has been shaped by the nature of the appeals that parents have brought forward. These appeals were launched through several channels:

- the appeal mechanisms provided in the education policy and legislation of the provinces

- legal provisions in place to guarantee human rights at the provincial level

- the Charter of Rights and Freedoms at the federal level

The appeals have taken one of two diverging themes: parents of students who have historically been segregated in contained classes or institutions are fighting for stronger guarantees that their children will be served in inclusive settings alongside their non-disabled peers; and parents of children who have been designated as gifted or as having a communication-related learning disability are battling to have their children removed from the regular classroom setting to receive intensive, specialized instruction designed for their learning characteristics. This division of opinion about the most appropriate placement for students with differing identifications continues to this day (McLaughlin & Jordan, 2005) and in part explains the provincial governments' lack of clarity on the official stance on inclusion.

A further influence that has also contributed to the current special education inclusion policies in various provinces is the simultaneous transformation of regular or general education. As Lupart and Webber (2002) note, at the beginning of the 1980s, a major impetus toward school reform and restructuring began. This resulted in part because the public no longer believed that the public education system was adequately preparing students for the workforce. Evidence of how North American students stood on international achievement ratings was used to support the claim that schools in North America were falling behind the achievement standards of other nations (National Commission on Excellence in Education, 1983; National Association of Secondary School Principals, 1992). Motivated by the growing number of students who were unable to meet graduation standards, and a visible increase in students with disabilities and students at risk of failure in the classrooms, the media and public believed that schools were not being held accountable and needed to be reformed. Thus began a period of market-driven reforms of the school system, including increased accountability of schools to their public, greater prescription and surveillance by government, and more competition for resources (Jordan, 2001).

FLORIDA BOARD PASSES CONTROVERSIAL MERIT-PAY PLAN

The Florida Board of Education Tuesday unanimously approved a new pay plan that starting next year will tie salaries and annual bonuses to student performance on standardized tests. Officials from the Miami-Dade and Broward districts say there's no way they'll be able to meet a June 15 state deadline for completely overhauling their salary systems.

—*The Miami Herald* (February 22, 2006)

Reprinted with permission.

Although Canada fared relatively well on some international achievement measures compared with the United States (e.g., TIMSS, 1999), the reform movement still swept across our education systems. A major initiative for reform was the introduction of standards of achievement in a prescribed curriculum, and high-stakes assessment of student performance to show how these standards were being met. However, this reform agenda worked directly against the principles of special education that were also represented in legislation (Lupart & Webber, 2005). Teachers found themselves caught between the demands of a defined, intensive curriculum to be completed by their students in order to achieve well on the provincial examinations, and at the same time, a requirement to adapt their teaching and the curriculum to meet a wider range of needs in their diverse classrooms (McLaughlin & Jordan, 2005).

Some of these issues came to a head in a court case that reached the Supreme Court of Canada in 1997. The Supreme Court addressed the serious question of whether *identification* (i.e., whether identifying a student as a member of a prescribed category of disability) resulted in attributing to the child "stereotypical characteristics" that would be discriminatory in relegating the child to a segregated placement. The Supreme Court interpreted the meaning of the equality rights clause, section 15 of the Canadian Charter of Rights and Freedoms, in favour of the school board's decision to place the child in a segregated class. While this was viewed as a blow to those who

support inclusion, the decision of the Court supported neither the identification nor placement criteria of the province. The ruling held that the Charter clearly provides for the equality rights of students with disabilities by providing differences in treatment where necessary to ensure equality of outcomes. The ultimate test of inclusion must be "a determination of the appropriate accommodation for the exceptional child...from a subjective, child-centred perspective, one that attempts to make equality meaningful from the child's point of view" (*Eaton v. Brant County Board of Education [1997] 1 S.C.R. 241at page 278, 142 D.L.R. (4th) 385, 31 O.R.(3d) 574n, 97 O.A.C. 161, 41 C.R.R. (2d) 240, 207 N.R. 171.*). The Supreme Court Justices are shown on the right, including John Sopinka (2nd from the right, bottom row), who wrote the decision in the Eaton case.

The Supreme Court further stated that "It is the failure to make reasonable accommodations, to fine tune society so that its structure and assumptions do not result in the relegation and banishment of disabled persons from participation, which results in discrimination against them. The demand for inclusion as a placement can result in reverse discrimination or stereotyping which, by not allowing for the conditions of the disability in the individual, forces him or her to 'sink or swim in the mainstream environment'" (ibid. at pp 272–3).

The Supreme Court's use of the terms "appropriateness" and "accommodations" are interesting. They are to be applied to the individual child in the individual circumstances in which the child is located. This does not support any overall preconceptions or presumptions in favour of a particular placement, or special education program or service (Bowlby, Peters, & MacKinnon, 2001). The onus is on society and the school personnel in particular to seek accommodations that maximize each child's "equality, from a child's point of view."

In other words, the Court maintained that the rights of students with disabilities are not secured on the basis of their identification as belonging to a category of disability, nor on being placed in a setting, inclusive or otherwise, without regard for what is taking place in that setting. Both the focus on identification as a means to qualify for special education resources and on placement as a means to satisfy individual students' rights are misleading, if not wrong.

Rights are preserved when accommodations are supplied that are appropriate to the individual needs of each child. Such accommodations, including the location in which they are delivered, must be identified on a case-by-case basis (McLaughlin & Jordan, 2005).

Currently, this litigious trend continues. Parents of students with autism spectrum disorders in Ontario recently won an Ontario Superior Court decision in which school systems were found to have violated the Charter rights of children with autism in refusing to pay for highly specialized behavioural treatments and interventions for these children after they reached school age (*Wynberg et al. V. Her Majesty the Queen in Right of Ontario, and Deskin v Her Majesty [2005 03 30] 00CV184608CM*). These treatments, Applied Behavioural Analysis (ABA) or Intensive Behavioural Intervention (IBI), were previously available without payment only to children who had not yet reached school age. The decision of the Superior Court extended these treatments beyond the date on which a child enters school. In July 2006, however, the Ontario Court of Appeal struck down the Superior Court decision. The question of who should fund treatment for children aged 6 and older with autism is currently unresolved.

Those who subscribe to inclusion, including those who wish to define inclusion as placement in a regular classroom setting and those who do not interpret inclusion as placement, will continue to press their cases through the courts and through the media. They will be countered by groups who believe that inclusion denies the services and supports that their children need. Because the issues are so complex, there is unlikely to be a simple resolution any time soon. As the Supreme Court of Canada implied in considering the Eaton case, perhaps every child is sufficiently unique as to belie any set formula for meeting his or her special education needs.

Study questions:

1. How far should teachers be held accountable for the gains in achievement that their students make?

2. Should there be mechanisms in place to ensure that teachers provide instruction at a high level of professional skill and competence? If so, how might this be done?

3. The Supreme Court ruling in the Eaton case emphasized the importance of addressing the needs of each child individually, rather than through school policies that define a child's needs through membership in a given disability group, or by policies that favour one type of placement, such as regular class inclusion, for all students with disabilities. Think of the policy for providing special education to students in a school with which you are familiar. Are there implications from this decision for this school's policy of delivering special education?

Inclusive models also vary considerably. The degree to which additional help is integrated with the curriculum being taught to the rest of the class depends on a number of factors. One is the extent that the student needs a program that differs from the curriculum set for the class or subject (termed "**curriculum modifications**"). Another is the extent to which the teacher collaborates with support personnel. Collaboration among school staff turns out

to be a very significant factor in how well inclusion and **integration** work. Seating may also be a factor. In very few classrooms, the students with disabilities may be effectively segregated by the location of their desks or tables relative to the rest of the class. There was one class where students with disabilities have their desks turned so that they face the Educational Assistant, with their backs to the rest of the class. In another case, a student with a complex disability was placed at the front of the room facing the teacher, with the remainder of the students in rows behind that student's desk. Again, the student was unable to see his classmates. Fortunately these instances of segregation within a regular classroom are not common. It is not uncommon, however, to see a student with an Educational Assistant (EA) working away from the rest of the class, on a computer or at a desk at the back of the room. Ideally, all students would be located within the seating arranged for the total class. Of course, consideration should be given to wheelchair access and to specialized equipment so the student can access resources, can be reached, and can be mobile within the larger group.

An inclusive delivery model requires that all the staff in a school—administrative, teaching, and support staff—work collaboratively to provide the classroom and subject teachers with as much support and as many materials and resources as needed to meet the variation in a given class. In most provinces and territories, the needs of students with disabilities and the services provided are tracked through an **Individual Education Plan** or **Program** (IEP or IPP) and need not fall into the trap of "formula remediation" or "cookie cutter solutions" as seen in Vaughn's resource rooms study. The emphasis should not be on placement, but rather on the whole school effort to meet the needs of all students on an individual basis. Research Box 1-6 related the picture of an inclusive school environment as described by Dyson and colleagues. Dyson et al. (2004, 2005) talk about the "ecology of inclusion" or the collective commitment shared by a staff to provide services to all students. This ecology is formed in the delicate balance between competing demands, policies, and resources.

Advantages:

- Students with disabilities form part of the variation in achievement, behaviour, social skills, and self-esteem that comprise a class

- Students are members of the classroom and school community

- The staff see their moral and professional responsibility to be working together to meet the educational needs of all their students

- For many, inclusion is more than a debate about setting and service delivery; it is the moral and professional responsibility of teachers and of society at large to reduce and remove barriers to participation for people with disabilities

Disadvantages:

- There is no consensus on the meaning of the term "inclusion"; for some, the term "full inclusion" is used to indicate that a student with disabilities should participate fully in all aspects of school life, within the classroom community of peers, while others believe it means meeting the individual needs of each student, as seen in the Supreme Court of Canada decision in Research Box 1-7

- At present, teacher training has failed to keep up with the demands of inclusive school systems, and teachers feel generally unprepared for inclusion and under-supported in attempting to include a range of learning needs in their classes

- The legislative and resource imperatives of the larger school system and society have created tensions in how schools implement delivery models; school staff may not be supported because of the lack of clarity about the benefits of inclusion, the roles of staff to promote inclusion, and the expectations of parents and community groups

- The funding structures for special education in most school boards and provinces are still based on the premise that students must be identified by category of disability, and served by placement

Until better methods of supplying resources are found, and until parents and the larger public are satisfied that there are better ways to serve students than through categorical approaches, there will continue to be debate and tension about inclusive delivery models.

Disability Categories

learning objective

1-7

Depending on the perspective held, therefore, the category of a student's disability is either: a crucial piece of information that opens the way to specialized educational resources; or a peripheral piece of information that is a useful starting point for assessing instructional needs but is not usually central to how and what the student is taught and how he or she progresses. It can assist a teacher to zero in on the needed assessments at the beginning of a school year that will lead to the design of appropriate interventions, particularly for students with curriculum-related disabilities. Labels are not themselves bad or dangerous; we are label-users from our very first words as infants. The dangers come from relying on the labels to "explain" a student's learning difficulty, to "predict" what the learning outcome will be for the student, and to absolve the teacher from having to act.

The final section of this module presents definitions of each of the disability categories commonly used in Canada. A commentary is included with each category that includes some of the characteristics of each disability; how these may be useful for teachers when they are planning instruction; or alternatively how the category definition can be confusing and misleading from an instructional or cross-category viewpoint.

The definitions do not equip readers to be diagnostic experts. The clinical skills needed to accurately diagnose a disability require more skill and qualifications than most teaching professionals possess. Teachers can and should, however, acquire the expertise to begin instruction with students with disabilities and to know where to find additional resources when a student arrives in their classroom. Knowing the diagnosed disability of a student equips a teacher with the ability to start the process of asking questions and forming hypotheses about teaching and learning for this student. Along with the just-in-time delivery of specialized resources from personnel available in most school systems, information from print and on-line resources, and resources from professional development courses, these skills will be sufficient for beginning work with students with disabilities, whatever these might be.

Prevalence Rates

Prevalence, or the number of people who are identified as having a disability, is reported by the federal Government of Canada from its Census and survey data. The federal government 2001 Participation and Activity Limitation Survey (PALS) report indicates that about 3% of Canadians aged 0 to 14 and 10% of Canadians aged 15 to 64 have a disability (http://www.sdc.gc.ca/asp/gateway.asp?hr=/en/hip/odi/documents/PALS/PALS003.shtml&hs=pyp; retrieved February 21st 2006). School systems, on the other hand, identify between 9% and 15% of students as falling within one of the categories of disability described in this section.

As noted by Sarason and Doris (1979) and others, defining students by category can lead to missing the uniqueness and diversity of their learning characteristics. Trying to count how many students are in each category is fraught with similar problems. Yet prevalence rates, or the rate at which people with this designation occur in the general population, are often needed for setting policies, funding, etc. The weakness of the science of defining disabilities by category can be seen when comparing the prevalence rate of people with disabilities from one agency to the next, or one country to another. In North America (the US and Canada), education agencies usually consider about 10 to 12% of the school population to have a disability. Of those designated as exceptional (i.e., having a disability) in Ontario, about 50% of the students are diagnosed as having a learning disability, while about 15% are identified as gifted. Between 12% and 15% of the students designated as exceptional are identified in one of the complex disability categories: multiple handicaps, or severe emotional, physical, communication, and developmental disabilities. In the United States, giftedness is not a category of exceptionality.

Review Think it Over 1-4 and survey results from Statistics Canada regarding the prevalence rates of disability in the Canadian population. Think about why the prevalence rates vary among social service agencies and those that fund programs for people with disabilities.

think it
over

1-4

think
it over

1-4

Incidence or Prevalence Rates of Disability in Canada

In the 2001 Census, 3.6 million Canadians living in households reported having activity limitations. This represents a disability rate of 12.4%. However, the prevalence rate varies with age. Statistics Canada reports that in 2001, in children from 0 to 14 years of age, the prevalence was 3.3%. Boys have a greater likelihood at 4% than girls at 2.5%. Between the ages of 15 and 24, the prevalence rate rises to 3.8% in males, and 4.0% in females. If we take into account that StatsCan data are self-reported and that people are reluctant to declare themselves disabled, particularly in some categories, then the prevalence figures may be underestimated. Nevertheless, they are markedly lower than the prevalence rates reported by school boards.

Examine the data at **http://www.statcan.ca/english/freepub/89-577-XIE/canada.htm**.

Discussion Questions:

1. What might account for the differences in incidence (prevalence) rates reported for disabilities? For instance, why might there be a variation between agencies or from one school system to another?

2. In the 1980s, Jane Mercer, a researcher in California, collected actual prevalence data by going door to door in the district of Riverside. She then compared the records of social service agencies such as the school system, nursery and daycare agencies, employment and welfare services, and medical and health agencies. She found that schools labelled students as mentally retarded significantly more than any other agency. This led her to suggest that mental retardation is a 6-hour condition commencing at 9 a.m. and finishing at 3 p.m. each day, and prevalent between ages 5 and 16.

3. What are your thoughts about Mercer's comments?

Conventions of Language

Before examining some common definitions of categories of exceptionality, there are some conventions for their use that are important to know.

1. **People first language**. When talking or writing about a person or group with a disability, the person is mentioned first. Thus we talk about people with disabilities, not disabled people. This convention correctly puts the respectful emphasis on the person first and the disability second. It is also helpful when talking about their teachers—gifted teachers is ambiguous!

2. **The migration of terms**. A term used to describe a disability is viewed as appropriate in one era in society while in another era it is derogatory. For example, several decades ago people with hearing impairments were termed "deaf and dumb." As the science of audiology and knowledge of hearing impairment progressed, it was determined that people with hearing loss can range from very little hearing to a great deal, and the hearing loss may distort sound in different ways for different people (see Hearing Impairment section). Since there is no single syndrome of "deaf," a term such as "hearing impaired" provides a less categorical and more accurate label. This is an example of the ways in which labels can lead to stereotypes that conceal the variety and individuality of a group of people who share one characteristic.

In addition, people with **prelingual deafness** acquired prior to birth or prior to the development of language have great difficulty learning to speak, read, and write English. But they are by no means "dumb" in the old sense of being unable to speak. A range of communication systems have been developed by and for people with prelingual deafness, and are described in the Hearing Impairment section. The problems people with hearing impairments have with mastering English are in part due to the phonological nature of English and how the spoken language is condensed into a 26 letter phonic alphabet that is very hard to decode without considerable knowledge of the sounds of spoken English. People without hearing difficulties, for example people learning English as a second language and people attempting to learn to read in English, may also struggle with written forms of English because of the lack of correspondence between how it sounds and how it is spelled.

3. **Derogatory terms**. Be aware of the derivations of terms that once had a technical meaning but have migrated and become subsumed under common terms of insult, such as "imbecile," "idiot," "dumb," and "retard." Wikipedia has a list of terms with negative connotations and an explanation of their misuse. Interestingly, "special education" is included. Find out what else is viewed as negative or at least euphemistic at http://en.wikipedia.org/wiki/List_of_disability-related_terms_with_negative_connotations

Smith, Salend, and Ryan (2001) provide a helpful article that explores the effects of certain kinds of language and how it is used on students with special needs.

4. **High vs. low-incidence disabilities; Mild vs. moderate vs. severe disabilities; Curriculum-related vs. complex disabilities**.

Incidence rates indicate how often a disability occurs, or the frequency of a disability in the general population. In the literature on special education, a distinction is usually made between "high incidence" (the most frequently occurring disabilities such as learning disabilities and mild developmental delay), and "low incidence disabilities" (the complex and less frequently occurring disabilities such as severe developmental disability). An alternative set of distinctions is therefore "mild" and "severe" disabilities, but this distinction once again falls into the trap of creating stereotypes. People who have Down syndrome, for example, have a chromosomal abnormality that often results in varying degrees of developmental delay, but this is not always the case. People in this category of disability do not share the same capacity for intellectual development, but instead vary considerably. The designation of Down syndrome cannot predict school success. Therefore an alternative terminology, which points to the functional abilities of the person rather than the neurological basis, may be more helpful for educators.

Curriculum-related vs. complex disabilities: Although these terms are not commonly used, they express the distinction between high- and low-incidence disabilities. Curriculum-related disabilities are high-incidence difficulties that are evident in **functional** skills, such as learning

to read and write, solving mathematics problems, remembering facts, organizing study material, etc. Complex disabilities involve major difficulties that are more pervasive, not only with learning in the curriculum, but also in communicating needs, managing life, and being self-supporting. These complex, low-incidence disabilities may be associated with other difficulties that stem from early neurological development or organic diseases.

Definitions of Disability

There are many differing definitions of each of the categories of disability. It may be helpful for teachers to go to their province's or territory's Ministry of Education website to view the definitions used in their school systems. The web addresses for each province can be found at http://www.edu.gov.on.ca/eng/relsites/oth_prov.html. There are also definitions preferred by organizations that serve the needs of people with disabilities. Rather than attempting to coordinate the information and the differences between these definitions, the definitions presented here are mostly those defined under the Education Act in Ontario. They serve as examples of the categorical definitions used throughout North America, and provide a basis for critical analysis of tone and content. The official definitions of the Ministry of Education of Ontario can be found at http://www.edu.gov.on.ca/eng/general/elemsec/speced/guide.html. Where there is a national definition, as is the case for Learning Disabilities, this definition is reported instead. A commentary section follows each definition.

There are five main categories of disability: communicational, intellectual, behavioural, physical, and multiple. There are 13 subcategories under these five main groups.

Communication

Autism/pervasive developmental disability (PDD)— Autism spectrum disorder

Definition

A group of difficulties termed **Pervasive Development Disorder** (PDD). These are a subcategory of communication, one of the five categories of exceptionality identified in the *Education Act*. **Autism** is defined as a severe learning disorder characterized by disturbances in:

- rate of educational development
- ability to relate to the environment
- mobility
- perception, speech, and language

Autism also includes lack of representational–symbolic behaviour that precedes language.

Autism/pervasive developmental disability (PDD)— Pervasive developmental disorders (PDD)

Definition

A plural umbrella term for several disorders and syndromes that may or may not have biological basis or causes. The World Health Organization's (WHO) International Statistical Classification of Diseases and Related Health Problems (10th Revision), also know as ICD-10, lists the following disorders under the PDD umbrella. Useful websites are added for each syndrome:

- childhood autism:
  Canada: www.autismsocietycanada.ca

- atypical autism:
  Rett's syndrome
  www.wrongdiagnosis.com/r/retts_syndrome/basics.htm;
  overactive disorder associated with cognitive impairment and stereotyped movements;

- Asperger syndrome:
  http://www.aspergersyndrome.org

  People with **Asperger syndrome** share some of the characteristics of those with autism, although without the language disabilities that mark autism. People with AS may have poor social skills, may lack of awareness of social cues, and may avoid eye contact with others. They may also have difficulty with transitions and a preference for predictability. Individuals with AS can exhibit a range of difficulties from mild to severe. The syndrome has only recently become identified, and prior to the 1990s, many children were misidentified as learning disabled, socially awkward, or uncooperative.

- other pervasive developmental disorders (such as Fragile X –http://www.fragilex.org/)

- pervasive developmental disorder, unspecified

Commentary

Autism Spectrum Disorders is the fastest growing category of disability in North America, and is cause for concern (Autism Society of America, 1999). The United States Government Accounting Office (2005) reports that the incidence of school-aged children with autism rose in the United States from 5,415 in 1991 to 118,602 in 2003, a 22-fold increase. Autism Spectrum Disorders typically appear in the first three years of life and are related to neurological factors. They affect both children and adults. As a spectrum disorder, autism takes different forms and affects different individuals to different degrees. The group of disorders are characterized by qualitative impairments in social interaction and communication, a failure to develop relationships with peers, and use of non-functional rituals and routines (DSM-IV, 1994). Intensive intervention based on behavioural feedback techniques (Applied Behavioural Analysis—ABA; Intensive Behavioural Intervention—IBI) and intensive one-to-one language intervention can successfully reduce the autistic behaviours, particularly if begun at a very early age (prior to Kindergarten). By the primary grades, the behaviours are harder to remediate. The responsibilities of school systems to provide the intensive behavioural intervention therapies after children reach grade school has been the subject of a recent Ontario court case (Wynberg v Her Majesty 00CV184608CM; and Deskin v Her Majesty, 99CV177616—Ontario Superior Court, March 30, 2005). However, the Ontario Court of Appeal struck down this decision in July 2006.

One key objective to accommodating students with autism spectrum disorders in inclusive settings is to assist them to develop meaningful participation with non-disabled peers. Some resources for regular classroom teachers who receive children with autism and similar pervasive developmental disabilities in their classrooms can be found in Safran (2002).

Deaf and hard-of-hearing

Definition

An impairment characterized by deficits in language and speech development because of a diminished or non-existent auditory response to sound.

Commentary

Students with hearing impairments differ considerably. If a student with hearing impairment is new to the school, the teacher should first find out the severity of the loss, and whether it is binaural (both ears). It is also useful to find out whether the student lost his or her hearing before (prelingual) or after (postlingual) the age of language development. People with prelingual hearing loss have more difficulty learning to decode and produce spoken English than those with postlingual hearing loss, who retain some language skills.

Another useful first step is to look at the student's audiogram. This tells the teacher the level of volume (decibels) required for the student to identify a sound at each of the frequency (cycles per second—cps) levels. Human speech requires recognition of sounds in a range of frequencies

from a high of 8000 cps where the "s" and "f" sounds of speech are registered, to a low of 250 cps, where the vowel sounds such as "ah" and "oo" are registered. The audiogram can tell the teacher if the student can hear speech sounds in some of the frequency ranges but not in others. A common audiogram pattern looks like a ski slope, indicating the student can hear the low frequency sounds but not the fricatives such as "s" and "f." From this, the teacher can conclude where the student might hear English with a distortion that favours low frequency and eliminates high frequency sounds. Other audiogram patterns suggest a uniform loss of volume but unchanged frequency, or a slope that distorts sounds to different degrees. The decibel or loudness value tells how much the person's hearing is reduced. Speaking in a loud voice or shouting do not compensate for this loss.

Teachers also need to know the communication system that the student has learned to use. Oral-aural communication combines lip reading and using the residual hearing skills of the student to receive spoken English and to communicate verbally. Signed English is a manual sign system that reflects the syntactic characteristics of spoken English, for example by indicating verb tenses. American Sign Language (ASL) is a manual communication system favoured by the deaf community as part of a cultural heritage. It has its own rules for syntax and does not map easily onto written and spoken English. Other types of communication systems may be used in conjunction with the systems mentioned above, such as fingerspelling in which each letter of the alphabet is represented by a hand configuration.

When working with a student with a hearing impairment, it is important to minimize the extraneous noise around the student. All sounds are amplified by a hearing aid or sound system, and therefore unwanted noises are likely to interfere with the student's attempts to distinguish amplified speech sounds. People with normal hearing have learned to ignore extraneous sounds and focus on target sounds, for example when talking to someone in a noisy room. People with hearing impairments often find this very difficult to accomplish. Try facing the student so that he or she can also use lip reading cues to assist with interpreting speech sounds. When the student is in a group, train the other students to face him or her. Think about alternative and supplementary ways of communicating that are visual, but remember that because speech is hard to understand, print versions of speech are even harder. It is difficult to learn to read without knowing the sound system on which print is based.

A useful source for teaching resources for teachers of student with hearing impairment, containing URL addresses for further research on the Internet, is Williams & Finnegan (2003). Moore also provides more extensive information in his 2001 book.

Language impairment

Definition

A learning disorder characterized by an impairment in comprehension and/or the use of verbal communication or the written or other symbol system of communication, which may be associated with neurological, psychological, physical, or sensory factors, and which may: a) involve one or more of the form, content, and function of language in communication; and b) include one or more of:

- language delay

- dysfluency

- voice and articulation development, which may or may not be organically or
  functionally based

Speech impairment

Definition:

A disorder in language formulation that may be associated with neurological, psychological, physical, or sensory factors; involves perceptual motor aspects of transmitting oral messages and may be characterized by impairment in articulation, rhythm, and stress.

- Dysarthria is difficult, poorly articulated speech, such as slurring.

- Aphasis is impaired comprehension or expression of speech and written language.

Learning disability

Definition

The official definition of learning disabilities, adopted by the Learning Disabilities Association of Canada on January 30, 2002, is as follows:

> "Learning Disabilities" refer to a number of disorders which may affect the acquisition, organization, retention, understanding or use of verbal or nonverbal information. These disorders affect learning in individuals who otherwise demonstrate at least average abilities essential for thinking and/or reasoning. As such, learning disabilities are distinct from global intellectual deficiency.
>
> Learning disabilities result from impairments in one or more processes related to perceiving, thinking, remembering, or learning. These include, but are not limited to: language processing; phonological processing; visual spatial processing; processing speed; memory and attention; and executive functions (e.g., planning and decision-making).

Learning disabilities range in severity and may interfere with the acquisition and use of one or more of the following:

- oral language (e.g., listening, speaking, understanding)
- reading (e.g., decoding, phonetic knowledge, word recognition, comprehension)
- written language (e.g., spelling and written expression)
- mathematics (e.g., computation, problem solving)

Learning disabilities may also involve difficulties with organizational skills, social perception, social interaction, and perspective taking.

Learning disabilities are lifelong. The way in which they are expressed may vary over an individual's lifetime, depending on the interaction between the demands of the environment and the individual's strengths and needs. Learning disabilities are suggested by unexpected academic under-achievement or achievement which is maintained only by unusually high levels of effort and support.

Learning disabilities are due to genetic and/or neurobiological factors or injury that alter brain functioning in a manner which affects one or more processes related to learning. These disorders are not due primarily to hearing and/or vision problems, socio-economic factors, cultural or linguistic differences, lack of motivation, or ineffective teaching, although these factors may further complicate the challenges faced by individuals with learning disabilities. Learning disabilities may co-exist with various conditions including attentional, behavioural, and emotional disorders, sensory impairments, or other medical conditions.

For success, individuals with learning disabilities require early identification and timely specialized assessments and interventions involving home, school, community, and workplace settings. The interventions need to be appropriate for each individual's learning disability subtype and, at a minimum, include the provision of:

- specific skill instruction
- accommodations
- compensatory strategies
- self-advocacy skills

The main principles of the 2002 definition adopted by Learning Disabilities Association of Canada are that a learning disability is neurobiological, genetic, lifelong, and affects all areas of life, not just education.

View a video outlining the controversy about the prescription of Ritalin for children with Attention Deficit Disorders (ADD). A video summary and discussion questions are also available on-line.

Commentary

As previously noted, between 6% and 15% of the school-aged population is thought to have a learning disability. Students with learning disabilities comprise about half of the students with disabilities in North American schools. The category and its definition are controversial and have been intensively researched. On the one hand there is a belief, reflected in paragraph 6 of the definition, that LD stems from neurological or other organically based deficits. On the other hand, there are those who believe that LD is a socially— or medically created disability that manifests only in difficulties with reading and writing, and that results in part from the way reading in the English language is taught.

One set of criteria for the diagnosis of LD is that there is a discrepancy between ability (typically the score on tests of ability such as IQ test) and tests of achievement (reading, writing, and other school-related skills). This "discrepancy hypothesis" has been challenged by several researchers (Stanovich, 1991, 1996, 2000; Siegel, 1992; Stuebing et al., 2002), who question the failure

of this criterion to discriminate between students with LD in reading and other low performing readers. Siegel claims that the IQ component is misleading and that LD is best defined in terms of weak skills in school related subjects. If LD is therefore defined as difficulty learning to read and/or write and/or compute, the definition is somewhat circular, and as the researchers point out, not worthy of an explanation of an underlying deficit with a neurological basis. It also raises doubts about the use of a grandiose label such as "dyslexia" to imply a brain-related deficiency.

There have been significant advances in the US—which are only now beginning to reach Canada—in developing ways to identify students with learning disabilities on the basis of their response to early instructional intervention, that increases in intensity as the student continues to struggle to learn. Instruction is intensively delivered at three stages or tiers through Kindergarten to grade 2 or 3. About half of the children who are initially identified as struggling readers, and therefore potentially identifiable as learning disabled, are able to make up the ground in reading delay through this method. This finding suggests that more pervasive reading disabilities occur in only about half of the struggling readers in the early grades (Vaughn, Wanzek, Woodruff, & Linan-Thompson, In press; Vellutino, Scanlon, & Lyon, 2002).

THINK IT OVER 1-5:

Learning Disabilities: Nature or Nurture?

Where do you sit in the debate about learning disabilities?

Do you think there is a physiological basis for difficulties in learning to read?

What evidence would you need to reach a conclusion?

How much do you think early experiences in learning to read contribute to later difficulties?

think it over

1-5

There are many websites that provide useful information for teachers with students with learning disabilities.

The Council for Exceptional Children has an extensive website for teachers and others working with students with disabilities, found at http://canadian.cec.sped.org/.

CEC also has a division devoted to assisting teachers with students with learning disabilities: http://www.TeachingLD.org/.

The Learning Disabilities Association of Canada (LDAC) has many resources for teachers, parents, students, and adults with learning disabilities.

It also provides links to many other resources: http://www.ldac-taac.ca. This well developed organization also has chapters in most provinces and territories that support children and their families, adults with learning disabilities, and teachers and others who seek help to work with people with learning disabilities.

LDAC and other sources indicate there are many people who have made important contributions to society who were thought to have a severe learning disability in their school years. These include scientists Albert Einstein and Thomas Edison, author Virginia Woolf, and politicians Winston Churchill (shown in the adjacent photograph), and Nelson Rockefeller. Successful artists with significant learning problems, perhaps disabilities, during their school years include Tom Cruise, Cher, and Whoopie Goldberg.

Intellectual

Mild intellectual disability

A learning disorder characterized by:

- an ability to profit educationally within a regular class with the aid of considerable curriculum modification and supportive services
- an inability to profit educationally within a regular class because of slow intellectual development
- a potential for academic learning, independent social adjustment, and economic self-support

Commentary

This definition is perplexing because the second clause seems to contradict the first by anticipating the removal of the student from a regular classroom as a condition for diagnosis. Yet there is no standard of "ability to profit from instruction" nor of the skills expected by a teacher in order for a student to profit, that allows us to decide that it is the child, rather than the placement, that has met the criterion of ability to profit from instruction. See the next definition for a proposed alternative to the model of delivering services.

Developmental or moderate intellectual disability

Definition

Defined as a severe learning disorder characterized by:

- an inability to profit from a special education program for students with mild intellectual disabilities because of slow intellectual development

- an ability to profit from a special education program that is designed to accommodate slow intellectual development

- a limited potential for academic learning, independent social adjustment, and economic self-support

Commentary

Again, the disability is defined in terms of the student's difference from the previous category, which is itself based on a student's inability to profit from instruction. These definitions allow the school system to draw the line between those students it is prepared to serve and those it is not. There are no standards for the level and extent of service to determine a student is unable to take advantage of the instruction. As such, it represents a deficit-based or pathognomonic approach to identifying students as intellectually disabled.

In a non-categorical model, there would be levels of intensive instructional intervention beginning at an early age, usually in Kindergarten, although it could begin at any age. In the three-tier intervention system, if the student did not respond to the intervention at the first level of intensity by a given date, for example by the end of the first school term, then a second, more intensive level of intervention would begin. Only when the student was unable to benefit from this second level of intervention would the student be deemed to need specialized help. This would lead to the development of an Individual Educational Program (IEP). The placement for the student would depend on where the resources to implement the IEP were located. It might be delivered in a variety of locations, including the regular classroom with peers for communicational and social development.

An important website is the Canadian Association for Community Living—www.cacl.ca. CACL promotes support and community services and education for people with intellectual disabilities across Canada. The website provides contact information for the provincial and territorial chapters of CACL.

In Montreal in 2004, participants at the Pan-American Health Organization (PAHO) and World Health Organization (WHO) Conference on intellectual disability signed the *Montreal Declaration on Intellectual Disabilities*, on behalf of the international community of people with intellectual disabilities. It can be found at http://www.montrealdeclaration.com/

In the opening video-clip of this module, you met Ashif, a young man with Down syndrome, on his way to university.

A resource that describes the development of services for children with intellectual disabilities is Vera Pletsch's 1997 book, *Not Wanted in the Classroom* (London, ON: Althouse Press).

Giftedness

Definition

An unusually advanced degree of general intellectual ability that requires differentiated learning experiences of a depth and breadth beyond those normally provided in the regular school program to satisfy the level of intellectual potential indicated.

Commentary

Like the two preceding definitions, the onus is on the student to be unable to profit from the learning opportunities available in the regular classroom. The question remains, who is responsible for providing the opportunity to learn, and is enough opportunity available?

Renzulli's (1978) definition of giftedness contains three criteria: ability, task commitment, and creative expression, and requires that all three be applied to a valuable area of human endeavour. School boards generally have identification criteria in place that include results of ability and achievement tests and evidence of task commitment and motivation, usually based on teacher report.

There are two main approaches to programming for gifted and talented students:

- **enrichment**—the regular curriculum is supplemented with more in-depth study

- **acceleration**—the student skips part or all of a grade level and advances to the next

There are numerous useful resources for working with gifted students. There are educational journals devoted to the subject (Journal of the Education of the Gifted, Roeper Review, GCQ [Gifted Child Quarterly] and Gifted International) and websites such as the Council for Exceptional Children (Teaching Gifted Students) http://ericec.org/gifted/gt-menu.html

The Gifted Canada website is http://www3.bc.sympatico.ca/gifted-canada/. This website links to provincial organizations for parents and professionals for students with gifts and talents.

The field of gifted education is not without its controversies. On one hand, critics accuse the education system of failing to develop the skills of potentially outstanding students in an increasingly competitive international marketplace, for example in high tech and athletics.

A category of students with disabilities recognized by school systems is "gifted learning disabled." One claim is that these students have been held back in a mediocre education setting to the point that they have ceased to develop their potential. On the other hand, there is opposition to favouring a subgroup of students with resources that are not available to other students who may develop similar characteristics if given the opportunity. Critics also claim that intellectual gifts may be accelerated at the expense of social and affective development. The nature–nurture debate again lies at the heart of this controversy. Proponents of inclusion for students with disabilities sometimes see an irony in the promotion of specialized services often delivered in segregated settings for students with intellectual gifts and other talents. There are possibilities for teachers to broaden their instructional repertoire to include such students in the regular classroom. Hutchinson (2002) provides a table of enrichment strategies that can be used for teaching gifted students (p. 69).

STUDENT POLL 1–1:

Should students with intellectual gifts, who are performing significantly beyond levels normally exhibited by students in the regular classroom, be taught in specialized, segregated classes?

Yes ☐   No ☐   Undecided ☐

student poll

1-1

Behavioural

Behaviour exceptionality

Definition

A learning disorder characterized by specific behaviour problems over such a period of time, and to such a marked degree, and of such nature as to adversely affect educational performance, and that may be accompanied by one or more of the following:

- an inability to build or to maintain interpersonal relationships
- excessive fears or anxieties
- a tendency to compulsive reaction
- an inability to learn that cannot be traced to intellectual, sensory, or other health factors, or any combination thereof

It is interesting to note the similarities between this definition and the definition for **emotional disturbance** in the United States. The Individuals with Disabilities Education Act (IDEA), Public Law 101-476, defines emotional disturbance as follows:

"...a condition exhibiting one or more of the following characteristics over a long period of time and to a marked degree that adversely affects educational performance:

- an inability to learn that cannot be explained by intellectual, sensory, or health factors
- an inability to build or maintain satisfactory interpersonal relationships with peers and teachers
- inappropriate types of behaviour or feelings under normal circumstances
- a general pervasive mood of unhappiness or depression
- a tendency to develop physical symptoms or fears associated with personal or school problems" [Code of Federal Regulations, Title 34, Section 300.7(b)(9)]

Another term used in Canada is **neurobiological disorder**, indicating a condition more closely identified with psychiatric and emotional disorders.

Commentary

Unlike cognitive and learning disabilities, people with behavioural and/or emotional disabilities are not represented by strong advocacy groups. They tend to be the hidden people in the disabilities movement. It is therefore interesting to note how the Ontario definition of a behavioural disability has an almost parallel definition in the United States under the label of emotional disturbance. Is there a distinction to be made between behaviours that are challenging and those associated with an emotional disability such as schizophrenia or depression? If there is, should the intervention prescribed be the same for both?

From mild disruptions that can escalate, to challenging behaviours associated with known disabilities, such as some autism spectrum disorders, these areas of exceptionality are often viewed as the most difficult for a teacher in an inclusive setting. However, there are many steps that teachers can take at various levels of intervention, from preventing the occurrence of challenging behaviours and identifying the causes of disruptive behaviours, to putting interventions in place that are effective in reducing or eliminating unwanted disruptions, and recognizing behaviours as indicators of more complex emotional disabilities. In this field in particular, an ounce of prevention is worth a great deal of intervention. Skills in anticipating and preventing discipline problems from escalating into disruptions are part of an effective teacher's toolkit. More specialized skills are also available to teachers and support people who can assist in planning strategies for the classroom. These might be developed collaboratively on a just-in-time basis for individual students. They include functional behavioural analysis, behaviour modification, knowing when and how to refer to specialists in psychiatric care, and other tools.

Although primarily established to provide resources for people with **Attention deficit disorder (ADD)**, CHADD Canada has a number of useful links to sites that address various aspects of challenging behaviours arising from anxiety, conduct disorders, fetal alcohol syndrome, etc. They can be found by clicking http://www.chaddcanada.org/links.php.

A useful site for teachers and parents is Conduct Management, a resource that serves both Canada and the United States: http://www.conductmanagement.com.

Physical

Physical disability

Definition

A condition of such severe physical limitation or deficiency as to require special assistance in learning situations to provide the opportunity for educational achievement equivalent to that of pupils without exceptionalities who are of the same age or development level. This group includes students with medical conditions that make them fragile, such as disease, **closed head brain injury**, and HIV-AIDS.

The photograph on the left shows Sam Sullivan, mayor of Vancouver, BC. He is a quadriplegic, who has achieved success not only in the political realm, but also as a leader and advocate for the physically disabled. He has founded six non-profit organizations related to this cause.

Commentary

A useful website for teachers of students with physical disabilities can be found at a general website, About.com: http://specialed.about.com/od/physicaldisabilities/

Also visit the US National Institute of Health: Physical Disabilities Branch: http://pdb.cc.nih.gov/.

The Bloorview MacMillan Children's Centre, a Toronto centre dedicated to children with physical and multiple disabilities, has a world-famous research centre for prosthetic devices. It also has a website with links to community resources: http://www.bloorviewmacmillan.on.ca/.

Blind and low vision

Definition

A condition of partial or total impairment of sight or vision that, even with correction, affects educational performance adversely. View the online video and meet Doug, a grade 12 student, who explains how the assistive software on his computer has helped him to be successful in his studies, and to pursue his aspirations to become a commercial artist. He demonstrates software that not only magnifies texts, but can read it to him, conduct searches, and perform other word processing routines to assist Doug to conduct research and compose (ZoomText, Kurzweil 3000, and WordQ).

Commentary

Like hearing impairment, vision difficulties can vary greatly. A helpful introduction to visual impairment and what teachers can do to assist students with vision difficulties in regular classrooms can be found in Cox & Dykes (2001).

A main resource in Canada is the Canadian National Institute for the Blind. Access their website at http://www.cnib.ca. Visitors have access to a digital library as well as many resources in both large print and **Braille**.

There are also resources at the New York Institute for Special Education at www.nyise.org/lowvision.htm

People who have visual disabilities include two outstanding artists, Andrea Bocelli, and Stevie Wonder, shown in the adjacent photograph.

Multiple

Multiple exceptionalities

Definition

A combination of learning or other disorders, impairments, or physical disabilities, that is of such nature to require, for educational achievement, the services of one or more teachers holding qualifications in special education and the provision of support services appropriate for such disorders, impairments, or disabilities.

Commentary

The term is usually reserved for people who have considerable as well as multiple disabilities. In this series, the term "complex disabilities" denotes both the severity of multiple exceptionalities, and the complexity created by the tendency for physical and neurological conditions to be compounded with each other. As noted in the section on prevalence rates, about 12% to 15% of the approximately 10% of students who are designated as having a disability are identified as having multiple exceptionalities; this represents approximately 1% to 1.5% of the school-age population.

Because each individual with multiple exceptionalities has unique characteristics and needs, it is likely that one or more people with specialized skills and knowledge has worked with each student and will be available to consult with school personnel when a student with a multiple exceptionality is registered. A team of specialists is then set up to advise and assist the school in accommodating the student's needs, and in recommending the specialized resources that he or she will need. These may include medical interventions and nursing care, educational assistants, specialists in communication, social, and behaviour training, among others.

There are considerable resources available to assist a teacher to prepare to work with students with complex disabilities. They should be available from resource staff, but a good source is *TEACHING Exceptional Children*, a magazine published by the Council for Exceptional Children (www.cec.sped.org), which features articles for and by teachers who work with students with complex disabilities.

TASH, the Association for persons with Severe Handicaps, publishes journals such as *Research and Practice for Persons with Severe Disabilities* (formerly *The Journal of the Association for Persons with Severe Handicaps*). TASH also conducts conferences and offers resources to teachers and others for people with severe handicaps. It can be found at http://www.tash.org.

The Council of Canadians with Disabilities consists of member organizations that advocate for people with disabilities in Canada. Its website is http://www.ccdonline.ca.

One of their members is NEAD, The National Educational Association of Students with Disabilities, which advocates for equal access for students with disabilities into college and university.

A unique Canadian public education website is offered by Child and Family Canada. Fifty Canadian non-profit organizations have come together under the banner of Child & Family Canada to provide quality, credible resources on children and families on this website. It is found at http://www.cfc-efc.ca/.

Summary

In this module, a framework was developed to look at teachers' responsibilities for teaching students with disabilities. The framework challenges the assumption that disability is a state of a learner, and instead suggests that disabilities are linked to challenges in accessing the resources necessary for learning. Teachers have a responsibility to find ways to reduce the barriers to access that are faced by students with disabilities.

The main concepts of this framework were presented:

Inclusive education is an international priority

- Including students with special education needs in regular classrooms is a world-wide movement and is here to stay.

The Canadian context

- Disability and underachievement are associated with many factors: high drop-out and failure rates at secondary levels, limited post-secondary opportunities, the impact of high-stakes assessment on teachers' priorities, and the quality of teaching.

- Social and systemic factors create barriers to accessing educational opportunities for people with disabilities.

Defining student and teacher responsibilities

Working with students with special education needs in inclusive settings involves extending and refining the best practices of regular teaching.

- People hold beliefs and assumptions about disability that range along a continuum.

- At one extreme, people with pathognomonic beliefs view disability as an internal and stable trait of an individual that is not responsive to change.

- At the other extreme, people with interventionist beliefs view themselves as being responsible for reducing barriers to access for people with disabilities.

In teachers, differences in beliefs are linked to differences in:

- their willingness to take responsibility for teaching students with disabilities

- their attributions about the causes of achievement and failure

- teacher efficacy

- their teaching philosophy

- their instructional practices in the classroom

Concepts of disability

- Labelling or categorizing someone as having a disability is not in itself negative. How the label is used may, however, have serious consequences.

- Categorical approaches to delivering special education depend on identifying students as belonging to a category, grouping students by category, and delivering instruction to the groups.

- Non-categorical approaches deliver special education on the basis of individual learning needs without reference to a student's category of disability.

- Cross-categorical approaches group students for instruction on the basis of their needs, using the assessment information about categorical features as a starting point for designing instruction. Teachers then apply the instructional cycle for these students as with other students in their classes.

Disability categories

- Prevalence rates for different categories of disability vary across institutions, agencies, and schools.

- The accepted conventions of language when referring to disability categories are:
  - people-first language
  - taking into account shifts in social meanings of terms
  - avoiding derogatory terms
  - complex vs. curriculum-based disabilities

Definitions of disability

- Thirteen categories are defined under five main groupings:
  - communication
  - intellectual
  - behavioural
  - physical
  - multiple
- The categories of disability are related to the dimensions of beliefs, the controversial issue in each field, and to resources that can be accessed electronically.

Complete the Module 1 post-test on-line to review topics covered in the module.

Glossary

Asperger syndrome or (Asperger's disorder)   A neurobiological disorder named for a Viennese physician, Hans Asperger, Asperger Syndrome may range from mild to severe. Defining characteristics are normal intelligence and language skills but a marked difficulty with social skills, transitions, or changes, and a preference for sameness. People with Asperger Syndrome may have difficulty reading body language and responding to social cues, and may be very sensitive to sensory cues such as sounds, light, and tastes. (p. 62)

Attention deficit disorder (ADD)   A condition resulting in inability to sustain attention. This condition does not yet have official recognition in DSM-IV. It is often used synonymously with Attention Deficit Hyperactivity Disorder (AD/HD). Physicians typically prescribe stimulant medications (Ritalin, Cylert, Dexedrine, or Adderall), although their prescription and use are controversial. (p. 75)

Attention deficit hyperactivity disorder (AD/HD)   A condition resulting in inability to maintain attention, impulsive behaviours, and/or motor restlessness. AD/HD is thought to be related to a neurobiological disorder resulting from problems in the dopamine neurotransmitter systems in the brain. Most cases are genetically inherited. If a parent or close relative has AD/HD, there is a 30% chance that a child will have AD/HD. The prescription of stimulant medications for this condition is controversial.

Autism   A severe learning disorder that includes disturbances in the rate of educational development, the ability to relate to the environment, and the development and use of language. (p. 61)

Autism spectrum disorders   A group of disabilities that may include disturbances in some or all of:
• the rate of educational development
• the ability to relate to the environment
• the development and use of language and mobility
The commonly known term for these disorders is Autism. (p. 63)

Braille   A method used to read and write by people who are blind or who have severe visual impairments. Braille consists of embossed arrangements of dots on a page that are identified through touch. It was invented by a blind Frenchman, Louis Braille, in 1829. Braille is comprised of a rectangular six-dot cell, with up to 63 possible combinations using one or more of the six dots. (p. 77)

Categorical   An approach to delivering special education that depends on identifying students as belonging to a category, then grouping students by the category and delivering instruction to the group. (p. 2)

Closed head (brain) injury   Injury to the brain that results from a trauma, such as a motor vehicle accident, in which the brain is compressed against the skull. The resulting damage may impair sensory, language, emotional, or other brain functions. (p. 76)

Complex disabilities   Significant disabilities that may be compounded by additional factors such as physical, psychological, neurological, and/or sensory impairments. Also known as "low-incidence" (infrequently occurring) disabilities. (p. 6)

Cross-categorical   Students are grouped for instruction on the basis of their needs, using the assessment information about categorical features as a starting point for designing instruction. However, functional skills determine how teachers then select instructional interventions for these students as with other students in their classes. (p. 2)

Curriculum modifications   Changes made to the content of instruction and/or to the performance level expected of the student that markedly differ from the standard level of difficulty or curriculum expectation set at the age appropriate level for the student. Curriculum modifications differ from accommodations, but both may occur together in a student's IEP. (p. 53)

Curriculum-related disabilities   Students who are underachieving in various components of the curriculum, including those who have difficulty with specified areas of the curriculum. Curriculum-related disabilities are high-incidence (frequently occurring); that is, they make up the majority of disabilities in the school-aged population. Compare with complex disabilities. (p. 6)

Developmental or moderate intellectual disability   Defined as relatively more severe than mild intellectual disability, requiring that the person has limited potential for independent living and self support. (p. 71)

Down syndrome   A genetic variation that usually causes delay in physical, intellectual, and language development. It is one of the leading clinical causes of cognitive delay in the world, although there is wide variation in mental abilities, behaviour, and physical development in individuals with Down syndrome. (p. 2)

Efficacy   The extent to which we are confident in our ability to make a difference in the learning of our students (personal efficacy); and also the expectation that teaching will have an impact on student learning despite ability and family background (general or teacher efficacy). (p. 33)

Emotional disturbance (US term)   Severe, pervasive, or chronic emotional/affective condition that prevents a child from performing everyday tasks. This condition is characterized by an inability to build or maintain relationships, inappropriate behaviours or feelings under normal circumstances, a pervasive mood of unhappiness or depression, or a tendency to develop physical symptoms or fears related to personal or school problems. See **Neurobiological disorder**. (p. 74)

Functional   Characteristics of the learner relating to how he or she currently functions—his or her current skills, knowledge, and learning characteristics. (p. 60)

High-stakes assessment   Periodic testing of all students at specified grade levels across a province, territory, or state, in order to monitor the achievement of students. These data may have several uses: supporting initiatives to raise achievement in given subjects such as literacy; holding teachers, schools, and/or school systems accountable for improving achievement in defined areas. (p. 15)

Incidence   These rates indicate how often a disability occurs, or its frequency of occurrence in the general population, over a given period or at a given point in time. It addresses the question of how often a disorder occurs, or the number of new cases per the population at risk of the disability during a specific period. Compare with prevalence. (p. 60)

Inclusion   The perspective that individuals with disabilities are entitled to an appropriate education that includes full participation with their peers and an educational process that allows them access to the same resources to learn as other students. Inclusion is also a school-based model for delivering programs and services that fulfil this perspective. (p. 7)

Individual Education Plan or Program (IEP or IPP)   Some Canadian provinces and territories require that school systems implement a process of designing and delivering individualized programs and services for students with disabilities. These may be documented in a prescribed format that informs teachers, parents, and others how best to meet the student's needs. (p. 54)

Instructional cycle   A continuous process used by teachers to assess student needs, tailor an instructional program, and evaluate student progress and achievement. The instructional cycle should be self-correcting by feeding back student achievement data that can be used to extend or adapt the program. (p. 45)

Integration   The placement of students with special needs and disabilities in the same school environment as their peers without disabilities. Integration may involve a range of placements within a school, grade, or class. (p. 53)

Interventionist   The belief that students' disabilities are not a condition of the individual person, but are in part the result of social restrictions in the world around the student, such as their interactions with a physical and social world designed for non-disabled living. These social restrictions create barriers that reduce the opportunities for these students to learn. Consequently, teachers with interventionist beliefs see themselves as responsible for removing barriers to students' access to learning, in order to facilitate their achievement. (p. 26)

Just-in-time delivery   Materials, information, resources, or tools are provided to teachers at the time when teachers need to use them. For example, a student with a complex disability has just been enrolled in the school. Information about the student's disability, his/her needs, and the materials and resources that will be useful to assist teachers to work with the student are delivered to the staff in the school at a meeting prior to the student's appearance. (p. 4)

Labelling   Designating a student as having a disability or exceptionality according to one or more of the categories of disabilities prescribed for use by an agency (e.g., a province's prescribed list of categories of special education needs). (p. 2)

Meta-analysis   An analytic research tool that statistically combines the results of several studies that address a set of related research hypotheses. Analyzing the results from a group of studies can allow more accurate interpretation of the data than from single studies alone. (p. 49)

Mild intellectual disabilities   Defined as a learning disorder manifesting across all learning situations, associated with slow intellectual development and not so severe as to limit the person's potential for eventual independent living and economic self-support. Compare with **developmental** or **moderate intellectual disability**. (p. 70)

Nativist   Characteristics of human traits and/or behaviour that are thought to be present at or before birth and are therefore attributed to factors of nature; that is, not susceptible to change post birth, during development. See also **nurturist**. (p. 28)

Non-categorical   Approaches that deliver special education on the basis of individual learning needs without reference to a student's category of disability. (p. 2)

Neurobiological disorder   An illness of the nervous system caused by genetic, metabolic, or other biological factors. Many illnesses categorized as psychiatric disorders are thought to be neurobiological, including AD/HD, autism, bipolar disorders, obsessive–compulsive disorders, schizophrenia, and Tourette syndrome. (p. 75)

Nurturist   Characteristics of human behaviour that are thought to be developed as a result of interaction with the environment (during the post birth or nurturing years), for example through the opportunity to learn. These may include genetically predetermined predisposition that must be triggered by specific environmental circumstances to emerge. Compare with **nativist**. (p. 28)

Pathognomonic   The belief, or tacit assumption, that disability is a stable, internal state of the individual, characterized by a medical–pathological condition, and therefore not amenable to instruction. It can be reliably diagnosed through medical and related procedures and/or through norm-based tests of behaviour and ability, such as IQ tests. (p. 25)

Personal efficacy   The extent to which one is confident in one's ability to make a difference in the learning of one's students. See also **efficacy**. (p. 30)

Pervasive development disorder (PDD)   Plural umbrella term for several disorders and syndromes that may or may not have biological basis or causes. These include autism, Rett's Syndrome, and Asperger Syndrome. See also Autism Spectrum Disorders. (p. 61)

Prelingual deafness   Deafness that is either present at birth or occurs as a result of a trauma or disease before the child acquires the skills to comprehend and produce language. Compare to post-lingual deafness in which a person has already learned to speak and comprehend language prior to losing his/her hearing. (p. 59)

Prevalence   The frequency of people, or how many people there are, who are identified as having a disability, expressed as a percentage of the population over time. Compare with **incidence**. (p. 56)

Pull-out   Term used in the U.S. for withdrawal programs in which students are taken to a resource or other room outside of their regular classroom for remedial assistance. (p. 43)

Regular education, regular classrooms   The subject and grade classes and programs that match the student's chronological age, and that are attended by the student's non-disabled peers. Also termed "general education classroom" (US). (p. 49)

Resilience   Some children overcome extremely difficult experiences and challenging environments to become achieving, independent, and successful adults. Researchers are studying the factors that contribute to their stamina or resilience. (p. 15)

Resource room   A room within the school to which students who are experiencing difficulties with learning and/or behaviour are withdrawn from their classes to receive additional instruction and support. (p. 46)

Resource teachers   Teachers holding qualifications in special education, who work either in the classroom alongside regular teachers or in the resource room, to provide specialized programs and services to students with learning difficulties. (p. 50)

Reverse integration   Students with disabilities usually receiving their instruction in a special education classroom are joined by students without disabilities for lessons or activities together. (p. 46)

Segregated or contained class   A classroom or class of students with learning difficulties and disabilities who spend the majority (typically more than 80%) of their school day together rather than in the regular classroom with their non-disabled peers. (p. 46)

Service delivery models   Schools have some latitude in determining how students with disabilities will be served. They may decide whether the students will be included in regular classrooms or served in a resource room or contained classroom. The roles that teaching staff, resource, and special education teachers play are influenced by the delivery model chosen. The delivery of specialized services and supports is also affected. (p. 45)

Special education class   Usually a segregated or contained class in a school or other setting, in which students with disabilities receive most or all of their instruction. (p. 46)

Special education resource   See **Resource room** (p. 49)

Teacher efficacy   The belief we hold about the influence that our teaching can have on a learner despite the influence of environmental factors. See also **efficacy**. (p. 30)

Three tier intervention system   Students who are struggling with pre-reading and other skills in Kindergarten, grade 1, 2, and 3, are given intensive instruction aimed at bringing them to grade level. Those who still lag at the end of the first year may receive further intensive intervention for one or two more grades. Increasingly, this process is used not only for remediation, but also as an assessment tool for identifying disabilities. (p. 41)

Universal access   Good instructional practice includes built-in flexibility that reduces or removes communicational and other barriers to learning for all students. This includes adapting teaching for students at various levels of understanding, and ensuring all students have a full opportunity to demonstrate their learning. (p. 4)

Withdrawal   A program in the school for students with learning difficulties in which they are taken out of their regular classroom to a resource or other room in the school for remedial assistance. See **pull-out**. (p. 43)

Additional Resources

UNESCO
Salamanca Statement and Framework for Action on Special Needs
Education: http://www.unesco.org/education/pdf/SALAMA_E.PDF

Canadian Charter of Rights and Freedoms
Section 15, 1985
http://www.justice.gc.ca/loireg/charte/const_en.html

Statistics Canada
In a number of Censuses, StatsCan has included a survey of the prevalence of disability in the Canadian population. The findings are available on its website:
http://www.statcan.ca/english/freepub/89-577-XIE/canada.htm

Esmerel
Esmerel's Collection of Canadian Disability sites contains a comprehensive collection of links to Canadian organizations that are involved with every form of disability for people in all age groups. It is available at
http://www.esmerel.org/canada/canada2.htm

Canadian Provincial Government Special Education Websites
Visit the various websites containing the provincial government policies and guidelines for special education. A list is available at:
http://www.edu.gov.on.ca/eng/relsites/oth_prov.html

Alberta
http://www.education.gov.ab.ca/k_12/specialneeds/ident.asp

British Columbia
Manual of Policies, Procedures and Guidelines:
http://www.bced.gov.bc.ca/specialed/ppandg/toc.htm

Manitoba
The School Support website:
http://www.edu.gov.mb.ca/ks4/specedu/

New Brunswick
http://www.gnb.ca/0000/anglophone-e.asp#ss
http://www.gnb.ca/0000/index-e.asp

Newfoundland and Labrador
Statutes: http://www.hoa.gov.nl.ca/hoa/chapters/1997/S12-2.c97.htm
The resources offered by the Student Support Services unit of the
Department of Education for students with special education needs can
be found at http://www.ed.gov.nl.ca/edu/dept/sss.htm

Northwest Territories
View the Strategic Plan for 2005–2015, and specifically the goal for the
Education of Children and Youth at:
http://www.ece.gov.nt.ca/Strat_Plan/Strategic_Planning/index.htm

Nova Scotia
Nova Scotia Department of Education Special Education Policy Manual:
http://www.gov.ns.ca/snsmr/publications/product.asp?numRecordPositi
on=7&P_ID=3604&strPageHistory=cat&strKeywords=&SearchFor=&PT_ID
=2832

Nunavut
http://www.gov.nu.ca/education/eng/index.htm

Ontario
The Ministry of Education of Ontario Special Education Guide can be
retrieved at
http://www.edu.gov.on.ca/eng/general/elemsec/speced/guide.html
A list of resources can be found at:
http://www.edu.gov.on.ca/eng/teachers/speced.html

Prince Edward Island
The web page for students with special educational needs is
http://www.gov.pe.ca/educ/index.php3?number=74836&lang=E

Quebec
Ministry of Education Plans of Action and ministerial policies including
documents related to adapting schools to the needs of all students:
http://www.meq.gouv.qc.ca/GR-PUB/menu-plans-a.htm

Saskatchewan
The minister's response to the report of the Special Education Review Committee is available at:
http://www.sasked.gov.sk.ca/branches/curr/special_ed/docs/review/strgthsupp.pdf

Yukon
http://www.education.gov.yk.ca/specialprograms/

References

Andrews, J. & Lupart, J. (2000). *The inclusive classroom: Educating exceptional students.* (2nd ed.) Calgary, AB: University of Calgary: Nelson Thomson Learning.

Artz, S., Nicholson, D., Halsall, E., & Larke, S. (2001). *A review of the literature on assessment, risk, resiliency and need.* Department of Justice: National Crime Prevention Centre, File No. 3510-U1. December 31st.

Ashton, P. T. & Webb, R. B. (1986). *Making a difference: Teachers' sense of efficacy and student achievement.* New York: Longman.

Bickel, W. E. & Bickel, D. D. (1986). Effective schools, classrooms and instruction: Implications for special education. *Exceptional Children, 52*(6), 489-500.

Blackorby, J. (2003, September). *Analysis for teacher quality: Update on the collaborative analysis from the Study of Personnel Needs in Special Education (SPeNSE) and the Special Education Elementary Longitudinal Study (SEELS).* Memorandum to Patricia Gonzalez, U.S. Department of Education. Menlo Park, CA: SRI International.

Booth, T. (2000). *Inclusion in education: Participation of disabled learners.* Executive summary: Thematic study for the EFA2000 assessment. Report to UNESCO.

Bowlby, J. & McMullen, K. (2002). *At a crossroads: First results for the 18 to 20-year old cohort of the Youth in Transition Survey.* Ottawa: Human Resources Development Canada and Statistics Canada. Retrieved December 14, 2005 from http://www.drhc-hdrc.gc.ca/sp-ps/arbdgra/publications/research/2002doc/YITS

Bowlby, B., Peters, C., & MacKinnon, M. (2001). *An educator's guide to special education law*. Aurora, ON: Canada Law Book.

Boykin, A. W. (2005). *Addressing achievement gaps: Progress and prospects for minority and socio-economically disadvantaged students and English language learners. Highlights from the ETS Symposium on addressing achievement gaps*. ETS Policy Notes: Notes from the ETS Policy Information Center. 13(1). December.

Burris, C. C., Heubert, J. P., & Levin, H. M. (2006). Accelerating mathematics achievement using heterogeneous grouping. *American Educational Research Journal, 43*(1), 105–136.

Chapman, J. W. (1988). Learning disabled children's self-concepts. *Review of Educational Research, 58*, 347–371.

Cox, P. R. & Dykes, M. K. (2001). Effective classroom adaptations for students with visual impairments. *TEACHING Exceptional Children, 33*(6), 68–74.

Crespo, M. & Carignan, N. (2001). L'enseignant-ressource en milieu urbain defavorise: Une intervention educative efficace. *International Review of Education, 47*(1-2), 31–58.

Darling-Hammond, L. (1998). Unequal opportunity: Race and education. *Brookings Review, 16*(2), 28–32.

Darling-Hammond. L. (2006). *Securing the right to learn: Policy and practice for powerful teaching and learning*. Presidential address; Dewitt-Wallace Reader's Digest Distinguished lecture. American Educational Research Association Annual Meeting, San Francisco, April.

DiBella-McCarthy, H., McDaniel, E. A., & Miller, R. (1995). How efficacious are you? *TEACHING Exceptional Children, 27*(3), 68–72.

Dyson, A., Polat, F., Farrell, P., & Gallannaugh, F. (2005) *Inclusion and achievement: School processes*. Paper presented to the American Educational Research Association Annual Conference, Montreal, 11–15 April.

Dyson, A., Farrell, P., Gallannaugh, F., Hutcheson, G., & Polat, F. (2004). Inclusion and Pupil Achievement (London, DfES). Retrieved May 10, 2006 from http://www.dfes.gov.uk/research/data/uploadfiles/ACFC9F.pdf

Fenstermacher, G. D. & Richardson, V. (2005). On making determinations of quality in teaching. *Teachers College Record, 107*(1), 186–213.

Finkelstein, V. (1980). *Attitudes and disabled people.* New York: World Rehabilitation Fund.

Florian, L. (1998). Inclusive practice: What, why and how? In C. Tilstone, L. Florian & R. Rose (Eds.) *Promoting inclusive practice* (pp. 13–26). London: Routledge.

Foorman, B. R. & Schatschneider, C. (2003). Measurement of teaching practices during reading/language arts instruction and its relationship to student achievement. In S. Vaughn and K. L. Briggs (Eds.), *Reading in the classroom: Systems for the observation of teaching and learning* (pp. 1–30). Baltimore: Brookes Publishing.

Fuchs, D. & Fuchs, L. S. (1994-5). Sometimes separate is better. *Educational Leadership, 52,* 22–24.

Gaarder, J. (1996). *Sophie's world.* New York: Berkley Books.

Gerber, M. M. & Semmel, M. I. (1984). Teacher as imperfect test: Reconceptualizing the referral process. *Educational Psychologist, 19,* 137–148.

Government of Canada (2004). *Advancing the inclusion of persons with disabilities.* Available at www.sdc.gc.ca/en/gateways/topics/pyp-puu-jyhshtml.

Gresham, F. M. (1984). Social skills and self efficacy for exceptional children. *Exceptional Children, 51*(3), 253–261.

Gresham, F. M. & Reschly, D. J. (1986). Social skills deficits and low peer acceptance of mainstreamed learning disabled children. *Learning Disabilities Quarterly, 9*(1), 23–32.

Haager, D., Gersten, R., Baker, S., & Graves, A. (2003). The English-Language Learner Classroom Observation instrument for beginning readers. In S. Vaughn and K. Briggs (Eds.), *Reading in the classroom: Systems for the observation of teaching and learning* (pp. 111–114). Baltimore: Brookes Publishing.

Hattie, J. (1992). *Self concept.* Hillsdale, NJ: Lawrence Erlbaum.

Heubert, J. P. (2002). First do no harm: How the misuse of promotion and graduation tests hurts our neediest students. *Educational Leadership, 60*(4), 26–31.

Heubert, J. P. & Hauser, R. M. (Eds.). (1999). *High stakes: Testing for tracking, promotion and graduation.* Washington, D.C.: National Research Council.

Hobbs, N. (Ed.). (1976). *Issues in the classification of children:* (a sourcebook on categories, labels, and their consequences). New York: Jossey-Bass Publishers.

Howard, S., Dryden, J., & Johnson, B. (1999). Childhood resilience: A review and critique of the literature. *Oxford Review of Education, 25*(3), 307–323.

Hutchinson, N. L. (2002). *Inclusion of Exceptional learners in Canadian Schools: A practical handbook for teachers.* Toronto: Prentice Hall.

Individuals with Disabilities Education Act (IDEA) (1990) Code of Federal Regulations, Title 34, Section 300.7 (b) (9).

Jordan A. (2002). Special education in Ontario: A case study of market-based reforms, *Cambridge Journal of Education, 31,* 349–371.

Jordan, A., Lindsay, L., & Stanovich, P. J. (1997). Classroom teachers' instructional interactions with students who are exceptional, at-risk and typically achieving. *Remedial and Special Education, 18,* 82–93.

Jordan, A. & Stanovich, P. (2001). Patterns of teacher-student interaction in inclusive elementary classrooms and correlates with student self-concept. *International Journal of Disability, Development and Education, 48*(1), 43–62.

Kagan, D. M. (1992). Implications of research on teacher belief. *Educational Psychologist, 27,* 65–90.

Kalyanpur, M., & Harry, B. (1999). *Culture in Special Education: Building reciprocal family-professional relationships.* Baltimore: Brookes Publishing.

King, A. J. C., Warren, W. K., Boyer, J. C., & Chin, P. (2005). *Double cohort study: Phase 4 report.* Ontario Ministry of Education. Retrieved Nov 6, 2005 at http://www.edu.gov.on.ca/eng/document/reports/phase4/index.html

Leicester, M. & Lovell, T. (1997). Disability Voice: educational experiences and disability. *Disability and Society, 12,* 111–118.

Lehmann, W. & Taylor, A. (2003). Giving employers what they want? New vocationalism in Alberta. *Journal of Education and Work, 16*(1), 45–67.

Levin, B. (2004). *Students at risk: A review of research*. Paper prepared for the Learning Partnership. April.

Looker, D. & Thiessen, V. (2004). *Aspirations of Canadian youth for higher education*. Final report: Learning Resources Directorate, Human Resources and Skills Development Canada. Retrieved October 27, 2005 at http://www.sdc.gc.ca/asp/gateway.asp?hr=/en/cs/sp/hrsdc/lp/publications

Loveless, T. (1998). *The tracking wars: State reform meets school policy*. Washington, DC: The Brookings Institute.

Lupart, J. & Webber, C. (2002). Canadian schools in transition: Moving from dual education systems to inclusive schools. *Exceptionality Education Canada, 12*(2&3), 7–52.

McGhie-Richmond, D. (2001). *Incorporating the affective to enhance the cognitive: A case study of exemplary teaching*. Unpublished PhD dissertation, University of Toronto.

McGhie-Richmond, D., Jordan, A., & Underwood, K. (2002). *Discovering the general in the particular: A case study of an exemplary teacher's beliefs*. Paper presented at the annual meeting of the American Educational Research Association, New Orleans, April.

McLaughlin M. M. & Jordan, A. (2004). Push or pull: The forces that shape inclusion in the U.S.A. and Canada. In P. Mitchell (Ed.), *Contextualising inclusive education*. London: RoutledgeFalmer.

Moore, D. (2001), *Educating the deaf: Psychology, principles, and practices*. Boston: Houghton-Mifflin.

Montecel, M. R. (1989). *The answer: Valuing youth in schools and families: A report on Hispanic dropouts in the Dallas Independent School District*. San Antonio, TX: Intercultural Development Research Association.

Montecel, M. R., Cortez, J. D., & Cortez, A. (2004). Dropout-Prevention Programs: Right Intent, Wrong Focus, and Some Suggestions on Where to Go From Here. *Education and Urban Society, 36*(2), 169–188.

Muijs, D. & Reynolds, D. (2002). Teachers' beliefs and behaviors: What really matters? *Journal of Classroom Interaction, 37*(2), 3–15.

National Association of Secondary School Principals (1992). *A leader's guide to school restructuring*. Reston, VA: Washington, DC: National Association of Secondary School Principals.

National Commission on Excellence in Education (1983). *A nation at risk: The imperatives of school reform.* Washington, DC: National Commission on Excellence in Education.

Nougaret, A. A., Scruggs, T. E., & Mastropieri, M. A. (2005). Does teacher education produce better special education teachers? *Exceptional Children, 71*(3), 217–229.

Oakes, J., Ormseth, T., Bell, R., & Camp, P. (1990). *Multiplying inequalities: The effects of race, social class, and tracking on opportunities to learn mathematics and science.* Santa Monica, CA.: RAND.

Oliver, M. (1990). *The politics of disablement.* Basingstoke, UK: Macmillan.

OSSTF (2000). Implementing secondary reform: A review of year #1. *Update, 27* (17), May 30.

Piers, E. V. (1984). *Piers-Harris Children's Self-Concept Scale (The way I feel about myself):* Revised Manual. Los Angeles: Western Educational Services.

Pressley, M., Wharton-McDonald, R., Allington, R., Block, C. C., Morrow, L., Tracey, D., Baker, K., Brooks, G., Cronin, J., Nelson, E., & Woo, D. (2001). A study of effective first-grade literacy instruction. *Scientific Studies of Reading, 5*(1), 35–58.

Rae, B. (2005). *Higher expectations for higher education: Postsecondary review.* Queen's Park, Toronto: Government of Ontario. Retrieved December 15, 2005 from www.raereview.on.ca/en/report/default.asp?loc1=report

Renzulli, J. S. (1978). What makes giftedness? Re-examining a definition. *Phi Delta Kappan, 3,* 180–184, 261.

Reynolds, C. R. & Fletcher-Janzen, E. (2000). *Encyclopaedia of Special Education. 2nd Ed.* New York: Wiley.

Rice, J. K. (2003). *Teacher quality: Understanding the effectiveness of teacher attributes.* Washington, DC: The Economic Policy Institute.

Rioux, M. (1997). Disability: The place of judgment in a world of fact. *Journal of Intellectual Disability and Research, 41,* 102–111.

Roehrig, A. D., Dolezail, S. E., Mohan-Welsh, L., Bohn, C. M., & Pressley, M. (2003, April). *The development of a tool to assess the quality of early-primary grade teachers' classroom practices.* Poster presented at the meeting of the American Educational Research Association, Chicago, IL.

Rosenshine, B. & Stevens, R. (1986). Teaching functions. In M.C. Wittrock (Ed.), *Handbook of research on teaching*, (3rd. ed., pp. 376–391). New York: Macmillan.

Rozenholtz, S. J. (1989). *Teacher's workplace: The social organization of schools*. New York: Longman.

Safran, J. S. (2002). Supporting students with Asperger's Syndrome in general education. *TEACHING Exceptional Children*, *34*(5), 60–66.

Sarason, S. & Doris, J. (1979). *Educational handicap, public policy, and social history: A broadened perspective on mental retardation*. New York: Free Press.

Scofield, J. (2004). Trades training for teens (Ontario Youth Apprenticeship Program). *Education Today*, *16*(3), 26.

Siegel, L. S. (1992). An evaluation of the discrepancy definition of dyslexia. *Journal of Learning Disabilities*, *25*, 618–629.

Slee, R. (1996). Imported or important theory? Sociological interrogations of disablement and special education. *British Journal of Sociology of Education*, *18*, 407–429.

Smith, R. M., Salend, S. J., & Ryan, S. (2001). Watch your language: Closing or opening the special education curtain. *TEACHING Exceptional Children*, *33*(4), 18–23.

Stanovich, K. E. (1991). Discrepancy definitions of reading disability: Has intelligence led us astray? *Reading Research Quarterly*, *26*, 7–29.

Stanovich, K. E. (1996). Toward a more inclusive definition of dyslexia. *Dyslexia*, *2*, 154–156.

Stanovich, K. (2000). *Progress in understanding reading; Scientific foundations and new frontiers*. New York: Guilford Press.

Stanovich, P. & Jordan, A. (1998). Canadian teachers' and principals' beliefs about inclusive education as predictors of effective teaching in heterogeneous classrooms. *Elementary School Journal*, *98*, 221–238.

Stanovich, P. & Jordan, A. (2004). Inclusion as professional development. *Exceptionality Education Canada*, *14* (2-3), 169–188.

Stanovich, P., Jordan, A., & Perot, J. (1998). Relative differences in academic self concept and peer acceptance among students in inclusive classrooms. *Remedial and Special Education*, *19* (2), 120–126.

Stuebing, K. K., Fletcher, J. M., LeDoux, J. M., Lyon, G. R., Shaywitz, S. E., & Shaywitz, B. A. (2002). Validity of IQ-discrepancy classifications of reading disability: A meta-analysis. *American Educational Research Journal*, *39*, 469–518.

Swanson, H. L. & Malone, S. (1992). Social skills and learning disabilities: A meta-analysis of the literature. *School Psychology Review*, *21*(3), 427–443.

Taylor, A. (2003). Finding the future that fits. *Eric Information Clearinghouse*, ED477494.

Taylor, A. (2005). "Re-culturing" students and selling futures: School-to-work policy in Ontario. *Journal of Education and Work*, *18*(3), 321–340.

TIMMS 1999 International Mathematics. Retrieved February 21, 2006 from http://timss.bc.edu/timss1999i/math_achievement_report.html

Tregaskis, C. (2002). Social Model Theory: The story so far. *Disability and Society*, *17*, 457–470.

Underwood, K. J. M. (2002). *Parents' understanding of disability: An exploration of the culture of special education in Ontario*. Unpublished M.A. thesis, University of Toronto.

Vaughn, S., Moody, S. W., & Schumm, J. S. (1998). Broken promises: Reading instruction in the resource room. *Exceptional Children*, *64*(2), 211–225.

Vaughn, S., Wanzek, J., Woodruff, A. L., & Linan-Thompson, S. (In press). A three tier model for preventing reading difficulties and early identification of students with reading disabilities. In D. H. Haager, S. Vaughn, & J. K. Klingner, (Eds.), *Validated reading practices for Three Tiers of Intervention*. Baltimore: Brookes Publishing.

Vellutino, F. R., Scanlon, D. M., & Lyon, G. R. (2000). Differentiating between difficult-to-remediate and readily remediated poor readers: More evidence against the IQ-achievement discrepancy definition of reading disability. *Journal of Learning Disabilities*, *33*, 223–238.

Wayne, A. J. & Youngs, P. (2003). Teacher characteristics and student achievement gains: A review. *Review of Educational Research*, *73*(1), 89–122.

Weisel, A. & Tur-Kaspa, H. (2002). Effects of labels and personal contacts on teachers' attitudes toward students with special needs. *Exceptionality*, *10*(1), 1–10.

Williams, C. B. & Finnegan, M. (2003). From myth to reality: Sound information for teachers about students who are deaf. *TEACHING Exceptional Children, 35*(3), 40–45.

Willms, J. D. (2002). Vulnerable children and youth. Findings from Canada's National Longitudinal Study of Children and Youth. *Education Canada, 42*,(3), 40–43.

Wilson, S. M., Floden, R. E., & Ferrini-Mundy, J. (2001). *Teacher preparation research: Current knowledge, gaps, and recommendations.* Seattle, WA: University of Washington.

Winzer, M. (1998). A tale often told: The early progression of special education. *Remedial and Special Education, 19*(4), 212–218.

Wotherspoon T. & Schissel, B. (2003). The business of placing Canadian children and youth "at risk". *Canadian Journal of Education, 26*(3), 321–339.

Getting Ready to Teach

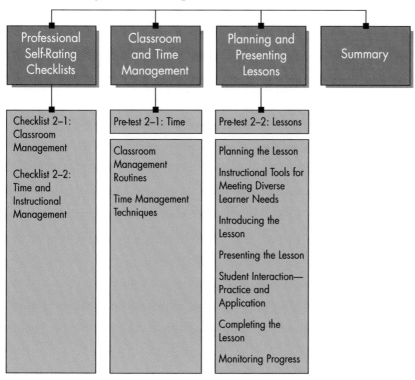

Learning Objectives

Section 1: Professional Self-Rating Checklists

In this section, readers will learn:

1. the essential prerequisite concepts and skills upon which adaptive instructional techniques are built, which is a necessary first step in differentiating instruction for learners with differing needs

2. a professional self-monitoring system that can be used now and at any time in their teaching career to examine and reflect upon their command of fundamental skills that are necessary for effective teaching

In the first section, a series of self-rating checklists allows readers to rate themselves on the fundamental skills of teaching: classroom management, conserving and using instructional time, and lesson planning and presentation. The intent of these checklists is two-fold: to allow readers to think about their areas of strength and the areas that are fundamental to effective teaching, and to review the concepts of the module in their simplest form. At the end of the checklists, readers are encouraged to reflect on their self-ratings and to identify one or more areas of priority for their own professional growth. This exercise is personal, however, and does not form part of the marking system; readers can rate themselves without being concerned that their record will be available to anyone else. The remainder of the module contains resources to help readers develop their understanding of and/or review these teaching fundamentals.

Section 2: Classroom and Time Management Techniques that Support Instruction

In this section, readers will learn:

3. ways to expand the instructional time available in a school day so they will have sufficient time to work with all students; this additional time can then be used for working with individual and small groups of learners who will benefit from adaptations made to their learning goals and instructional objectives

4. how to establish an orderly and predictable flow of activities in the classroom to be able to predict disruptions and difficulties almost before they happen, and take preventive steps to eliminate them

5. develop a community in the classroom in which students take a role in managing their own activities, and where they can develop a sense of self-direction and independence in managing their own learning time, assist other students, and take responsibility for their accomplishments and those of their peers

The second section reviews principles for the effective use of time, including techniques for classroom and time management. These techniques enable the teacher to redirect instructional time away from managerial and disciplinary tasks by establishing a classroom community in which each person has a part to play in ensuring that lessons and routines flow.

Section 3: Planning and Presenting Lessons

In this section, readers will learn:

6. to identify instructional objectives and learning goals, curriculum

expectations and standards, and distinguish the characteristics of instructional objectives that are well-designed compared to poorly designed

7. to identify the components of an instructional objective, so that, in Module 3, they will be able to adapt it with accommodations and change it to meet curriculum modifications

8. design instructional objectives to reflect various types of teacher knowledge and student knowledge, that will then provide the basis for designing Individual Educational Plans and Programs (IEPs) for students with exceptional needs

9. how to design goal-related performance criteria, using rubrics, that permit teachers and students to monitor students' progress and adapt instructional outcomes for differing learner needs

10. consider a range of pedagogical techniques that engage diverse learners

The third section examines the principles of teaching and learning that lead to decisions about how to design, develop, present, and complete a lesson and monitor the effectiveness of instruction. The section contains the following sub-topics:

- planning lessons

- introducing lessons

- presenting new material (the expository part of a lesson)

- practising and application (the interactive activities of a lesson)

- completing the lesson

- keeping track of student achievement and monitoring progress

Woven through each of the subtopics will be activities and research boxes about:

- writing instructional objectives

- different theories of how students learn and how teachers teach (direct instruction, strategy instruction, constructivist teaching, guided discovery learning)

- rubrics, a system for developing and sharing with students the objectives and standards for student performance on a lesson or unit

Opening Vignette

D r. Jon Van Loon is a Professor Emeritus with a long and distinguished career. He is the author of six books, has been instrumental in advocating for environmental change, and has worked through UNESCO in many countries. Yet, Dr. Van Loon has a significant learning disability that has profoundly affected his life and his concept of himself. View an interview with Dr. Van Loon on-line.

After viewing the video, consider the following questions:

1. What has been the impact of having a disability on Dr. Van Loon's understanding of his own skills in the following:

   • cognitive

   • social

   • self-concept?

2. Compare the video of Jon Van Loon with the Ashif Jaffer video sequence in Module 1. Why do you think these two people have arrived at such different understandings of themselves as achievers? What factors have contributed to their differences?

3. Do you think that an early diagnosis would have made a difference to Dr.Van Loon's life, and if so, in what ways?

4. Dr. Van Loon advises young people with a disability to follow a set of principles. What are these?

Module 2 introduces the concepts, skills, and knowledge of teaching that are essential prerequisites to adapting instruction to individual learner needs. Much of the material to be discussed in this module may be familiar to teachers since it is a review of concepts that are fundamental to all aspects of good teaching: principles of teaching practice and lesson design. Most textbooks on special and inclusive education either present these concepts as they describe the processes needed to adapt instruction, or the authors assume that the reader is already familiar with them. For example, to design learning goals and instructional objectives that accommodate learner differences, teachers must first be familiar with the anatomy of an instructional objective, and be able to build progressively more complex objectives into a system for tracking student progress, such as a rubric.

These prerequisites have been collected here in the form of a review. The module is in three sections. The first section contains a self-rating checklist of fundamental skills for effective teaching. Whether or not readers are conversant with these skills, they may want to examine them and even print them off as handy tools for their own professional self-monitoring. The checklists include a comprehensive set of effective teaching skills that cover the basics in classroom and time management and lesson design and presentation. They also provide an invaluable synopsis of effective teaching skills that readers can use as a self-guided reference at various stages in their career. The second section of the module examines classroom and time management in greater depth. Without these skills, teachers will struggle to get around to all the students in their classes. The third section examines the initial skills needed for designing and presenting lessons and units that accommodate learner differences. These skills are then further developed in Module 3.

Because the module is delivered electronically, it allows readers to take a short pre-test at the beginning of Sections 2 and 3. If the concepts and ideas in Section 2 on managing and conserving instructional time are already familiar, and readers therefore score a high percentage of correct responses on the pre-test, they can skip over this section of the module and move on to the next pre-test. Section 3 introduces concepts of lesson planning and design, and once again, if readers do well on the test they may skip the material and move on to the end of the module. Readers can choose to review the materials at any point, and there are links in the Section 1 checklists to allow them to skip to related material later in the module.

Section 1: Professional Self-Rating Checklists

learning objective

2-1–
2-2

The following checklists ask readers to rate their skills in classroom management, use of instructional time, and lesson preparation. If the results of this self-rating lead readers to want to review the material in greater detail, it is included in the following sections. These checklists are for readers' personal use only, and they may choose to print and save them for later reference. When finished, readers should continue to the next section by taking Pre-test 2–1 on using instructional time effectively.

Self-Rating Checklists 2-1 and 2-2: The Organization and Management of Instructional Time

(Adapted from Englert, C.S., Tarrant, K. L., & Mariage, T. V. (1992). Defining and redefining instructional practice in special education: Perspectives on good teaching. *Teacher Education and Special Education*, 15(2), 62–86.)

checklist
2-1

Name: _____ Date: _____ Class/Subj/Grade: _____

Number of students: _____ Support personnel present: _____

CHECKLIST FOR CLASSROOM MANAGEMENT				
Instruction	Excellent 5 4	Satisfactory 3 2	Needs Work 1	My Notes
Beginning of year/semester/course:				
Arranges physical space to maintain minimally disruptive traffic patterns and procedures				
Has established rules and procedures for **non-instructional** events (e.g., movement about the room, student talk, distribution materials, bathroom, etc.)				
Has established rules and procedures for **instructional** events (getting ready for lesson, roles of instructional groups, obtaining help, seatwork procedures)				
Has established rules that involve respect for members of the class and provides verbal reminders to students about how to treat each other				
Clearly states in advance what behaviour will be tolerated and what will not				
Introduces rules, procedures, and consequences (e.g., rules are stated and posted; has provided discussion of rules, defined contexts in which rules apply, stated consequences in advance)				

CHECKLIST FOR CLASSROOM MANAGEMENT CONTINUED				
Instruction	Excellent 5 4	Satisfactory 3 2	Needs Work 1	My Notes
Demonstrates what behaviour is acceptable by presenting examples and non-examples of target behaviour				
Ongoing through year/semester/course:				
Monitors rule compliance and provides feedback				
Provides consequences for rule non-compliance quickly; cites rule or procedure when dealing with disruptive behaviour				
Positions self in room to provide high degree of visibility (e.g., can make eye contact with all students)				
Scans class frequently				
Uses non-verbal signals when possible to direct students in non-disruptive manner when teaching other groups of students				
Administers praise contingently, and uses specific praise statements				
Includes students in the management of their own behaviour and cues self-regulation (e.g., self-monitoring, self-evaluating)				
Provides behavioural corrections to students to indicate how they can control themselves				

CHECKLIST FOR TIME AND INSTRUCTIONAL MANAGEMENT

Instruction	Excellent 5 4	Satisfactory 3 2	Needs Work 1	Notes
a) Time Management:				
Allocates generous amounts of time for instruction (limits time spent on behaviour management, non-academic activities)				
Keeps transition times between lessons short				
States expectations for transitions to/from seatwork in advance				
Establishes lesson routines that signal a clear beginning and end				
Prepares students in advance for transitions by stating behavioural expectations and informing them when lesson is coming to a close				
Monitors transitions by scanning and circulating among students				
Gains students' attention at beginning of large group and expository activities and maintains it at 90% level				
Maintains student attention during seatwork at 80% or higher				
Establishes seatwork procedures for early finishers and students needing help				
Demonstrates 'with-it-ness' by monitoring seatwork students through scanning and provides correction through signals				
b) Lesson Presentation: *i. Introducing the Lesson* Provides review of previous day's concepts at beginning of lesson; actively tests students' understanding and retention of previous day's lesson concepts				

CHECKLIST FOR TIME AND INSTRUCTIONAL MANAGEMENT CONTINUED				
Instruction	Excellent 5 4	Satisfactory 3 2	Needs Work 1	Notes
Provides a clear overview of the lesson (explains task in terms of teacher's and students' actions) and tells students what they will be accountable for knowing and doing				
Involves students in setting goals				
States the purpose and objective of the lesson				
Introduces a new learning task and activates prior experience and knowledge relevant to the topic, strategies, and skills to be learned				
Relates lesson topics, concepts, or strategies to other concepts, strategies, and existing knowledge				
ii. Presenting New Material				
Provides a framework to help students organize the lesson information (e.g., text structure, diagram, concept map, semantic web, etc.)				
Points out distinctive features of new concepts and uses examples and non-examples to show relevant and irrelevant features of the concept				
Models task-specific learning strategies and self-talk that will help students achieve (e.g., rehearsal strategies, problem-solving routines, retrieval strategies, etc.)				
Tells students what the lesson strategy is, how to perform the skill/strategy, when it can be used, why it is beneficial to students (what learning outcomes result), and how it can be adapted				
Points out organization, relationships, and clues in learning material that elicit learning strategies				
Maintains a brisk pace during the lesson				

CHECKLIST FOR TIME AND INSTRUCTIONAL MANAGEMENT CONTINUED				
Instruction	Excellent 5 4	Satisfactory 3 2	Needs Work 1	Notes
iii. Interaction – Practice and Application				
Provides frequent questions to evaluate students' mastery of lesson concepts; repeats practice opportunities until students not making errors				
Requires overt and active participation (reading text aloud, writing a response, working with peers)				
Delivers instructional cues and prompts to maintain high accurate responding				
Maintains high success rate in teacher-led activities (70–90% accuracy)				
Provides error correction procedures, using prompting or modelling, following errors rather than telling answers				
Re-teaches and makes instructional decisions on the basis of students' performance				
Instructs students to generalize and apply knowledge across settings, situations, and conditions				
iv. Completing the Lesson				
Gives summary of lesson content and integrates lesson content with other lessons and experiences				
Provides error drill on missed concepts during and at the end of the lesson				
Summarizes the lesson accomplishments of individuals and groups				
v. Monitoring Progress				
Supplies assignment/evaluation criteria and explains how assignments are to be completed				
Forecasts upcoming lesson content				
Provides daily, weekly, and monthly reviews				
Maintains continuous graphs and records of students' achievement				
Communicates results of evaluation activities to students				

How did you do?

In reflecting about the ratings that you gave yourself, what did you find were your strengths?

Note two things:

_____

_____

_____

What areas are possible targets for your next stage of professional growth? Jot down the top two priorities for your professional wish list:

_____

_____

_____

Section 2: Classroom and Time Management Techniques that Support Instruction

This section begins to address the major objection that teachers raise when asked to include students with diverse learning needs in their classrooms: there is insufficient time to teach everyone. Some educators claim there are too many students competing for too little class time for the teacher to be able to do an effective job of meeting the needs of all students, particularly those whose needs diverge from those of the rest of the class. Module 3 discusses techniques for maximizing instructional time through grouping, peers as tutors, and use of paraprofessionals and other adult resource people. However, the ideas presented in Module 3 rely on the assumptions about the conservation and use of classroom time presented here. First, take the Pretest 2-1 on-line to see whether you have already mastered this material or whether you will benefit from a brief review.

pre-test

2-1

Access Pretest 2–1: Time on-line.

learning
objective

2-3

In Case Study 2–1, Lisa's classroom is a profile of a modern urban Canadian classroom. It demonstrates the dilemmas faced every day by teachers. How should they allocate instructional time? Should they act like triage doctors in emergency rooms, using their time with the students they know will leap ahead? Or do they work with individuals who are struggling to stay afloat? Will a little of both fail both groups? Just what are teachers supposed to know about the various difficulties and disabilities that their students are encountering, and how are they supposed to work with them? How much attention should students with difficulties and disabilities receive and at what level, given the constraints of curriculum standards, students with greater achievement potential, and their parents' expectations?

case
study

2-1

Read about the class that Lisa teaches in Case Study 2–1: Lisa's Class.

case study

2-1

Lisa's Class[1]

One of Lisa's grade 4 students tackles a math problem. It requires him to identify which series of containers in the picture holds more: seven containers each drawn as small pails with 1 litre labels, or three larger pails each of which is labelled 2 litres. The student doesn't stop to compute, but points to the drawings of the larger pails, and says "Those are bigger so they hold more." This is not a misunderstanding of the problem or an incorrect computation. He is functioning at what Piaget (1952) would term "pre-operational thought" in which the size of the pail is the only salient variable in his repertoire of problem-solving skills. In similar tasks, he shows that he does not understand the concept of volume, nor even of number. He is persuaded only by the visual appearance of each problem, estimating from the apparent size of each rather than from its properties. This level of understanding is usually exceeded by children at around 5 or 6 years of age.

Lisa surveys her class of 32 students. In her class, one-third live below the poverty line. Eight live with one parent, one with grandparents, and two are in foster care. Eleven come from homes where English is not spoken, and they represent five languages. Four students have recently arrived from a war-torn country where they suffered traumatic experiences. They huddle together, speaking their first language. Another four students are designated as speaking English as a second dialect. Four racial groups are represented in the class. Six students are new to that school and four will relocate to another school before the end of the school year.

There is a five grade spread in reading achievement. Only six students are at or above the curriculum standards set for grade four. One student has been identified as having a developmental disability, three are designated as learning disabled, and one is achieving at grade level and mobile in her wheelchair. There are nine students in the class for whom an IEP has been prepared. A social services agency is monitoring two students because of suspected abuse at home. For one of these students, the school staff are on alert to prevent the child's father from entering the school because a restraining order has been issued prohibiting the father's access.

Lisa considers her choices. She could give the rest of her class "busy work" and concentrate on one-to-one tutoring of the boy who doesn't understand volume. Or she could attempt to teach the whole class, giving this child some time and attention whenever she gets a moment. Finally, she could ignore this student and use her stretched time and resources to teach where it will have the most impact—with those students who are capable of higher achievement.

Fuchs, Fuchs, Mathes, and Simmons (1997) suggest that in most classrooms, the teacher feels like a triage doctor in M*A*S*H, choosing who to attend to on the basis of who has the best chances of long term survival. Inherent in Lisa's class is a "zero-sum game" (Brown & Saks, 1981, 1987; Gerber & Semmel, 1984). Fuchs et al.

---

[1]This case study was written by combining elements of several authentic cases that were documented in classrooms.

(1997) comment that, although one is initially struck by the considerable diversity of the students in a typical classroom, and the multiple obstacles (e.g., poverty, abuse, instability) that the students must overcome to achieve some semblance of school success, less obvious is the breathtaking range of the students' cultural and experiential backgrounds, knowledge, and skills to which the teacher must respond. An unavoidable question is how the teacher might reach out to everyone.

This is a dilemma faced daily, even hourly, by teachers in classes like Lisa's. With limited time and resources, where do they put their efforts? Do they give everyone a little attention? Or do they concentrate on doing a good job with fewer students at the expense of the rest? This is a deeply painful moral and professional dilemma. It has become exacerbated in recent years with the introduction of province-wide curriculum standards and high-stakes assessments, where class achievement averages are made available to the public and teachers are held accountable for the assessment outcomes.

Cook, Tankersley, Cook, and Landrum (2000) asked teachers to consider their attitudes toward their students by nominating them to one of four categories: **attachment** (high achieving students who were a pleasure to teach), **concern** (students who teachers felt could be assisted by their teaching), **indifference** (students whose presence in the classroom is often overlooked), and **rejection** (students with behavioural, social, and motivational problems who were beyond help). The surprising finding was that teachers were able to rate their students into these groups—akin to "triage"—to determine who would most benefit from the teacher's efforts and who to leave alone. Further, the researchers showed that in practice, teachers gave differential attention to the students in each group, suggesting that attitudes were closely allied with teaching practices, and therefore with the opportunities that students received to learn.

The triage option ensures that the class averages are optimized, since concentrating on the better students has greater "payoff" than spending time with lower achievers. On the other hand, one of the reasons why people become teachers is to contribute to every one of their students in ways that will significantly impact the rest of their lives.

There must be ways that give Lisa more options than to become a triage teacher!

Discussion Questions:

1. What are the pros and cons of the triage system that allocates students to different levels of instructional treatment?

2. Instead of conducting a triage on her students, what are some of Lisa's options?

One important assumption of these special education modules is that all teachers have the readiness and ability of Lisa, the teacher featured in Case Study 2–1, to cope effectively with such diversity in the regular classroom. They do not have to make dramatic decisions about triage; they will need to balance their time with different individuals and groups. By "thinking outside the box" of traditional teaching practices, Lisa and her colleagues can reach every one of the students in their classes, at least to a degree that will give each student the opportunity to progress.

The sections that follow introduce teachers such as Serena, Emma, Keith, Keiko, Maria, Wilma, Ben, and Jill. These real teachers illustrate that not only do highly effective teachers conserve their precious instructional time, they also practise these techniques every day. They demonstrate how to use that time to calibrate instruction to individual student needs, and to draw upon resource people to work with them in novel ways.

Classroom Management Routines

learning objective
2-4

Teaching time is inversely proportional to the amount of time a teacher spends on management. The more time spent on orchestrating people's movement, getting ready for a lesson and packing up, and on discipline, the less time there is for instruction. It seems that teachers who are able to provide large amounts of instructional time can do so because they have already established the organizational and managerial skills required to free up this time. This is done by relegating the managerial and organizational tasks of running the class largely to students. Effective teachers are very much the coordinators of their classes, but they do not have to be the pivot around which the class functions. A sense of community and mutual support also needs to be in place so that the students take on the managerial tasks as a partnership in a community of learners.

How do they do this? The process begins before the start of each new school year, and continues as a high priority during the first weeks of the new term. It is often called "survival," but these skills are more that that. They are a key ingredient to a teacher having a wide **Zone of Responsibility** for the students in the class.

Arranging physical space

The goal is to make sure that traffic flow is optimized. This includes locating materials so that students can readily access them without coming to the teacher, and arranging furniture so that students can move freely around the room and the teacher can see and reach each student.

Establishing classroom rules

Class rules are usually set up early in the school year and often posted. Rules may be developed jointly by the students and teacher and posted, or they may reflect the school code of behaviour together with the teacher's preferred routines for having students leave the room, assist each other, and other behaviours that contribute to the smooth running of the classroom. The purpose of the rules is to free the teacher from having to deal with behaviours that interfere with instructional time. Collectively devising and monitoring rules is part of handing over responsibility (though not ultimate control) for classroom conduct to the students. There is a sense in the class that students have autonomy in accessing what they need to get on with the task.

Diagram 2–1a: A teacher who is central to every classroom decision is a busy person.

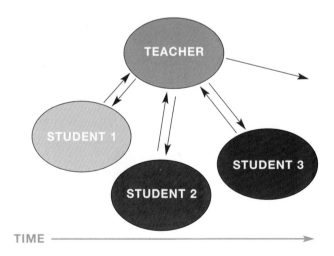

Diagram 2–1b: A teacher who delegates the organizational decisions has more time to supervise learning.

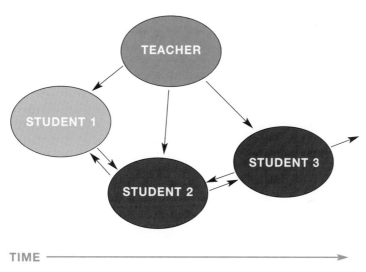

In the first part of Diagram 1, one teacher is at the centre of managing every student, and as a result is very busy dealing with student requests. The second teacher has established the expectation that students will make some of the decisions about routines, accessing information, and assisting each other. As a result, this teacher has more time to oversee the class and can select whom he or she wants to spend time with.

Teacher visibility and visual monitoring

Enforcing the collectively developed rules requires teachers to have fair and just leadership skills. These skills include quickly providing consequences for student non-compliance of a rule, for example by citing the rule or by using "the look." This "look" includes eye-contact and a semi-bemused look with which the teacher targets a disruptive student until that student settles down. It is associated with "the periscope," the ability of a teacher to look up from his or her work in order to scan the room, usually every few minutes, to identify what is happening

on the periphery of the class. Teachers also use proximity to subdue some student behaviours. They continue to teach, but move to where the unruly student is seated. In the 1970s, Kounin (1970) termed the skills of being aware of one's classroom space as "**with-it-ness**," a term that has stuck.

Administering praise

Brophy and Good (1986) conducted a study of teachers' use of praise. Their findings indicated that students look for authentic praise that is given for deserved achievements. It is specific to individual students and to particular task accomplishments. It is neither broad, general praise that has the tone of cheerleading, nor is it the withholding of praise. It can be very effective in motivating students to risk responding, such as those who struggle to generate a response. In classrooms in which teachers' questioning routines have been observed, withholding praise is relatively common.

Effective teachers have various techniques for rewarding achievement and effort. In its simplest form, praise is a word and a smile. In some classes, more elaborate systems are used that may involve a points system where students earn privileges for their group or for themselves. In other classes, teachers effectively use checklist charts for individual students that result in free time or notes home. Of course, these methods vary with grade level and age of the students, and systems that pit individual students against each other competitively should be avoided. Systems that allow students to earn points for a group or team are preferable, since they build on cooperation and a sense of community.

learning
objective
2-5

Time Management Techniques

Interviewer: What is your most important goal?

Teacher T: Expectations and relationship. Because if you can get that set up, then you are golden for the rest of the year, like that makes life just so much easier. Because they trust me more, they're willing to take risks, they're willing to get me a bit of space. You know it all…it all benefits me. That's why I do a lot of it.

Teacher S: I think it's two things. One is routines should not come through me, and the other is that learning doesn't always have to come through me. If all the routines go through me then I waste exorbitant amounts of time doing stuff like "Can I go to the bathroom?" And prior to this year, our [previous grade] teacher was exactly the opposite to me, so the kids would come to me in September and it would take months to get them through the idea that they don't have to ask to go to the bathroom. Now they come up and it's like "Oh yeah! I can go to the bathroom" and they just scoot out the door....So if things always go through me, then I'm not free to do what I really need to do, which is *What are you thinking?, Where are we going with this?*, organizing learning. So routines, I do not want them to go through me for a whole variety of reasons; one is laziness, and it interrupts teaching.

I don't think the learning has to go through me either. I much prefer that I would say, "Here's what I need you to go work on. Here's some different ways of doing it. Let me know what you come up with." And so I become instead the... I don't know... the [pit]stop at the race tracks. So they stop in with me, like the race car, and they get some new tires, and out they go again. Rather than it coming from me, just all from me, because that's too much pressure.

Teachers should be protective of the precious instructional time that they have created. Yet in many schools, it is not well respected. An **expository teaching** event is interrupted by the school announcement system. Since the students are busy, a parent or colleague walks in during seatwork to chat about something, disregarding the important work of the teacher with individuals and small groups. The teacher in the next room sends a student to borrow something. The healthy snacks are delivered. The resource teacher arrives mid-lesson to return a group of students, causing the teacher to backtrack in order to catch up this group with the task at hand.

The management of time, and the apparent lack of it, is in part a reflection of a long history of viewing teaching as an art, rather than as a small s "science." Yet teachers are very much scientists, developing their own theories of learning and teaching, and experimenting with how to enhance student achievement. In the classrooms in which excellent inclusive practices are used, teachers' well-developed theories have in no way detracted from their caring, their dramatic flare for engaging students, and their sense of creativity. But it has made them protective of their time so that they are able to do what they know they are capable of doing.

The adaptation of instructional materials, techniques, and delivery to the individual needs of each student is a more time-consuming process than teaching in a **transmissive** or "broadcast" manner to the whole class. In

Module 1, the beliefs and practices of teachers were characterized as lying along a continuum from "pathognomonic" to "interventionist." In that module, differences in assumptions and beliefs about teachers' roles and responsibilities for teaching students with special needs were examined, as well as how these assumptions and beliefs are strongly related to differences in teachers' practices. The most effective teachers not only show that they can create lots of instructional time, but that they can also use it very effectively to meet the diverse needs of **all** students, including those with disabilities.

The major theme of **time management** includes making the lesson, its objectives, and the teacher's expectations for student achievement totally understood and transparent to the students. This teaching skill establishes the students as co-partners in being responsible for meeting the achievement, social, and behavioural expectations for the class. By making the learning experience agenda and its objectives available to students, the teacher transfers the management of student attainment to the students, yet without relinquishing control of steering the process. The instructional time usually taken by managerial activities such as repeating instructions and managing students is consequently reduced and made available to the teacher for instruction.

Time management skills include:

- stating the lesson expectations in advance

- notifying the students when the lesson is beginning and ending, and when transitions to other classes or breaks are imminent

- monitoring the transitions by circulating and establishing routines for transition (who will collect work, what to do when finishing work early or late, how to prepare to leave or switch subjects)

These routines minimize the amount of "down time" that students need to start, complete, and change activities, thus contributing to the teacher's instructional time.

Many of the above routines will be familiar to you as the "old chestnuts" that are taught in teachers' college methods courses as survival skills for beginning teachers. Some commentators claim that these skills are passé, that they belong to the mechanistic perspectives of researchers in the 1960s, and that their intent was to raise the efficiency of teaching along the lines of factory production lines (in general education, see Brophy & Good, 1986; Doyle, 1986; Rosenshine & Stevens, 1986; in special education see Bickel & Bickel, 1986; Rieth & Evertson, 1988). Indeed, this is where these skills were first identified. But they continue to be the foundation upon which modern pedagogical techniques are based.

Studies of highly effective teachers (Berliner, 2001; Berliner, Mangieri, Collins, & Block, 1994; Bereiter & Scardamalia, 1993) show how teaching has many of the attributes of other kinds of skilled performance. Teachers learn to coordinate the multiple activities in the classroom, scan it frequently, and select ways to respond and make decisions at a fast and frequent pace. Clark and Peterson (1986) estimated that on average, teachers make a decision about interacting with students every two minutes. As experience develops, teachers monitor the flow and hum of the class, enabling them to detect clues and early warning signs that unanticipated events are about to occur. They are then able to be proactive rather than reactive, responding to anticipated interruptions and changes before they occur, so that the flow of the class activity continues without disruption.

For a case study of a group of teachers who are experts in engaging their diverse students in their inclusive classrooms, review Case Study 2–2: Expert Teachers below.

case
study

2-2

case study

2-2

Expert Teachers

Meet Serena, Keith, and Emma[1]

In a large research study of inclusive practices (Jordan, Lindsay & Stanovich, 1997; Jordan & Stanovich, 2001), these teachers stood out from their peers as being exemplary in meeting the diverse needs of students in their classrooms. As a result, the researchers wanted to document their thinking about themselves as teachers, and to learn about their philosophies of teaching and how these were reflected in their actions in the classroom. The researchers returned to these three classes to observe the teachers, recording their lessons on audiotape by having each teacher wear a radio-frequency microphone that transmitted to a tape recorder. The taped material was then available to assist each teacher to recall various instructional decisions and actions that had taken place during the lessons. This prompted them describe the reasons for their instructional decisions and actions, and to link them to their philosophies and beliefs. This study was reported in Stanovich & Jordan (1999).

Serena, teaching a grade 3 class in a geographically large rural school system, had taught all grades at the elementary level during her 24-year career. Her class contained 29 students, five of whom Serena nominated as being at-risk and who would likely be referred for subsequent placement in special education. This school system starts such a process in grade three for placement in grade four.

Emma, a veteran of 26 years, had also taught all elementary and intermediate grades (for the last six years at grades 6 and 7), in a school system serving a mid-sized town. Grade 7 groups rotated daily through her language arts program. There were 27 students in the observed group, three of whom had been designated as exceptional, including K., who had been identified as having a moderate intellectual disability.

[1]The case studies are based on real situations. The names of the teachers and some details have been changed.

Keith had taught for 9 years in a metropolitan school system that served a portion of a city of four million people. A total of 54% of the students in this board were from non-English speaking home backgrounds. Twenty four percent of residents in the area served by this school system were members of racial minority groups. Keith taught a grade 10 English class in which nine of the 28 students had been formally identified as exceptional, and two further students were designated as gifted. Three of the nine identified students attended a withdrawal program for part of their day before joining Keith's English class. Five students had not been formally identified but were considered by Keith to be at-risk of needing further intervention at a later point in their school career. C. and S., male students, had been formally designated as disabled learners because of severe emotional and behavioural difficulties.

Research Findings

All three teachers had four characteristics in common, each based on and building on the previous one.

1. Maximize teaching time to work with individuals and groups

Emma is able to maximize her own teaching time, particularly on seatwork activities in which she circulates and pays attention for sustained periods of time to individual students or small groups of students engaged in a similar or cooperative task. Similarly, Serena expects that all students will receive her individual attention and instructional support until they feel able to continue their work independently. When Serena is working with one student, all other members of the class respect that individual student's time with the teacher as a priority over their own immediate needs, unless a crisis arises. In order to use her time equitably, Serena makes sure that she works with all students over the course of a day. She maintains a class list that she annotates to keep track of her work with every student.

Keith spends large amounts of time with students who are having difficulties. He places them around a table at which he is also seated. Other students bring their work to the table for him to check. Every so often he leaves this table to hold conferences with students who have not come up to his "command centre." He describes himself as monitoring at-risk students "out there on the periphery" while freeing up a lot of time to work one-to-one with the exceptional students. Keith is careful to emphasize, however, that this table is not to be associated with students' difficulties. He rotates students frequently and deliberately selects students to join the table who are doing well, to assist them to further extend their thinking. "It's supposed to be a place for safety and help...it's a place to be encouraged and to be respected as opposed to a place to be told you mustn't do that."

2. Encourage independent learning and risk-taking

One of the outcomes of the managerial skill of each teacher is that every student is aware of the objectives of the lesson and how to be a participant in the learning process. All three teachers forecast upcoming transitions and preview future tasks. Each teacher uses time judiciously to maximize student involvement in the task. The theme of encouraging students to venture into the learning process is echoed by all three teachers. Serena states that her primary objective is to promote in her students a sense of independence as learners. This objective has many facets, both cognitive and affective.

Serena: Independent problem solvers would have to be one of the most important things I'm looking for in my kids.

Interviewer: By independent problem solving, what I'm hearing is giving them a sense that they're in charge of their learning. Is that correct?

Serena: Yup, definitely....I'm not looking at the right answer always. I'm looking at how they solve it, and they know there are so many things in the room that they can use.

In order for a learner to reach this self-knowledge, the classroom has to be a safe environment in which to risk trying new skills. For students with a history of failure and labelled as exceptional, the need to feel safe is enormous and difficult for the teacher to meet. The teachers therefore emphasize the process of learning rather than the outcome. They are careful to praise effort and not to demean students' efforts. They further model this behaviour and expect other members of the class to behave similarly.

Keith: Yeah. And the kids here, they'll know if they don't do something well but that they haven't labelled themselves and some of the labels that they felt they had in the past...C. has been one of the biggest problems in the whole school but you'd never know that. He's very rambunctious...And S., he's very bright and he's had a horrible write up and report cards, personality, and I can't even go through it. In the class I had last year we had two kids that, these kids would pale in comparison, but it just depends on how you treat them and how you get along. For instance, I'll give you an example. They're so used to doing put downs and taking things very personally; that's why I'm always in a way...if I make a mistake... instead of just...if I were helping you instead of just saying, "can you get a dictionary for me?" I'll make an announcement. "Can somebody get me a dictionary please because I can't remember that word?" So now they know that when I do that with them they don't feel stupid.

A relaxed, accepting, and light-hearted atmosphere pervades each classroom. Emma laughs aloud at her students' antics, but signals that it cannot go too far. Serena takes the role of learner, making her students giggle as they attempt to straighten out her thinking. All three teachers share personal anecdotes and reflections on their own childhood experiences.

3. Calibrate instruction to learning

All three teachers use the time that they allocate to students who are experiencing difficulty to assess and calibrate their instruction to the current level of understanding of each student. This calibration process is not limited to academic and conceptual cues supplied by the students, but also to their emotional status at that moment. The teachers often engage in the complex process of fine tuning their instructional dialogues to a student's current conceptual and cognitive characteristics.

Interviewer: It seems to me that you don't give away answers the way I'm tempted to do. You wait for them to come up with the answers. You have a real patience for that.

Emma: I call it nudging ...and it's a perfect term for what we do in teaching. We just up the ante, and then back off if you have to back off.

Interviewer: But you don't give clues.

Emma: Sometimes you do. Sometimes you put them in the track and you nudge them right along the track. For instance, with K., I did a lot of that.

The sliding tracks are similar for all students in the class, irrespective of their designation or grouping. Emma describes a process akin to Palincsar and Brown's (1988) and Palincsar's (1990) "scaffolding," whereby each student is located along each track which leads to one or more of the lesson objectives, through a series of probes and questions from the teacher, listening for cues from the student's responses to fine-tune the calibration of instructional comments and questions. The teacher then "nudges" or pushes the student along the track. Emma holds five or six tracks in her head at any given time.

All three teachers exhibit the skill to follow the student's lead when holding a dialogue about the topic at hand, dialogues that we term "cognitive extension." In these exchanges, the teacher does not supply answers or comment on the correctness or incorrectness of a student response. The focus is on engaging the student in the process of learning rather than the arrival. There is a high proportion of questions in the teacher's talk and a willingness to follow the students' leads in searching for answers. Teachers see the students' answers as vehicles for teaching rather than as evidence of products or outcomes. This permits a wider set of acceptable responses from the diverse students in the classroom, since each response can signal not only mastery but also an index of where to calibrate subsequent questions in the nudging process.

4. Encourage moral responsibility through preserving dignity and enhancing self respect

All three teachers use a method of handling students' moral development that avoids a confrontational challenge. Talking to Keith, the interviewer says:

Interviewer: I can't remember which kid it was. I think it may have been S. and he may have been at the back of the room and you said to him, "Are you getting on with what you're supposed to be doing? Please answer yes so that I can praise you." And he said, "Yes." And you said, "Good for you." And of course he wasn't doing what he was supposed to be doing...

Keith: Yes. But he got the message and I didn't make it negative.

Lickona (1991) discusses the elements in a school culture that contribute to the moral character and values education of students. They include a school-wide sense of community, democratic self government, and a moral atmosphere of mutual respect, fairness, and cooperation that pervades all relationships. All three teachers demonstrate these characteristics in the confines of their classroom. They create the safe and positive classroom climate that allows each student an opportunity to take the risks needed to discover the value to the community of his or her own contributions.

Keith: And it's just because there are people saying "ain't" and there are people from backgrounds where they don't use helping verbs. So they speak...they write how they speak. So I just try...it's pure modelling. That's the whole thing. And there are certain norms that are in society but they're not norms at home. So when you're walking down the hall, "please take your hats off." At home, "I can wear my hat at home." "Yes, but not here please." So it's pure modelling, pure repetition, and you find that as the year goes on, when people are approaching me they start to use...well they stop themselves and say, "May I go to the washroom Mr. D?" And that seems like no big step but for a student to stop something that's ingrained, he's been saying for years, is a [big] step.

All three teachers seem to have a clear understanding of how to share the responsibility for learning and behaviour with their students. They do not attribute blame to the students for failure to learn or for misbehaviour, but they also do not see themselves as solely responsible when students fail. This balance of responsibility will vary from student to student, but all three teachers handed back to students, time after time, new opportunities for assuming that responsibility.

SUMMARY

The three teachers described here have multiple images not only of the lesson and the way it should proceed, but also of each student's characteristics and where each fits into the skills sequences implicit in the lesson and the process of achieving the lesson objectives. Such images are not static, but are modified by the conditions of the moment. The teachers also have beliefs about their own roles in and responsibilities for maximizing the opportunity of each student to progress. This includes modulating the expectations that they hold for each student on the basis of their prior knowledge of the student, his or her circumstances and history, and also their ongoing observation of the cues that indicate a student's current emotional well-being.

Adaptations are covert wherever possible in order for each student to maintain dignity as a fully contributing member of the class. Teachers press students to assume responsibility for their own learning and achievements.

When reflecting about how they make adaptations for individual students, each teacher articulates a belief about adapting their expectations for individual students. This does not entail, however, lowering the requirements of the lesson or providing materials and tasks that differ from those used by the remainder of the class, common adaptations in many inclusive classrooms. Instead the teachers move back to prior skills in the implicit skills sequences and then nudge the student forward. This form of adaptation is cyclical, and can vary as a result of the teachers' beliefs about the learning potential of that student and the student's mood and willingness to risk or expend the effort needed to succeed. This adaptation is also relatively invisible to other members of the class, since all students are similarly taught.

All three teachers had considerable teaching experience and cared deeply about their students, elements that Pressley, Rankin, and Yokoi (1996) include in their discussion of outstanding teachers. But these elements alone are not sufficient conditions for the exemplary practices that were witnessed. Possible contributing factors include a strong sense of self efficacy (perhaps resulting from a history of success with difficult-to-teach students), a strong sense of moral authority for themselves and beliefs in the moral responsibility of the classroom community to include students with disabilities, along with considerable reflection about their craft.

Discussion

Undertake your own mini-research project on teacher expertise by examining some of the following studies.

There are different genres or strands of research. This literature represents diverse starting points and theoretical lenses (Berliner, 2001). One strand of this literature has examined the cognitive processes of teachers. Based on research of information-processing theory in psychology, these studies have drawn parallels between effective teachers and skilled operators in other professions. For example, like skilled drivers, teachers learn to anticipate upcoming problems such as behavioural challenges in the classes, and do so with sufficient foresight to be able to make adjustments to their teaching to head off potential disruptions without interrupting their lessons. They develop routines which they put into action at a level that is almost subconscious or automatic to maintain their attention on the larger curricular and programming objectives of the lesson (Bereiter & Scardamalia, 1986, 1993; Sternberg & Horvath, 1995).

Other strands of research have examined the career stages through which teachers develop over the course of their careers (Berliner, 1994; Shulman, 1986, 1987), while others use case study to examine expert teachers' thinking and actions in depth (Berliner, 2004; Orland-Barak & Yinon, 2005; Poulson & Avramidis, 2003). Several studies compare expert with novice or less effective teachers, (Berliner, 2001; Carter, Cushing, Sabers, Stein, & Berliner, 1988; Copeland, Birmingham, DeMeuille, D'Emidio-Caston, & Natal, 1994).

Discussion questions:

Several of the themes from Module 2 are reflected in the case study.

1. What did you learn about the time management skills of the three teachers?

2. How does each teacher encourage risk-taking?

3. What are the overall objectives of the teachers for students with learning difficulties and what strategies do they use to achieve them?

4. Describe in your own words what Emma means by "nudging." How would nudging appear in a subject that you teach? Give an example.

5. Encouraging moral responsibility that each teacher describes consists of what kind of teaching actions?

Section 3: Planning and Presenting Lessons

In this section, each of the phases of a lesson is reviewed, starting with planning the lesson, and ending with monitoring student progress. Several themes can be found throughout these phases. The design of a rubric, for example, has implications for each of the phases of lesson planning through implementation and completion. Details of rubrics, of different types of learning objectives, and of different types of instructional approaches can be found in the linked boxes on your way through this section.

Start by taking the pre-test to see if you feel you should proceed directly to the next module. Access Pre-test 2–2: Lessons on-line.

Planning the Lesson

Read Interactive Exercise 2–1: Emma's Adaptations for Kamleh. Emma describes her instructional process and how she adapts it for two of her students with special needs.

interactive
exercise

2-1

Emma's Adaptations for Kamleh[1]

Emma, a veteran of 26 years in teaching, has taught all elementary and intermediate grades, and for the last six years has been teaching grades 7 and 8. Two grade 7 groups were observed. The two groups rotated daily through Emma's Language Arts program. There were 27 students in one group, three of whom have been designated as exceptional. Kamleh, a female student, had been formally identified as exceptional. Several of Emma's other students were termed "at risk" of failing the grade, including Tom, a student who had a very low opinion of his own ability and a fear of failing, and Nathan, who also lacked confidence in his ability. Emma is teaching a Language Arts unit to her grade 7 class. She has adapted her curriculum from Nancy Atwell's (1998) writing program for the intermediate grades. Emma is in the midst of a unit which she has designed to teach the skills for persuasive writing.

Emma: (in a loud voice to address the whole class, quite fast pace) OK, this morning we are going to continue the unit on persuasive writing. As we see on the rubric wall chart, your written work will have three parts to it: introducing your proposition or claim, developing your case by presenting three arguments, and a summary and conclusion. You will continue to develop your outline on the worksheet.

[1]This case study is based on a real classroom event. The names of the participants however have been changed.

NOW IS THE TIME TO STOP

Arguments:

1. _____

   _____

2. _____

   _____

3. _____

   _____

Emma: Most of you have chosen your proposition or your claim statement and written it on your work-sheet. John has written "Now is the time to stop alcohol abuse." Joanne has "…to stop child labour." And Kyle has written "…to stop smoking." Your job today is to develop those claims. You are looking for three good reasons or arguments that you can make to support your claim that "Now is the time to stop…" whatever you have chosen for your claim.

I will assign you to groups. One group will go to the library where our librarian, Mrs. Grant, and Ms. Parisi, our student who is with us from the college, are waiting for you. They will help you use the Internet to research your arguments. One group will stay here and work together to help each other develop the arguments. There are some magazines and newspapers on the back table to help you with this.

One group will work with me at the set of desks that we moved into a square. Each group has a half hour for this part of the lesson, and then you will move to the next task. I will let you know five minutes before you need to move to the next task. We have a period this afternoon to finish the task, so you will all get to do all three tasks, and by then you should all have developed three good arguments for your claim and be ready to write them as paragraphs. Some of you may even start this today. OK, your groups are on the overhead: Don't move till I say 'Go'….

Later Emma is discussing the lesson with the researcher, Anne.

Emma: I chose Kamleh to join me at the desks, together with Nathan and Tom. They are all struggling with the English program. But I want different outcomes for each of them. I don't expect Kamleh to develop three arguments to sustain her proposition that "Now is the time to stop child abuse." I'll be pleased if she can come up with three facts or pieces of information about the prevalence, nature, or outcome of child abuse. She is not very confident about herself as a learner, but with encouragement and support, she will find three facts. Obviously, prolonged dialogue with me will be embarrassing to her as she will feel singled out. She likes and responds well to Nathan, so I asked Nathan to assist her to find her three facts.

Anne: As I watched you, it seemed to me that you don't give away answer the way I'm tempted to do. You wait for them to come up with the answers. You have a real patience for that.

Emma: I call it nudging. ...and it's a perfect term for what we do in teaching. We just up the ante, and then back off if you have to back off.

Anne: But you don't give clues.

Emma: Sometimes you do. Sometimes you put them in the track and you nudge them right along the track. For instance, with Kamleh, I did a lot of that. She had a big thing about abuse, so we narrowed it down, narrowed it down, so now I'm nudging her along the track (toward three facts about child abuse).

Anne: Do you apply this selective nudging to other students who are having difficulty too? Tom has been unable to state his main premise in the claim he is preparing.

Emma: Tom is a bit of an enigma to me. I think he has lots of capabilities, lots of topics. He'll be a fine thinker eventually, but he's still not thinking well. He's very concrete, but I think it'll come. I have a sense that with him it'll come. We're in a transitional stage with him. With more education, more thinking, more exposure to stuff, he'll come along, but he's still very concrete. I will nudge him when he is ready, but I think that he must make the first decisions.

Anne: So you're not thinking of him like Kamleh where if he could get three topics you'd be happy.

Emma: Right! I'm hoping he can get more than that. But if he could just think around a topic right now that would be a big step for him. It's very abstract for him. For Kamleh, child abuse seems much more concrete. "I know what physical is; I know what sexual is." But for Tom it's an abstract concept.

Discussion Questions:

1. Emma uses a metaphor for how she perceives the instructional process. She calls it "nudging." She speaks of using "tracks," and of "up-ing the ante" and "backing off." In your own words, describe these processes.

2. Emma selectively "nudges" Kamleh and Tom. How do you think this process differs for each of them?

To review these concepts further, you can complete a quiz on-line.

Each year, teachers must decide what, where, when, and how to teach, while keeping the particular needs of their students in mind. This type of decision making requires careful planning. Before choosing what to teach, teachers must first set some goals to determine where they are going. What are the curriculum standards they seek to have their students achieve, and in turn, what are the learning goals and instructional objectives that map these standards onto the content and skill of the course materials?

Diagram 2–2

Diagram 2–2 illustrates the relationship between achievement standards, curriculum expectations, learning goals, and instructional objectives.

Instructional objectives

When planning the curriculum dimension, the teacher decides what to teach, selecting the entry points to the curriculum that are needed for the range of students in the class. In order to engage in curriculum planning, teachers must have a clear idea of the curriculum goals and of the objectives that these goals will become when the curriculum content is selected. For example, looking at Interactive Exercise 2–1, Emma's goals are as follows:

- Students will understand and use the principles of persuasive writing, including generating a proposition statement or claim and supporting arguments.

- Students will write an expository written assignment with an appropriate structure for developing a persuasive argument.

- Students will use library resources to conduct research, which can be used to develop arguments in support of the chosen proposition.

By choosing a pedagogical technique of concept webs, and a lead-in statement "Now is the time to stop…", Emma translates the curriculum expectations into learning goals, selecting controversial social causes as content to carry the goals. The specific instructional objectives for the series of lessons then flow from these goals and the content that will carry them. In Research Box 2–1, Emma's specific instructional objectives are displayed.

For a look at how to design good instructional objectives, and an amusing look at some less useful ones, examine Research Box 2–1: Designing Instructional Goals and Objectives.

research box 2-1

Designing Instructional Goals and Objectives

The design of lessons and units of study and the development of plans for implementing them depend on teachers having a clear statement of their learning goals and instructional objectives. There is an art and a science to designing goals and objectives. They need to contain sufficient information so that student progress can be monitored and evaluated. This information includes:

- a description of the skills, behaviours, and/or knowledge that the student will demonstrate once the objective is accomplished

- a description of the conditions under which the learning will occur

- the level of performance that will be needed to demonstrate that mastery has been reached

In Think it Over 2–1, the similarities in the definitions of types of knowledge are included. The distinctions between types of knowledge are crucial for understanding what to include in a good instructional objective.

Popham (1999) notes that there are three ways to frame the goals or objectives that comprise a given instructional domain, two of them detracting from and one supporting a teacher's ability to monitor and evaluate how much students are benefiting from instruction.

The overly specific objective

An instructional objective can be highly task-specific within a given domain, so specific that the teacher and the students judge mastery by the demonstration of that skill alone, and not on the class of skills that this one skill should be representing in sampling student outcomes. For example, the goal for Emma's grade 7 language class might be to understand the form and effect of persuasive writing and to design an essay that illustrates the claim and its supporting arguments. If Emma prepared an overly specific instance of this objective in order to communicate it to the class, it might look like this:

Students will write a one-paragraph rationale for the claim that "Now is the time to stop child abuse." The rationale will consist of the three reasons that they have selected from the list of arguments generated by the class and posted on the wall. Each reason will be written as follows: The first sentence will describe the reason. The second sentence will say why it is important. The student will write a concluding sentence that summarizes the three reasons....

This type of objective is not very useful instructionally because it specifies the content and the student's performance in so much detail that it fails to guide students to participate actively in the learning process. It de-emphasizes the skills needed to accomplish the objective. It takes much of the activity out of students' approximating the major goal, which in Emma's case is to lead her students to understand and design their own persuasive claim and formulate the arguments that support it. In beginning the persuasive writing unit, an overly specific objective may result in the students failing to understand the larger instructional purpose as they focus on the mechanics of the exercise. If they have reached the end of the unit, they will believe that the product, and not the process of getting there, is their teacher's main lesson objective. Further, this objective leaves no latitude for Emma to modify it to allow one student to identify three facts instead of arguments, or to accommodate the writing difficulties of another student by allowing pairs of students to work together.

The hyper-general objective

Popham's second type of less-than-useful objective is more common in our experience. The "hyper-general objective" is at the opposite extreme from the overly specific objective. It usually takes a form such as:

> Students will write superior essays in which the claim and its arguments are genuinely persuasive. Inferior essays will fall far short of this, and adequate essays will be somewhat convincing but less so than superior ones.

> The difficulty of teaching from hyper-general objectives is that there are no criteria that allow teachers to evaluate how well the students have reached the target instructional domain. Further, they are not helpful to the teacher in designing and fine-tuning instruction for individual students. They also fail to communicate to students the expectations for their performance. They produce arbitrary criteria for student performance that are not shared by the class community because they are inaccessible and rest entirely in the teacher's judgement.

The skill-focused objective

The third type of objective, like good porridge in the Goldilocks nursery tale, is "just about right." It specifies how student performance can demonstrate that the objective has been reached. In other words, the knowledge and skills that it samples are related to the target instructional domain. For Emma's unit in Interactive Exercise 2–1, it might be:

> A good persuasive article will convince the reader that a claim is justified. Students will write a persuasive article to support a claim that begins "Now is the time to stop..." They may choose their own claim.
> Step 1 – Researching the claim. Students will use the library and Internet resources, along with resources and ideas from people in class and at home, to develop three arguments to support the claim. Each argument will provide a good reason for the claim, and will differ from the other two arguments. These will be recorded on the concept web chart.
> Step 2 – Writing the Persuasive Article. The web chart will then be used to write a persuasive article in five paragraphs. The first paragraph states the claim, developing why it is important. In the second, third and fourth paragraph, each of the arguments that support the claim are to be presented and developed. The fifth paragraph summarizes the claim and the arguments.
> Marks will be given for the depth of research, flow of the finished article, the strength of each argument, and the extent to which the reader is persuaded by the claim.

Experienced teachers are usually able to articulate and justify their selection of instructional objectives, but novice teachers often have great difficulty describing why they are engaging students in learning activities. Novice teachers' descriptions tend to focus on a general need to expose the students to prescribed material. Perhaps some of the confusion about setting instructional objectives has arisen because teachers have a mandate to teach across curricular domains and integrate traditionally separate content areas. When carefully planned as a series of objectives that are understood by students, each with its own set of criteria for mastery, several instructional domains can be combined. However, this takes considerable planning, and requires using a foundation of learning objectives set for each of the component areas that share similar thinking skills, rather than content. It takes more than adding an art activity with no inherent objective to a math or language arts lesson, or adding a musical accompaniment to physical education to meet the instructional outcomes demanded in each instructional domain.

In Module 3, Sandi Batista's science lesson with her third grade class will be presented as an example. Sandi asks students to match the animals with their winter habitats. The primary instructional objective is to have students develop inquiry skills about why animals interact with their habitats in the ways that they do. For example, the beaver lives in a hut that is accessed through water that freezes; Sandi wants her students to think about why an animal might choose to live in such a place. Sandi uses this content as a basis for reviewing principles of physics (the qualities of insulation of ice, the effect of salinity on water freezing) while aiming toward her objective of having the students think

and ask questions about phenomena (in this case, animal adaptations to cold temperatures). This contrasts with other lessons in which students complete piles of work sheets under the guise of receiving individual programs.

Future modules will consider the importance of well-formulated instructional objectives as the basis from which the teacher adapts instruction. It will be evident that clearly formulated instructional objectives are a prerequisite to accommodating learner differences and to generating modifications and alternate programs for students who are receiving **Individual Education Plans**. The importance of objectives will also recur when state- and province-wide mandates for curriculum-based, high stakes assessment are considered.

STUDENT POLL 2–1:

Predesigned curriculum goals and instructional objectives can lock a teacher in to having to teach in a predetermined, mechanistic way and restrict the spontaneity of the lesson.

Yes ☐   No ☐   Undecided ☐

student poll 2-1

Formulating Instructional Objectives

The design of clear, well defined instructional objectives is central to effective teaching. The objectives are the small learning steps that occur along the way to reaching larger goals, which are usually part of the imposed curriculum. A teacher's first task in planning is therefore to translate a curriculum area into a series of lesson objectives. These objectives can provide important information to the students about what is being taught. To do this, objectives should represent various components of students' learning. It is important to recognize that fostering meaningful learning, knowing both what to do and why, can help students expand their understanding of the material at hand. In addition, remembering related ideas is easier than remembering isolated facts. When students are involved in active problem solving, they are trying to make sense of the tasks and devise solutions for them. This entails reorganizing their thinking, rather than merely accumulating information (Cobb et al., 1991). When teachers focus on problem solving and reasoning, students can begin to construct their own understandings and procedures.

learning objective 2-7– 2-8

Effective instructional objectives should be developed to represent the three types of knowledge students will demonstrate. The first type is known as **declarative** or **content knowledge**. It is the "what" of the subject material through which the teacher conducts the lesson and the student demonstrates mastery of it, such as the facts, the names, or the rote material. Second is **procedural knowledge** or **task-specific skills**. This knowledge includes the concepts and skills needed to undertake a task. The third type of knowledge is **conditional knowledge** or **information-handling skills**, the process by which students develop new connections between new and/or previously acquired concepts. Additionally, these lesson objectives should be related to previously learned concepts and ideas, and apply to new instances.

For a more in-depth review of types of knowledge, read Think It Over 2–1: Types of Knowledge.

Types of Knowledge

Instructional objectives are embedded in a broader set of goals that make up the overall lesson or unit objectives. These are themselves embedded in the objectives or expectations of the prescribed curriculum. The teacher must translate the broad curriculum objectives into specific lesson content through the medium of topical materials associated with subject areas (history or mathematics or physical education, etc.). Instructional objectives make the curricular expectations into operational units. Lesson objectives can consist of different kinds of instructional objectives: acquiring declarative or content knowledge, task-specific strategies or procedural knowledge, and conditional knowledge, which is also called transferable or metacognitive strategies.

Benjamin Bloom (1956) is credited with being the grandfather of the instructional objective. He originally distinguished five types of objectives in what he termed the cognitive domain, according to their progressive levels of cognitive complexity (and student engagement). Bloom noted that learning proceeded better when objectives targeted students' higher order thinking skills at the higher levels of the taxonomy, rather than simply requiring them to memorize and reproduce facts.

- **Knowledge:** At its lowest level, an instructional objective requires the recall of specific information.

- **Comprehension:** At the lowest level of understanding, the objective requires material be understood.

- **Application:** The objective requires students to both understand and apply a rule or a principle to the material.

- **Analysis:** Students are required to break apart the material into the component facts and concepts and to describe their relationship to each other.

- **Synthesis:** The objective requires students to combine the component parts of an idea or concept, or to combine ideas and concepts from different sources, to generate new knowledge.

- **Evaluation:** At the highest and most complex level, students must be sufficiently knowledgeable about the context in which the material is applied, and its component concepts, skills, and strategies to be able to make judgements about it.

Morrison, Ross, and Kemp (2004) provide the following examples of the taxonomy of cognitive objectives.

TABLE 2-1: Taxonomy of cognitive objectives

Level of Bloom's Taxonomy	Course: Chemistry Topic: Gas Laws	Course: Fundamentals of Electricity Topic: Connecting a Three-Way Switch
Knowledge: Recall of specific information	Define pressure.	List the tools required to wire a three-way switch.
Comprehension: Lowest level of understanding	Describe the relationship between pressure and volume.	Explain the purpose for each of the three wires used in connecting a switch.
Application: Application of a rule or principle	If you have a fully inflated basketball and you add more air, what is the effect on pressure inside the ball?	Sketch a diagram for connecting a three-way switch to an existing circuit.
Analysis: Breaking an idea into component parts and describing the relationships	Explain why an automobile's tire will not appear under-inflated after being driven several miles at a high speed.	Determine the gauge and length of wiring needed to connect a three-way switch to a junction box.
Synthesis: Putting the parts together to form a new whole	If you double the absolute temperature of a gas and double the pressure of the gas, what is the effect on volume?	Develop a plan for converting a dining room chandelier on a single switch to a three-way switch.
Evaluation: Making judgements about materials and methods	Before you is a container of water vapour with a temperature of 150° and a container of oxygen at 150°. Which gas is more likely to behave in accordance with the gas laws?	Given a diagram of an existing two-way switch for a dining room light, determine whether it can be converted to a three-way switch.

What kinds of knowledge should be the subject of instructional goals and lesson objectives?

Declarative or **content knowledge** is the *what* of subject material through which the teacher conducts the lesson and the student demonstrates mastery of it. Declarative or content knowledge should seldom constitute the total lesson objectives, except occasionally in the early grades. Usually the content is the vehicle through which the objectives are reached. For example, the subject domain might be history, and the lesson might be the war of 1812. The overall objectives of the lesson are unlikely to be "to know and be able to recite the dates and sequence of events of the war of 1812." Rather than recite the *what* of the war of 1812, the events might serve as the vehicle through which students understand how wars evolve, or how the causes of current wars are linked to those that occurred historically, or how the war of 1812 played a role in the constitution of the United States, or how the aboriginal peoples of North America have played a role in developing our society as it is today. The objectives, then, are more likely to be of the second and third types: procedural knowledge in which students come to understand *how* the war came to be, and conditional knowledge, in which students come to know *when*, *where*, and *why* the war of 1812 serves to tell us about recent history and current events.

The objectives of a mathematics lesson could consist of declarative knowledge. Indeed, the *what* of mathematics are the numerical conventions that we as a society have consensually agreed represent our numerical world. Times tables, generated from these conventions, are useful when learned to automaticity (i.e., learned by rote) as short cuts to the computational manipulations needed to think mathematically. But most teachers of mathematics would not view these as instructional goals for mathematics learning (except perhaps in novels about Victorian schoolrooms). Rather, they would wish their students to acquire **procedural knowledge** of mathematics: to know *how* to use times tables to compute, measure, apply to problems, etc.; and **conditional knowledge**: to know when, where, and why to use the properties of times tables.

TABLE 2-2: Types of learning objectives, and the forms of teacher's instructional objectives and questioning techniques related to them

Learning Objective	Knowledge Type	Instructional Objective	Questioning Format
Declarative or **content knowledge**, just the facts, related facts	Facts, names, rote material such as times tables, table of the elements	Know, recall, recognize, select, state, recite, label, name, point to, list, demonstrate, underline, highlight, identify, show, tell	What? Which? How many?
Procedural knowledge or **task-specific knowledge and skills**, differences between facts, concepts	Concepts (clusters of facts with a structural relationship) and skills that are needed to undertake a task	Understand, explain, relate, analyse, compare, contrast, distinguish, apply, derive, construct, synthesize, solve, calculate	When? Where? How? Why? How does? Under what conditions? What belongs and what doesn't?

TABLE 2-2: continued

Learning Objective	Knowledge Type	Instructional Objective	Questioning Format
Conditional knowledge or information-handling, or **higher order thinking**, or **metacognitive skills,** rules and laws	Developing new connections between new and/or previously acquired concepts; applying algorithms and heuristics to organize and expand one's conceptual framework	Abstract, infer, construct, generalize, interpret, appreciate, imagine, relate	Why do you think? What next? What implications? How would you respond, develop, relate? What do you think, feel, believe, infer, imagine? What if? What is the rule? What principle, law governs..?

Content knowledge is the facts, the basics for all tasks and subject areas (Bloom's *knowledge* and *comprehension*). Memorizing the facts can be very important, for example learning letter-sound relationships, times tables, and the table of chemical elements. In the introduction to a new subject area or skill domain, students usually master the terminology and factual material used in that field. These provide essential first steps for the material that become a vehicle for learning *how, when, where* and *why* to use it. *Learning objectives*, however, should usually, though not always, be framed in terms of task-specific and information-handling or *higher-order thinking skills* rather than in terms of content (Bloom's *application, analysis, synthesis,* and *evaluation*). If students are to remember new concepts and skills, they will need to take an active part in connecting the new terms to their existing understanding, and then to create or extend their **conceptual frameworks** to accommodate the newly encountered material, and to link it with other ideas and concepts. They identify relationships between new and already-learned strategies as they become familiar with the workings of that subject: procedural or task-specific knowledge and skills. Beyond this, however, students "learn how to learn" and handle information. This is variously termed conditional knowledge ("if x happens, y follows," "the rule/principle/law that governs them is.."), information handling strategies ("If I do x, I can achieve y") or **metacognitive strategies** (thinking about how to remember, process, recall, and apply new concepts to create novel applications and solve problems).

Kame'enui and Simmons (1999) have an alterative list of knowledge forms that looks somewhat similar to Bloom's (1956) taxonomy of instructional objectives.

TABLE 2-3: Kame'enui and Simmons' (1999) knowledge form (adapted)

1. Just the facts	Simple facts, verbal chains and discriminations	Letters of the alphabet Atomic weight of hydrogen
2. Related facts	Sequences of successive related simple facts	Days of the week Names of the oceans
3. Differences between items	Discriminating differences between two items	Convex vs. concave Volume vs. area Radius vs. circumference
4. Concepts (best taught through comparing examples and non-examples)	Objects, events, actions, or situations that are part of a class that shares a defining characteristic	Family structures, genus, phylum
5. Rules and laws	An if-then or cause-effect relationship	When supply goes up, demand goes down Mathematical equations

The differences among the various types of knowledge provide reasons why teachers must be skilled at calibrating instruction to individual learner differences in learning thresholds. All students, including those with disabilities, can acquire higher-order thinking skills, at least in the material that matches their current levels of understanding, their experiences, and their conceptual framework. Adapting instruction does not entail reducing the level of knowledge expected to be demonstrated by the students from rules to concepts, or from concepts to facts. Instead, skilled teachers adapt instruction by keeping their expectations high that students will master and apply concepts, strategies, and higher order thinking skills to material that is adapted for their level of language, understanding, and experience. As a result, instructional objectives need to reflect these expectations. In Module 3, the differences between instructional adaptations such as modifications and accommodations will be discussed.

If you think about it, it doesn't make much sense to expect struggling learners to recall content, while more proficient learners acquire thinking skills. Students do not simply absorb new material like a sponge. We have all "cribbed" for examinations, filling our short-term memories with information that barely carried us through the examination, then promptly forgetting most of it. To consolidate new information into long-term memory, it has to be organized, catalogued, and welded into our existing (and unique) framework of understood and meaningful concepts.

As human beings, we cannot possibly be efficient information archivists for all the facts that we encounter, so a major part of learning is to acquire the routines and strategies that enable us to process information efficiently. This consists of organizing and collapsing information into "chunks" in our personal mnemonic cataloguing system. We relate it to previously learned material, tagging the chunks for later retrieval from memory. We reconfigure it in ways that are novel for us, by generalizing its underlying principles, its organizational characteristics, and the characteristics that generate novel representations of it. These strategic information-handling skills are more important components of our learning than the memorizing of content through which they were learned, because they not only enable us to organize, retrieve, or recreate the content of previously acquired information, but they can also be applied or transferred to new bodies of related information.

Metacognitive strategies involve knowledge about one's own stock of task-related strategies, and about one's thinking processes (Pressley, Woloshyn, et al., 1995). Such strategies allow the learner to create novel applications, to make inferences, and to create new connections among existing conceptual frameworks. They are the "stuff" of learning, and the major accomplishment of our school experience.

As will be apparent, students with cognitive disabilities and special learning needs—unlike students without disabilities—typically do not acquire these skills and strategies spontaneously, by using guesswork and trial and error or by realizing that there are implicit strategies to be found. So teachers need to make these skills and strategies explicit by describing them, modelling them, and allowing lots of opportunity for students to practise them. This is the topic of Research Box 2–2: Strategies for Engaging Diverse Learners.

Discussion Questions:

Metacognitive strategies are not apparent before the age of 5 years. Younger children seem not to be aware of the limitations of their memories and thinking capabilities. As they develop, they become increasingly aware, and therefore learn to become active participants in learning by applying strategies to help them cope with limits in memory, recall, and information processing.

1. Can you recall a childhood event in which it dawned on you that you had to actively work at learning something in order to remember it? For example, learning to ride a bike, to swim, to remember your phone number and address, to recite a poem or tell a joke?

2. How do you currently memorize names? Telephone numbers? How do you study in preparation for multiple-choice tests? Take a poll of your friends or classmates to find out if they have different ways of doing these compared with you.

Although teachers may not necessarily write down in behavioural terms what their objectives are, they do need to have planned them in order to communicate them to students. Communicating them, or letting students participate in understanding and working toward the lesson objectives, is a prerequisite for effective teaching and will be discussed further in the next section, Introducing the Lesson.

To practise writing instructional objectives, review Interactive Exercise 2–2: Writing Instructional Objectives.

interactive exercise
2-2

interactive exercise
2-2

Writing Instructional Objectives

An instructional objective should specify the following:

• What will the student do (specific behaviours)?

• Under what circumstances?

• At what level of performance or accuracy?

Devise two instructional objectives for each of these cases.

A. Jillane walks into class late, slumps into her seat, and scowls at the neighbours who glance her way. It's the fourth time in two weeks that she has been late.

Write two instructional objectives for Jillane. To compare your objectives with examples, view the suggested responses on-line.

1. _____

_____

2. _____

_____

B. Sammy works very slowly, making sure his work will be completely accurate. As a result, he loses marks on his weekly math quiz by completing less than 50% of it.

Write two instructional objectives for Sammy. To compare your objectives with examples, view the suggested responses on-line.

1. _____

_____

2. _____

_____

Instructional Tools for Meeting Diverse Learner Needs

If the prospect of designing learning goals and instructional objectives that focus on learner differences in acquiring and applying cognitive and learning strategies seems daunting, take heart. There is a limited set of such strategies with which students struggle. There are endless applications of these strategies to curriculum material, but there are only a fairly small number of categories of cognitive challenges for students with diverse learning needs. For example, Baker, Kame'enui, and Simmons (1998) propose that students with diverse learning and curricular needs differ in terms of four types of cognitive processes: memory skills, strategy knowledge and use, vocabulary knowledge, and language coding.

Kame'enui and Carnine (1998) and Kame'enui and Simmons (1999) propose that excellent teachers use six high-quality instructional tools to involve the diverse learners in their classes. The teachers design their lessons with these six principles in mind.

• Primed background knowledge	• Scaffolding
• Big ideas	• Integrating strategies
• Conspicuous strategies	• Judicious review

Primed background knowledge

Make sure learners are "in" on the upcoming material and how it links to what they already know, and why it is important.

Pierre begins the class with a review of the key concepts that he taught last class. He then links these concepts to the exercise that he has assigned for homework, explaining how they will be important for the lesson today. Pierre conducts this part of the lesson from his table at the front of the room, around which sit the four students who normally have difficulty catching on to the lesson. In this way, Pierre can monitor their work and quietly point out the parts of their worksheets to which he was referring.

Pierre reviews the principles of punctuation with his group of students in their alternative learning program. "They're boring" one student declares. Pierre projects a cartoon on the screen. It shows three work-men talking to each other.

Diagram 2–3: The importance of punctuation

Pierre points out how difficult it can be to understand spoken language when transcribed into print because print lacks the stress sounds and non-verbal intonations that spoken language provides. The opposite is also sometimes true: punctuation can add or alter meaning to printed utterances that speech alone cannot convey, as in the cartoon. Having piqued their interest, Pierre leads the group to further discuss the relationship between print and speech.

Big ideas

Focus on the essential principles of learning, on concepts and skills that are broad and deep, and that anchor smaller ideas, facts, and details.

For example, in science, big ideas are those that represent central scientific ideas and organizing principles, have rich explanatory and predictive power, motivate the formulation of significant questions, and are applicable in many situations and contexts common to everyday experiences (NRC Standards, 1993). Grossen, Carnine, Romance, and Vitale (1998) illustrate this with the Convection Cell Model that explains the relationship between dynamic pressure and heating and cooling. This principle can be applied to water boiling in a pot, the circulation of air in a room, the currents of the ocean, and weather forecasting.

Antonio completes the lesson with his Grade 11 class on the relationship between Hinduism and Buddhism. In the remaining five minutes of class, he asks his students to think how the similarities between the two religions have their parallel in Christianity and Islam, the topics of the course in the previous term. Sam replies that the role of prophet is a theme in each of them.

Conspicuous strategies

*Plan to talk about how to think. Model and describe the steps that are needed to accomplish the task. One useful teaching strategy is **self-talk** or "**think aloud**" in which the teacher talks aloud about his or her thinking processes while demonstrating to the class each of the steps for completing the skill, task, or problem. For example, the teacher solves a mathematical equation on the board while describing aloud how to tackle each step in the process.*

Mr. Francis solves a mathematical equation on the board while describing aloud how to tackle each step in the process. He then assigns the next problem to pairs of students and instructs them to work together to solve it, using the think aloud strategies he has modelled. While they do so, he moves to Jack and Janelle's desks to listen in and provide support.

Maria conducts a lesson on finding the area of irregular geometric shapes. The students have already learned how to find the area of rectangles and triangles. Maria puts an L-shaped figure on the overhead projector.

Diagram 2–4: Using diagrams during "think alouds"

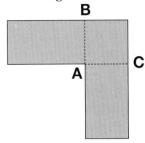

She asks for ideas from the class about how to find its area. Tina suggests bisecting the figure between A and B. Then she uses her knowledge of the area of a rectangle to compute the area of the two figures and adds them together. George wants to divide the between A and C. He then applies Tina's steps to solving the problem.

Scaffolding

Plan to set large group questioning, seatwork, and group tasks that allow the teacher (and others) to differentially guide and support differences in individual students' understanding.

Scaffolding is a multi-stage process that guides the students from their initial introduction to a new concept or skill to the point where they can apply the concept or demonstrate the skill independently. There will be more about this instructional strategy later in this module, and more about scaffolding instruction in Module 3. Also in Module 3, readers can view video sequences of scaffolding in both an elementary and secondary school class.

Integrating strategies

Plan to link big ideas across units and lessons. Demonstrate how to transfer strategies taught in other lessons. Link together related concepts. Strategic integration is the combining of essential information learned in one context in ways that apply in other contexts to produce new and more complex knowledge.

Sandi reads a story to her class on Friday afternoon. She pauses to point out how the names in the story reflect the spelling rules that the class learned earlier in the week.

Jolene extracts the main rules for using tenses from the unit for her French class. She writes them on a handout and adds examples, then makes the handout available to any students who want to use it to prepare for the next test.

Janice teaches her struggling readers how to identify the vowel sounds in the words pain and pane. She teaches the component parts, ensuring that her students can recognize /ai/ in gain, pail, etc. In the last lesson she reviewed the long vowel sound of /a/ modified by the silent /e/. She then puts the words pain and pane on the board and asks, "What strategies do we need to use to figure out these words? What do you notice about them?" The group begins to consider how spelling patterns can be a clue to meaning.

Judicious review

Plan for opportunities for students to recall and apply their newly learned information, during or at the end of the lesson. End the lesson by recognizing accomplishments of individuals at all levels of success. Review the important concepts and skills periodically through the year.

Maria and her class complete the unit on finding the measurement of area of irregularly shaped figures. She praises Marc's particular contribution. He devised a novel strategy for finding the area of an L-shaped figure by extending its vertical lines to form a rectangle, then subtracting the area of the rectangle he had created outside the original figure from the whole rectangle that enclosed the figure to find the area of the original. He came up with this idea when she first introduced the lesson and demonstrated how to bisect the L-shape to create two rectangles that could be measured and added together. Maria thinks about how capable Marc is when faced with mathematical problems that he can visualize. However, his math test scores don't do justice to his abilities, perhaps because of the high reading content that he is reluctant to tackle.

Judicious review is the lesson step that is least-often accomplished. Teachers often run out of time and simply do not get to review the big ideas and main concepts of the lesson and how students have fared with them. Yet it is an important step to consolidate students' understanding, particularly for those students who are uncertain about their accomplishments. It is important to plan to leave sufficient time for a final review and summary of accomplishments.

Kame'enui and colleagues expand upon these six principles in their 1998 book. Review Research Box 2–2: Strategies for Engaging Diverse Learners, to see a summary of these ideas and examples of their use.

Strategies for Engaging Diverse Learners

Kame'enui, Carnine, and colleagues (1998) propose that students with diverse learning and curricular needs differ in terms of four types of cognitive processes: memory skills, strategy knowledge and use, vocabulary knowledge, and language coding. They discuss the learning implications for each of these sources of learner differences, and they also suggest instructional options that teachers can use to address them.

1. Memory

The researchers suggest that, when considering diverse learners, teachers should notice how students differ in:

- working memory skills: rehearsing and categorizing information
- long-term memory skills: storing information permanently
- naming objects, recalling and recognizing items, and repeating sentences

  The implications of these differences for instruction are that teachers need to:

- engage students in explicit instruction of memory strategies such as categorizing and recalling
- emphasize long-term memorizing of important content
- engage students in actively using new information
- emphasize connections between concepts
- connect new learning to learner experiences
- monitor retention and recall over time

  Monisha is frustrated with her inability to do well on the social science quizzes. It isn't because she doesn't care; in fact this is her favourite subject. She knows the big concepts in the unit on social psychology, but she can't remember who has done what in the illustrative examples of experiments given in the textbook. She talks to her teacher, Mrs. Khan, about her frustration. Together they design a chart that lists the key concepts, keywords about the experiments that illustrate each concept, and three details of each experiment. Monisha learns to extract keywords and to update the chart on the lab's computer so that she can e-mail it to herself at home. She will then use the charts in preparing for the next quiz.

2. Strategy knowledge and use

Teachers should monitor how students differ in:

- ability to monitor learning and adjust to task demands

- being focused and goal-directed

- ability to use learned strategies

- use of different strategies to compensate for difficulties

- willingness/unwillingness to give up basic strategies for more powerful ones

  Instructional implications for teaching include:

- ensuring that underlying and prerequisite skills for learning a new strategy are firmly in place

- providing lots of exemplars of how to use a particular strategy and non-examples of what doesn't work

- breaking down a new skill or strategy into component steps and having students be proficient at each one, as well as at combining them to master the whole set

Shane, Viktor, and Ricardo are studying a novel together in English class. They have been assigned the task of writing an article to be published in the next student newsletter. It will be a critique of the novel, highlighting why other students should read it and addressing any difficulties it poses for readers. Their teacher assists them to set up a checklist so they can monitor their analysis of the novel. After reading each chapter together, they discuss the following strategies and record how they did. Shane monitors their comprehension by checking off the following:

- Did we learn the most important points of the chapter?

- Can we recite the most important information?

  Viktor records the quality of their work by checking off:

- Did we read the entire chapter?

- Did we read it accurately?

Ricardo records notes about the group's opinions of the best parts of each chapter and any difficulties they had to prepare for writing their critique.

3. Vocabulary

Teachers should monitor differences among learners in terms of:

- difficulty with both the number of words and the depth of knowledge; vocabulary breadth and use may get worse over time

- lack of opportunity to be exposed to new words and to hear newly learned words in use

- reading levels and quantity, thus compounding students' limited exposure to reading strategies and new vocabulary

    Instructional implications for teaching include:

- setting goals to allow students to learn many words at basic levels and fewer words at complex levels

- matching vocabulary goals to instruction

- having students link new vocabulary to their own experience

- encouraging as much reading as possible at students' levels as a basis for developing vocabulary

Wesley was a "non-reader." At age 13 he still had few reading skills and little interest in reading. This began to change when he was given a book of Calvin & Hobbes? comic strips. Although there was little print on each page, Wesley needed to read each caption accurately in order to get the jokes. From his perspective, this was the first time that he had understood that print conveys meaning. Some of his friends now rely on him for his interpretation of other cartoons, and this has encouraged him to begin designing and captioning his own cartoons.

4. Language coding in reading

Teachers should monitor differences among learners in terms of:

- reliance on semantic (meaning) features to code language; average learners rely primarily on phonological features

    Instructional implications for teaching include:

- providing rich and varied experiences in discussion, reading, and writing that involve the sounds and meanings of words

- providing opportunities to connect sounds in words and their phonological and alphabetic equivalents

Kyle is struggling in the college transition program because so much of the work requires that he read and integrate knowledge. Since as far back as he can remember, reading has been a big headache for him and he has consequently avoided it as much as he can. But he really wants to get into the laboratory technician program next September.

In the 1980s and 1990s, many teachers were trained to teach reading through what was termed the "Whole Language" or "psycholinguistic" approach (Goodman, 1976; Smith, 1978). The essential assumption in these approaches was that skilled readers were less reliant on graphic cues (such as grapho-phonemic correspondence between written words and their spoken sounds), and more reliant on meaning (semantic comprehension). Their higher speeds of reading were attributed to less need to decode words and more skills in extracting meaning and relating it to their own experiences. These approaches caught on like wildfire. Teachers were expected to reduce or eliminate the teaching of phonics and grapho-phonemic correspondence and base their reading programs largely on comprehending meaning. As a result, a generation of readers grew up with poor decoding skills. By about grade 3, many of these students were being diagnosed as reading disabled.

In retrospect, some of them failed because they had not developed the strategies needed to tackle new vocabulary words in texts that, from grades 3 and 4 on, departed from their own lived experiences and were designed to take them into new learning. In fact, as we now know, the assumptions of those early approaches were wrong. Struggling readers depend on meaning while skilled readers have accomplished high levels of vocabulary development and word decoding skills to the point of automatic application, and as a result have increased their speed in reading.

Introducing the Lesson

Once you have completed planning the lesson, it is time to share it with your students. This first impression is important, as the manner in which new information is presented can set the stage for failure or success, and is particularly significant when considering students with special education needs. So, what do effective teachers do when teaching a lesson? Research has shown that to increase learning, at least three important components need to be included when introducing the lesson. To begin, effective teachers gain the attention of every student by focussing them on the upcoming task. This is followed by a review of the skills and concepts that have been previously learned and on which the new material is built, and then finally, the teacher presents a preview of the new instruction that is about to take place (Berdine & Cegelka, 1995).

Task focus

With each new lesson, effective teachers focus interest on the task at hand. Teachers use many strategies to gain student attention. They may employ a verbal cue or a physical signal, such as a hand in the air, or they may use a focus activity (e.g., a journal entry) or partner discussion. Additionally, environmental factors, such as background noise, distractions in the room, people coming and going, and items on a desk, need to be reduced or eliminated. Successful teachers monitor student attention on a regular basis and refocus and redirect individuals as necessary throughout the day.

Reviewing previous concepts

As noted above, by reviewing a previous lesson, students refresh their memories, build confidence, and can anticipate what they will be learning. Furthermore, the review helps to provide a context for the new learning, as it allows the students to link new information with information they already have. With a deeper understanding of the "big picture,"students will feel more confident and approach new tasks with a positive outlook.

Previewing the lesson

Once the review is complete, an outline of the new lesson can be presented. Effective teachers focus on one point at time, explaining the relevance of the skill to everyday life, and linking it back to prior learning. Remembering related ideas is easier than remembering various isolated facts. Clearly stating the academic goals for learning and achievement will help students understand the expectations. It is also important to involve students in the evaluation process so they can be guided toward making realistic goals for improvement. At the same time, teachers can check for understanding and make changes to their instructional strategies if necessary.

Assessing and evaluating what students will learn

In Module 1 the relationship between instruction and assessment was proposed. The **instructional cycle** consists of phases that are self correcting; the goals set at the beginning are monitored, and if not accomplished by the end, then the structure and presentation of the lesson or unit should be reviewed and revised accordingly. Educators can use assessment results to help determine how well they are meeting instructional goals, as well as to alter instruction so that these goals can be better met. But, if the content and format of the assessment do not match what is taught, the results may be meaningless. As suggested in Module 1, lack of learning should not be attributed automatically to student inability.

Traditional assessment vs. performance assessment

Traditional assessment, such as paper and pencil tasks, standardized tests, and rote memory work, tend to provide the teacher with a limited picture of students' progress. This approach views learners as passive absorbers of facts and skills provided by the teacher. Traditional assessment compares students with one another to rank achievement. Typical tests tend to

over-assess student knowledge and under-assess student know-how with knowledge, or what can be seen as intellectual performance (Wiggens, 1992).

In contrast, performance assessment integrates instruction and assessment and progress is monitored on a consistent basis over time. Performance assessment is concerned with the degree to which students can demonstrate knowledge and skill in a certain field. The purpose is to allow students to show what they can do. Some examples of performance assessment include observing students learn, peer evaluations, demonstrations, portfolios, and rubrics. Effective performance tasks engage students in the authentic application of skills. There are a number of uses for classroom-based performance assessment. It can help teachers with instructional decision-making, provide feedback to students and parents, and evaluate students' learning and progress.

The rubric

Rubric scoring is one type of performance assessment. A useful rubric identifies specific performance-based criteria and incorporates student input. By clearly outlining the instructional objectives, the rubric acts as a tool to facilitate meaningful learning and communicate the standards for academic success for a particular concept or skill to be learned.

In her examination of teachers' use of rubrics, Kathleen Montgomery (2000) discovered that there are many advantages associated with using rubrics. Rubrics help teachers measure products, progress, and the process of learning. Assessing student work with a rubric helps the teacher to clarify the critical learning that should take place and increases the chances that the students will produce quality work. Furthermore, teachers also need to provide a way for students to take ownership for their work and a means for them to reflect on why they may or may not need to improve a completed assignment. The rubric involves students in creating and understanding the evaluation criteria, and therefore allows them to participate fully in the processes needed to reach the objective. Students should be encouraged to refer to the rubric throughout the teaching process and when working on the new skill or concept, thus encouraging them to take responsibility for their learning.

For a more in-depth examination of the importance of rubrics for instructional planning and evaluation, refer to Research Box 2–3: Rubrics.

Rubrics

One important way to generate and display instructional goals and objectives is through a rubric. Rubrics are charts that map the learning objectives for a new unit of study, and that specify what kind of performance will represent varying levels of success in mastering the learning objectives. A well-designed rubric provides students with a guide to how to participate in the unit, allowing them to be self-directed and self-reliant in reaching the instructional objectives and to take responsibility for their own learning. The rubric specifies both the goal to be achieved and the means by which the students will demonstrate that they have reached it. The partitioning of these two components also helps the teacher to take the short step of designing an accommodation for the means to demonstrate achievement for one or more students without compromising the instructional objective itself. Thus a rubric can be an excellent tool for specifying standards that are clear and transparent to everyone, and for tailoring independent work to a range of student needs.

So what does a carefully planned rubric contain? It tends to focus on instructional objectives that specify the learning *skills* to be achieved rather than the content of the instructional domain, although at times the content might be an important part. It is sufficiently specific to allow the teacher to monitor the progress of both the class and of individuals in it. It also allows students to participate fully in the processes needed to reach the objective.

Rubrics are sometimes designed at the beginning of a new lesson or unit, with students working with the teacher to specify the nature of the students' performance and the amount of credit that each level accomplishment will yield. The finished rubric might then be posted on the classroom wall, printed and distributed, or sent by e-mail to students as an ongoing guide for them to follow. Students can see for themselves from the beginning of the lesson or unit and while they work, just what the outcomes are to be.

Castner, Costella, and Hess (1993) developed the following framework for designing a rubric. The learning outcome for a segment of a lesson unit is communicated by the teacher to the students. The teacher identifies the criteria that fulfil the outcome, then collectively the class designs the performance descriptions that fit the criteria using the following descriptions:

> 4 = exemplary (fully meets criteria)
>
> 3 = proficient (adequately meets the criteria)
>
> —————————— Mastery line ——————————————
>
> 2 = approaching proficiency (sometimes meets criteria)
>
> 1 = evidence of attempt (seldom meets criteria)

Popham (1999) proposes five rules for designing good rubrics:

- Make sure the skill to be assessed is significant. Skills that are scored should reflect important accomplishments and not trifling ones.

- Make sure all the rubric's evaluative criteria can be addressed instructionally. Don't set out to evaluate something that hasn't been or can't be directly taught.

- Employ as few evaluative criteria as possible. Focus on three or four evaluative criteria. It is overwhelming to attempt to teach and evaluate (or learn) a dozen or more.

- Provide a succinct label for each evaluative criterion. One word, easy-to-remember labels help both the teacher and students to communicate and to achieve the criteria.

- Match the length of the rubric to your own tolerance for detail. Popham says "I'm most interested in the *impact* on instructional planning that a rubric has. And rubrics that aren't created by teachers 'because they're too much work' or rubrics that aren't used by teachers 'because they're way too long' will obviously have no impact on teachers' instructional planning."

You may want to review Popham's suggestions for writing instructional objectives that are part of rubrics. See Research Box 2–1: Designing Instructional Goals and Objectives.

For students who experience learning difficulties, the initial objectives and the performance criteria may be the same as those chosen for the class, with accommodations to how they are communicated or to the content of the material to be used to demonstrate mastery. Alternatively, a personal rubric might be designed to match the objectives in the student's IEP, possibly with a modified scoring criteria. This allows the teacher or assessor to explain to the student the criteria that will be used to evaluate his or her work. Student self-assessment can thus be incorporated into the rubric's framework, fulfilling the purpose of enhancing self-direction and self-regulation in the student's learning.

In the lower grades, for example, a teacher might require that students colour a drawing or illustrate a piece of writing when the objective is the form of the writing itself. Students in a math lesson, for example, may spend a majority of their time colouring a fish shape, on the back of which is a single addition problem that they had completed in the first few minutes of their seatwork. If the instructional objective is to teach addition, then the associated seatwork and homework should practise that skill and show how it had been grasped by application to similar mathematics problems. This does not mean that the activity should not be fun. But the main objective of practising addition problems should be the major activity for the seatwork task. The teacher could have students generate their own addition problems, for example, and have a partner solve them.

In higher grades, students might be required to make a display or diorama to illustrate the central event in a novel, when the objective could be much more quickly accomplished by writing a paragraph or even drawing a cartoon sequence. Time spent on reaching an objective is a major concern in effective instruction. As examined in Module 3, it is important for teachers to offer universal accessibility to lesson objectives, but the form this takes should not compromise the efficient use of instructional time.

The objectives and rubric for Emma's writing lesson might look like this (see Research Box 2–1):

- A good persuasive article will convince the reader that a claim is justified. Students will write a persuasive article to support a claim that begins "Now is the time to stop..." You may choose your own claim.

- **Step 1** – Researching the claim. Students will use the library and Internet resources, and resources and ideas from people in class and home, to develop three arguments to support the claim. Each argument will provide a good reason for the claim, and will differ from the other two arguments. These will be recorded on your concept web chart.

- **Step 2** – Writing the persuasive article. The web chart will then be used to write a persuasive article in five paragraphs. The first paragraph states your claim, developing why it is important. In the second, third and fourth paragraphs, each of the arguments that support your claim are to be presented and developed. The fifth paragraph summarizes your claim and the arguments.

- Marks will be given for the depth of your research, flow of the finished article, the summary, the strength of each argument, and the extent to which the reader is persuaded by the claim.

	Exemplary	Proficient	Approaching proficient	Attempted
Extent of research	Each argument contains ideas from several sources—from library research and opinions of others	Each argument is based on at least one library source and one opinion	Each argument contains ideas from at least one source—library or opinion	A good argument statement is presented
Strength of arguments	Each argument is supported by a strong base of evidence and opinion	Each argument is well developed and based on some evidence	Each argument is well explained and some evidence is included	The argument statement is clearly presented
Uniqueness of each argument	The three arguments are clearly different from each other	The three arguments follow from each other	There is some overlap in the arguments	The three statements are different
Flow of the article	The paragraphs relate smoothly to each other	The paragraphs follow each other, although transitions are abrupt	The paragraphs contain evidence that can be applicable to all the arguments	The introduction, three paragraphs, and summary are evident
Summary	A concise statement of the claim, its main issues and arguments, and, outstanding evidence is presented	The summary repeats the claim, main arguments, and some evidence	The summary does not encompass both the claim and the arguments and evidence	No summary but specific points are made
Overall persuasion	A strong and well-developed case for the claim	A strong case for the claim	The claim and argument are evident but not yet presented concisely	The main facts are evident

Presenting the Lesson

After the lesson has been introduced, the next step is to present the new material, the expository component of the lesson. How will the teacher convey the specific lesson objectives to the students? Much research has focused on the idea of learning styles and how learning may be improved when instruction is tailored to match these perceived differences. In fact, as discussed in Research Box 2–4: Learning Styles: Are They a Myth?, the various theories of learning styles have not been definitively supported by evidence that people differ in their learning "styles." One style that has been purported to vary from one person to another is modality-specific; the ability to learn better from material that is presented through hearing rather than through vision, or conversely to learn better from visual than auditory channels, or even to be "kinesthetic learners" who learn best through touch. Another theory invokes brain hemisphere differences as the source of learning style; that some people learn better from information that is associated with the left hemisphere or "left brain" (verbal, sequential) and others from information that is associated with the right hemisphere, or "right brain" (spatially and simultaneously presented). There are many sources of advice for teachers on how to design instructional tasks that differ along these and other dimensions that reflect differences in learners' purported "styles." The evidence of the benefits of these instructional approaches is, however, weak at best. In general, teaching to one specific modality is not good teaching practice. Until we know for sure that some people are better able to process information in a specified modality or benefit from information of a specified type, the best bet is for teachers to draw on multiple ways to present information and to allow students to respond in a variety of ways, as suggested above in the principle of universal access. Further, the majority of learning tasks require learners to integrate information from a variety of sources and modalities. Take reading as an example. Being a "visual learner" could be disadvantageous when trying to map graphemes (print units) onto their corresponding phonemes (sound units of speech). Conversely, being an "auditory learner" would make it difficult to identify the units of print, particularly since the English language is represented by such irregular spelling patterns! The task of reading requires that one integrates visual, auditory, experiential, and linguistic knowledge, and sometimes pictorial information also. Being instructed in one modality or with one type of information would be counterproductive for developing effective reading skills.

Methods that engage students in the concepts and skills are preferable to methods that leave the students at the receiving end of the information, but even then, sometimes these techniques are the only efficient and practical way to introduce formulae, vocabulary, and prerequisite factual knowledge. For example, it is more practical for a teacher to demonstrate a skill by showing how to do it while talking through the steps (self-talk or "think-alouds") than by hoping that students will discover the skill for themselves. As a result, effective teachers use as many methods as possible to increase access to and understanding of the skills and concepts to be learned.

Review Research Box 2–4: Learning Styles—Are They a Myth? below.

research box 2-4

Learning Styles—Are They a Myth?

A lot of concepts in education are not based in evidence. They are often promoted as the latest thing in educational folklore one month, and then replaced with something else the next month. One of these is "learning styles." Unfortunately, this term means many different things to different people. Some associate it with preferences for learning through an auditory, visual, or **kinesthetic** modality, a concept generated in the 1960s by a test that purported to distinguish the strong and weak modalities of test takers (Kirk & Kirk, 1978). Subsequent studies showed these claims to be unfounded (Hammill & Larsen, 1974; 1978).

This modality-based interpretation of a learning style was then replaced by a concept of learning styles as a preference for simultaneous (right brain) or successive, sequential (left brain) information. Ayers and Cooley (1986) cast doubt on this notion. Yet the "neurological antecedents" explanation is still very much a part of the thinking of some educators, reinforced by publications in recent years that purport to explain disabilities as imperfect or underdeveloped neuronal networks in one or another part of the brain (e.g., Sousa, 2006a, b, c). Unfortunately, the evidence to support these claims is at best in its infancy. It has the potential to be interpreted simplistically or without the necessary caveats for an area of new research. As a result, the evidence may be misleading, and may contribute to **pathognomonic** thinking.

Currently, there are some who think of learning styles in terms of preference for learning through direct instruction or through independent discovery. Still another understanding of the term is preference for working in a large group, a small group, or alone (Department of Education, South Africa, 2005). Personality styles have also been swept up under the general umbrella of learning styles, with claims made that students whose personalities match those of their teachers will learn more than those whose personalities do not match.

To take a look at the variety of learning characteristics that have been claimed to be associated with learning style differences, try typing "learning styles" into Google. You will find many pages of links to websites. Here are a few of them:

http://www.indstate.edu/ctl/styles/model.html

The University of Indiana website has a comprehensive list of the categories of so-called learning styles and links to each. This list includes:

- instructional preferences

- social interaction models

- information processing models including Gardner's (1983) seven learning styles

- personality style models such as Myers-Briggs (1985)
  http://www.career-lifeskills.com/index.php?main_page=index&cPath=5

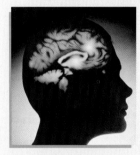

The most popular versions of learning styles, however, are associated with differences in sensory processes, and particularly auditory and visual preferences or styles of receiving information, or with hemispheric dominance theories. Auditory versus visual styles of learning and the claim that these underlie learning disabilities are the subject of this website:

http://www.ldpride.net/learningstyles.MI.htm

Learning style also refers to the claim that there are left brain dominant and right brain dominant ways of learning. These styles of learning assume that the left brain is primarily associated with language, logic, and the sequencing of information, while the right brain is associated with spatial and visual information, and creative and intuitive skills. You can take a 19-item test to receive an estimate of your brain dominance at **http://www.mtsu.edu/~studskl/hd/learn.html**. However, be cautious about what you are told. Many of these claims are based on assumptions that have not been supported by evidence. They assume that differences in people's aptitudes are related to their performance at school and at work. The argument goes that if we identify students' strongest aptitude and treat that aptitude as their primary learning mode by designing instruction (or treatment) to match it, students should be able to make greater learning gains. For example, a child who suffered from otitis media (middle ear infections) that affected their hearing in early childhood might be assumed to arrive in Kindergarten with a preference for and greater aptitude in the visual modality. This deceptively simple idea has prevailed since the 1950s, even though a series of important and rigorously conducted studies that addressed this "aptitude-treatment interaction" found no evidence for it (Cronbach, 1957, 1975). In the latter article, Cronbach wrote that the aptitude-treatment interaction notion should be replaced by explanatory concepts that focus on how to integrate multiple sources of information, or as he put it, "that will help people use their heads" (p. 126).

Two meta analyses (Fuchs & Fuchs, 1986; Kavale, 1990) are consistent with Cronbach's earlier findings (Reschly, 1996). They show that the relationship between the classification of students as having intellectual disabilities (developmental challenges)—that is, their aptitude, and their placement (i.e., treatment) in a class for students with intellectual disabilities—was negligible. The relationship was also weak between the classification of students as having curriculum-related learning disabilities (i.e., aptitudes), and placement in a class designed specifically to address visual or auditory learning difficulties (i.e., specifically designed treatment). The only strong effects were for students classified as having behavioural problems who were provided with well-conducted behavioural interventions. Of course, no one has yet claimed that behavioural problems are a style of learning!

On the other side of the coin are studies that have examined just how instruction addresses the presumed learning style differences of students with learning difficulties. Reynolds & Lakin (1987) examined IEP goals for reading, writing, and mathematics and found that they are typically prescribed for all students with disabilities, regardless of how students were labelled. King-Sears (1997) writes, "The best academic practices for inclusive classrooms are the methods that have the greatest desired impact in affective, psychomotor and cognitive areas of academics for students with and without disabilities who are receiving most, if not all, of their differentiated, individualized and appropriate learning, social and instructional experiences together" (p. 2).

Questions:

1. What is the aptitude-treatment interaction? Give some examples from your own experience.

2. An example of the use of the concept of "learning styles" to market learning materials to parents can be found at

   https://www.homeschoolingbooks.com/pages/learningprofiledefinitions.asp

   Another site with a sales pitch is **http://www.howtolearn.com/personal.html**

   Take a look at these sites.

   • What differences do the sites claim to be learning styles?

   • Do you think these are reflected in how students learn? In how they should be taught?

   • How credible is the evidence for learning style differences that the websites provide?

Model, demonstrate, and dialogue

One successful way to teach new content is to model and demonstrate the associated concepts and learning strategies. Teachers can show students how to perform various strategies, providing insights into the cognitive and **metacognitive processes**. Labelling the actions being performed and using strategies such as self-questioning and "think alouds" or self-talk all describe the thought processes used to help students to make decisions.

When discussing effective instructional delivery, Berdine and Cegelka (1995) point out that it may be necessary for teachers to pre-teach the critical steps or define new vocabulary before trying to model the concept or skill. For example, teaching early writers how to edit a piece of writing may require defining terms such as draft, proofread, edit, revise, and final copy. At least two examples of each concept should be provided, and to ensure mastery, non-examples should also be provided to contrast with the examples and to make the essential characteristics of the examples clear. Each time an example is presented, the teacher should outline the characteristics and demonstrate using self-talk. Forcing the students to verbalize the concepts can help the teacher ensure the new skills have been mastered, and also assists in determining if any adjustments to the method of instruction are necessary.

Visual aids

In addition to modelling and talking out loud, effective teachers also use props such as pictures, videos, and the chalkboard to show how the learn-

ing process takes place. To demonstrate, a teacher may use chart paper to create a flowchart that outlines the parts of an essay (e.g., introduction, topic sentence, body, conclusion). Students are then able to see the example in writing. They can also refer to the chart paper while working on their own essay, checking to make sure they are meeting all of the requirements.

Teaching pace and comprehension

Proceeding in small steps and checking for understanding along the way also ensure that students are mastering the new material. The speed of the lesson should be tailored to the needs of the learners. Swedish researchers in the 1970s noted that teachers set their teaching pace by monitoring their "steering group," a small subset of students ranging in achievement levels from the 10th to the 25th percentile of the class, that the teacher uses as an informal reference group to make decisions about pacing the lesson or unit (Dahllof & Lundgren, cited in Clark & Peterson, 1986).

By verbalizing each step, describing the thought process aloud, and explaining what comes next, the teacher demonstrates how to tackle the instructional material and how to make decisions about problems to be solved. From the teacher's modelling, the students learn the steps of the learning strategy, as well as gain insight into the thinking that directs the process (Berdine & Cegleka, 1995). Along the way, effective teachers interact with students to look for signs of comprehension, using eye contact, head nods, completed homework, and participation in discussions. By asking questions, correcting errors, and reviewing new material, teachers allow students a chance to strengthen their understanding before practising on their own.

Guided practice

Critical at this point is the opportunity for students to participate in guided practice. As the term indicates, it simply means the teacher and students work together as a group to perform the task. As students become more proficient, there is a gradual reduction of teacher support until they are able to practise and perform the skill independently. Guided practice reveals how much students understand and allows the teacher to provide immediate feedback to correct mistakes. The longer a student practises mistakes, the more difficult it will be to correct them at a later date (Rosenshine, 1997).

Deciding what approaches to teaching work best under different circumstances is complex. The strategies should not be prescriptive, but should offer a range of practices from which teachers can choose, keeping the students' development and individual needs in mind. Some additional examples of specific instructional strategies are **direct instruction, strategy instruction**, scaffolded instruction, guided discovery, and mastery learning.

In the late 1990s, Swanson and colleagues collected all the studies that had examined the relative effects of different instructional methods on the learning of students with disabilities. The meta-analysis was conducted on 180 previously reported studies to address a number of controversial questions in the field of teaching students with learning difficulties and disabilities. One such question was whether students learn better when teachers direct the instruction, a form of teaching often criticized as being too transmissive, compared with when teachers teach the underlying strategies needed for students to tackle the material. What did they find? The results are reported in Research Box 2–5: Direct vs. Strategy Instruction on the next page.

research
box

2-5

Direct vs. Strategy Instruction

One claim made extensively in modern education is that teachers who present information directly to their students in a one-way direction from teacher to student (transmission) are less effective than teachers who engage their students in the lesson by pointing out strategies for learning, modelling these strategies, and prompting students to attempt the strategies themselves (strategy instruction). This argument is problematic for students with disabilities, since a number of studies have indicated that students with disabilities need a more direct, expository form of instruction if they are to make up the ground in achievement between them and their non-disabled peers. One of the findings of Swanson's large scale meta-analysis addressed this question.

A meta-analysis is a procedure that finds all the previously reported studies on a topic, discards those that do to provide statistical evidence of their claims such as the size of the effects, statistically transforms the major trends in the remaining studies so that they can be compared, then computes the overall results. Some of the findings from Swanson et al.'s meta-analysis were presented in Module 1 (Swanson, 1999; Swanson, Hoskyn, & Lee, 1999). In one of their comparisons, the relative influences of segregated, resource withdrawal, and inclusive settings were examined.

Swanson and colleagues synthesized the results of 180 intervention studies that, in addition to setting, predicted effect sizes of the different instructional strategies that are recommended for students with learning disabilities. They compared direct instruction, strategy instruction, a combination of direct and strategy instruction, and instructional approaches with neither direct nor strategy components.

The instructional techniques used in the 180 studies were classified into 45 components that influence student outcomes. These were recoded into 20 clusters of components for analysis and assigned to either Direct Instruction (DI) or Strategy Instruction (SI). The components of each intervention technique therefore comprise an operational definition of DI and SI.

Direct Instruction (DI)

- breaking down a task into small steps

- administering probes

- administering feedback repeatedly

- providing a pictorial or diagram representation

- allowing for independent practice and individually paced instruction

- breaking the instruction down into simpler phases

- instructing in small groups

- modelling a skill or behaviour

- providing set materials at a rapid pace

- providing individual child instruction

- asking questions

- presenting new materials

Strategy Instruction (SI)

- providing elaborate explanations (systematic explanations, concept elaborations, a plan to direct perform-ance)

- modelling from teachers (verbal modelling, questioning, demonstration)

- giving reminders to use certain strategies or procedures (students were cued to use taught strategies, tactics, and procedures)

- providing step-by-step prompts or multi-process instructions

- including dialogue (in which teacher and student talk back and forth)

- asking questions

- providing assistance only when needed (Swanson, 1999, p. 29-30)

Swanson and colleagues then analysed each cluster of studies to see which forms of instructional interventions resulted in the greatest learning gains in reading, mathematics, spelling, and writing performance. The teaching techniques with the greatest impact on the outcome measures of students with learning disabilities were components of both direct instructional methods and strategy instruction. Direct instruction, explicitly aimed at teaching knowledge and skills in a systematic fashion, and strategy instruction, aimed at explicitly teaching learning strategies and metacognitive skills, each contributed to significant increases in student learning outcomes. The meta-analysis revealed that no single technique for instruction was superior overall, even in the contentious area of reading instruction.

In Think it Over 2–2, a related controversy is explored. There are differences of opinion about whether teachers should transmit knowledge during teaching or should structure learning so that students construct the knowledge for themselves. Review Think It Over 2–2: Should We Teach the Way They Learn? on the next page to explore these claims further.

Regardless of the instructional methods employed, students need to be actively engaged. Teaching at a brisk pace to hold students' attention, reminding students of their successes, and allowing ample opportunities for improvement will build confidence and increase motivation to continue learning.

Should We Teach the Way They Learn?

There is considerable literature that claims that students must be taught using one or another specific teaching method because, we are told, this is how learning naturally occurs. For example, we know from Vygotsky's (1978) contribution to theories of learning that learners need to interact with others to learn the socially constructed concepts that we as a society have agreed to use, such as mathematics to the base 10, alphabets for reading English, or the syllabary in printed Inuktitut. We know from investigations of memory that learners need to be active participants in learning since they assimilate new material into their cognitive frameworks as part of a process of actively constructing links between previously learned and new material. Do these theories and facts justify matching how we teach to how students learn?

According to constructivist pedagogy (Brophy, 2004), effective teachers are presumed not to transmit knowledge but to co-construct it through dialogue with students. It is claimed that teachers who are constructivist in their teaching style view learning as centred in the development of skills and knowledge in the child, while those who are transmissive are focused on the delivery of curriculum and on the efficiency of information flow to the learner (Torff, 1999, 2003; Torff & Sternberg, 2001). Olson & Katz (2001) also claim that curriculum-centred, transmissive techniques of instruction that maximizes the flow of knowledge to the learner are negative instructional techniques derived from an erroneous view of learning based in trait psychology.

So should teachers avoid broadcasting facts and knowledge in a transmissive fashion because learners need to interact with the material and construct their own reality? Should we all be "constructivist teachers" (Brophy, 2004) and design instruction that permits learners to discover the links between new material and what they know?

Heward (2003) claims there are 10 faulty notions that hinder the effectiveness of special education. Three of these faulty notions concern the direct instruction vs. constructivism debate. Heward suggests that there is no basis for believing that:

- structured curricula impede true learning

- drill and practice limit students' deep understanding and dulls their creativity

- teaching discrete skills ignores the whole child

In examining scaffolded instruction, the initial phases of this technique are highly transmissive. They involve self-talk in which the teacher models how to think about the task. In considering learning to read, it was noted that decoding the form that English (and most other Western languages) takes in print requires a great deal of knowledge of the letter-sound correspondences that we have assigned to represent our language. It cannot be discovered, although some learners have a facility for languages that others do not. Does this mean that we are wrong to teach grapho-phonemic awareness and word segmentation skills, as some proponents of the Whole Language approach to teaching reading claimed in the '80s?

Yet the claim prevails that direct instruction is undesirable, not student-centred, and antithetical to the development of higher order thinking skills in students, if not potentially damaging to them.

Discussion Question

What do you think?

Student Interaction—Practice and Application

Following guided practice, the interactive component of the lesson entails involving students in rehearsal and application. This phase of the lesson is concerned with whether students can apply new learning strategies and demonstrate understanding at a level independent from the teacher.

Long-term memory

Skilled learners are able to do more than recall the facts. They are able to effectively transfer and store new information in their long-term memory. In their book, *Differentiating Instruction in Inclusive Classrooms*, Haager and Klinger (2005) point out that there is a connection between prior knowledge and long-term memory. Students need prior knowledge to make connections and store information in long-term memory. The more prior knowledge a person has, the easier it will be to make connections that attach new knowledge and skills to their existing conceptual framework. Thus, it falls upon the teacher to facilitate the transfer of learning through examples, such as relating new material to students' personal lives, providing context, and helping to build associations between concepts.

Organizing information around different concepts can help students recall it easily. For example, a primary class studying frogs may begin by brainstorming what they already know. The teacher records all of this information and then discusses ways to classify the information into categories (e.g., where frogs live, what frogs eat, what frogs look like, etc.). The teacher can then use these categories for further writing assignments. By starting out with a brainstorming activity, the teacher is helping the students elicit any prior knowledge they have about frogs.

In another example, to explore the concept of buoyancy, a secondary school science teacher may ask students to think about things that float and things that don't. The students may think of anomalous substances that might float depending on other factors, such as the oil in salad dressing, the effluent from an oil spill, whether large corks float as well as small ones, whether a boat built of concrete will sink. Then, by creating a visual organizer and "chunking" the information into different categories, the teacher makes it easier for the students to store the concept of buoyancy, to ask questions about it that lead to its underlying properties, to generalize these to unfamiliar material, and to conduct experiments as necessary. Finally, by using this information to generate further academic activities, the teacher provides the students with sufficient knowledge of the topic to allow them to successfully record their experiences.

Scaffolding

The technique teachers use to help the students store information in long-term memory is known as *scaffolding*: teachers provide the assistance necessary for students to achieve success. Klinger and Haager (2005) break the process of scaffolding into three steps. Step one is when the teacher models the new task. Step two is when the teacher provides opportunities for the students to practise the new skill with ongoing support. Step three is when the teacher monitors the student performing the task without assistance. Module 3 examines scaffolding again in more detail, and Harris and Graham's six-step process is described.

During the interactive component of a lesson, the effective teacher is actually engaged in checking to see if students have successfully understood the concept, learned the requisite skills, and stored the new information in long-term memory. By providing opportunities for more independent rehearsal, the teacher is able to monitor understanding. At the same time, the teacher provides ongoing support as necessary. For example, the teacher may ask students to summarize, explain, give written responses, complete a homework assignment, or pair with a peer. Additionally, providing reviews on a daily, weekly, and monthly basis will increase retention. To further ensure success, it is necessary for the teacher to continue to make overt connections to prior knowledge and to clearly explain the purpose of the task at hand.

The guided practice and interactive stages of the lesson provide the teacher with the opportunity to circulate among the students. It is during these phases that the teacher can begin performance assessment, checking on the progress of individuals and groups of students as they work toward the instructional objectives. If the lesson has been designed carefully, this phase should provide the teacher with time to check in on most of the students, and to linger with some to guide them further. In some classrooms, it seems a waste of this most important instructional time when teachers use this phase to sit at their desks to catch up on paperwork or marking.

STUDENT POLL 2-2:

Reflecting on your experience as a learner, along with Research Box 2–4, do you believe that people have different skills sets that lead them to learn in different ways, or to prefer certain styles of learning over others?

Yes [ ]   No [ ]   Undecided [ ]

Completing the Lesson

The final part of a lesson involves finishing off the lesson and assessing how well each student has done on the learning and performance objectives set at the beginning. Skilled teachers will take a few minutes at the end of a lesson to do three things:

- Review the big ideas and main concepts and skills that have been central to the lesson

- Select one (or more) of the concepts and skills that has been difficult for some students to master during the lesson and conduct drills on how to tackle it

- Forecast the upcoming lesson objectives and content, including reminding students where the lesson started, how it has developed, and where it will lead

Dedicating time to independent study provides students with a means to review and practise the big ideas, main concepts, and skills they need to master. Essays, homework, peer practice, and seatwork assignments are all examples of independent activities. Teachers who commit to using a variety of instructional methods will be better able to assess their students' learning and provide additional support if necessary. Cegelka and Berdine (1995) point out that rather than teaching a new skill, the purpose of engaging students in independent work is

to develop fluency and reinforce the learning goals. Teachers should consider variables such as selecting work that is meaningful, establishing routines around the completion of assignments, and providing consistent feedback about the independent work.

It is interesting that few teachers take the important final step of forecasting the upcoming lesson objectives and content. Most rush to get everyone finished and materials put away before the bell rings! Yet by bringing the focus of the lesson back to its main objective, students are able to carry the "big picture" away with them and understand where they are going. They leave with the overall objective and direction for their work as the last thing they remember. This is Kame'enui and Simmon's principle of judicious review: providing the opportunity for students to recall and apply their newly learned information in terms of why it is important and where it will take them.

Praising individual task accomplishments

Skilled teachers accomplish the final step in various ways. They may point out examples from students' work, praising individuals for their task accomplishments as well as allowing the class to see good examples. The rubrics discussed earlier also provide a tangible reference for the teacher, as he or she points out examples that meet the criteria for success. Modified curriculum objectives can also be a part of this summary, in which students demonstrate what they have done and explain how it meets their learning goals.

In Case Study 2–3, Michelle outlines the stages of her Grade 9 Applied English lesson on the literary devices in poetry. She leads students through a review of the devices (alliteration, analogy, simile, metaphor, hyperbole, imagery, repetition, rhyme, personification, and onomatopoeia), and then uses a bingo-style game to help them find these devices in a poem," Short-Order Cook" by Jim Daniels.

case
study
23

How the stages of a lesson outlined above are reflected in Michelle's lesson plan are described in Case Study 2–3: Michelle's Poetry Lesson Plan.

<table>
<tr><td>case study
23</td><td>Michelle's Poetry Lesson Plan</td></tr>
</table>

Curriculum Expectation:

- Combine knowledge of literary devices and form and apply to analysing poetry

Instructional Objectives:

- To develop definitions for each of the literary devices on the list
- To identify examples of each device in single statements
- To correctly identify examples of devices in the poem "Short-Order Cook" by Jim Daniels
- To explore how literary devices and the form of a poem can influence the reader's understanding and enjoyment of a poem

Plan

As students enter:

- Distribute literary devices bingo cards
- Board work: write a sentence to illustrate onomatopoeia

Introduction and review: Prior lesson on literary devices and form

- Whole class review of forms of a poem: title, rhyming, structure, line length, etc.
- Whole class questioning of devices and what they mean: (alliteration, analogy, simile, metaphor, hyperbole, imagery, repetition, rhyme, personification, and onomatopoeia)
- Group work: each group to complete the definitions of each device by trading definitions with other groups

Devices (bingo):

- Each student to mark off a literary device on bingo card when I read a statement containing a device selected randomly from bag of statements

Scaffolding:

- Apple analogy: Each student describes their apple to partner, bites in and re-describes, eats to core and re-describes. Discussion of how this analogy holds for poem—1st , 2nd, and 3rd readings
- 1st reading: I read poem and "think aloud" about its form and meaning
  Discuss their reactions
  From overhead, discuss poem title, illustrations, form

- 2nd reading: individual silent re-read
  Identify figurative language, underline devices

- 3rd reading: Student volunteer to read poem
  Discuss any new meanings, nuances

Practice:

- Students to work in pairs on a second poem—scaffolding steps 2 to 4 above—continue for homework

Review:

- Forms, devices, and how they contribute to meaning

Monitoring Progress

A great deal has been written on how to track student achievement and to communicate the results to students. The topic of assessment and evaluation will be taken up in a later module. However, the following points are useful for this review.

Provide assignments for evaluation

Skilled teachers supply students with the evaluation criteria and explain how assignments are to be completed in order to meet them. Again, without belabouring the point, a well-designed rubric contains this information without giving so much detail that the students do not have to strive to integrate the knowledge and skills, nor with so little detail that the students are left in the dark about performance expectations until after their marks are returned.

Maintain continuous graphs and records

Teachers have different systems for keeping track of students. Some maintain separate files for each student, annotating or checking off completed assignments. Others use complex systems in which the teacher writes notes about behaviour and motivation to add to records of completed assignments and marks or credits earned. Portfolios have also become a popular way to track performance assessments. The tracking system most typically reported by teachers, however, is "in the head" anecdotal records, particularly at the elementary level. This can be onerous on one's memory, however, and subject to error. Also, students are less likely to be participants in a system in which the teacher's anecdotal record is the sole indicator of progress. Kame'enui and Simmon's principle of judicious review (see Planning the Lesson) is applicable here. Review is judicious because the expectations for accomplishments are shared with the students throughout the teaching and assessment cycle.

Teachers may also provide periodic reviews throughout the instructional year, for example through tests and quizzes, as a way to keep important objectives fresh and to link current to previously learned material.

Communicate evaluation results to students

This step completes the instructional cycle: assess student needs, intervene with programs and services, assess outcomes, and plan next steps. This cycle, introduced in Module 1, will re-appear in later modules.

Review the options initially jotted down for Lisa (Case Study 2–1). The following case study (Case Study 2–4: Maria's Class) describes how Maria tackles Lisa's problem, in a similarly complex class.

case study

2-4

---

case study

2-4

Maria's[1] Class

We left Lisa at the beginning of this module wondering how she could possibly cope with the diversity of her class. Should she give busy work to some and concentrate her time with those who would likely do well on the provincial assessments? Or should she try to spread her teaching time across the range of levels of need and hope that everyone would get at least a little of what they need to learn?

In the module, some of the answers to Lisa's dilemma are provided. Many techniques, skills, and even ways of thinking or personal philosophies and beliefs will need to be incorporated into the final answer. This will take us beyond the scope of this review module and into techniques for adapting instruction to meet different learner needs. However, here are some of the possibilities for Lisa's class and the many other classes like it that have already been reviewed.

Maria teaches a split grade 6 and 7 class. Like Lisa's, Maria's class consists of a wide range of skills levels, and has a high proportion of students with special needs. Ten of her 32 students work from or are in the process of being assessed for an Individual Educational Program (IEP). Four of the students were new to the school in September. A number of students have known and others unknown difficulties in the community and at home.

---

[1]This case study is based on a real classroom event. The names of participants have been changed.

Maria's description of teaching her class and the practices that she selected for the observed mathematics class said a great deal about how she copes with their diversity. A classroom observer first notices how Maria's classes are scheduled. By teaming with her colleague, a specialist in English and language arts, Maria concentrates on teaching mathematics to this and two other grades. Together they cover the two core subjects for grades 6, 7, and 8. This allows for some flexibility in how students are grouped. Maria has at hand mathematics curricula that span three grades. She can therefore move some students forward at an accelerated pace, while others can be grouped for more in-depth review and re-teaching of difficult concepts and skills. Maria has arranged the desks in her room into five groups, each group forming a U-shape that allows verbal interaction among the group and also a view of the blackboard. Groups are of mixed ability and at various levels in the curriculum. Students with IEPs are interspersed among the groups with students who have strong records of achievement.

The special education resource teacher and an educational assistant spend up to three half-hours a week in Maria's classroom. The segments of the lesson that review previously learned concepts and that introduce new material are presented during times before the extra staff are available in the room. When they arrive, Maria has assigned seatwork so that the extra staff can use their time to circulate around the groups, assisting students who need the most help.

Maria creates instructional time in many ways. She prepares her lessons so that she spends little time on setting up tasks. She uses an overhead projector and translucent materials to review previously learned skills for computing the area of geometric shapes. A calculator and a timer are adapted for the overhead projector so that students can watch as Maria computes the areas. She sets the timer for the practice component of the lesson so that students can see how much time they have left for their assigned tasks. Maria's review of previously learned material and her presentation of new concepts are fast-paced. She models her thinking, talking aloud as she bisects an irregular L-shaped figure to create two rectangles, and then computes their area using the reviewed formula for the area of a rectangle. She asks multiple questions, extending students' thinking: "Who can find another way to compute the area of this shape?" (bisecting the L-shape along another axis). "Is there a third way?" (enclosing the L-shape in a rectangle, computing its total area, and then subtracting the area beyond the L from the total).

Maria has established a cooperative ethic in the classroom. She trains her students to work together, to help each other out when they are struggling. During the practice component of the lesson, they "ask three before me;" that is, they consult with three other students when they have a lesson-related question before they take their question to the teacher. During this seatwork, Maria also has a "command centre," a round table where she convenes students who need extra help. She announces to the class at the start of their seatwork activity that anyone who has a problem with the work, and who has asked their group for help but is still unclear, may join her at the table until they have an answer to their question.

Jack's voice rises as he works in his group. His neighbour starts to leave his seat. Maria glances up and quietly calls their names. She stays still, a slight smile on her face as she fixes her gaze on them until they settle back to their task.

At the end of the lesson, Maria points out how each group has tackled the seatwork assignment. She praises the student who contributed the third method for solving the area of the irregular L shape, and, because he is shy, asks a colleague in the group to report the answer that they derived. She notes that Jack completed the exercise. She reminds students of the homework assignment and of how it relates to the rubric chart. At the bell, as the students leave the room, Maria stands at the door and quietly chats to them individually as they leave.

Her goal, she says, is to make everyone feel comfortable enough to risk trying, to feel that they are in charge of their own learning. That means working hard at the beginning of the year to establish cooperation and support as a community expectation. It means demonstrating by modelling for the students how to accept everyone's contribution without negating it, how to preserve dignity, how risking a response and being wrong won't mean being ridiculed. It means reducing competitiveness and reminding students that they have agreed to respect one another and to work together.

Summary

The first section of this module provided a synopsis of all the skills that teachers need to be effective in planning and executing teaching routines. The checklists (2–1 and 2–2) can be used as a self-evaluation tool for monitoring teaching skills and growth over time.

The remainder of the module reviewed the principles of effective teaching. These represent the foundational concepts and skills that will be needed to adapt instruction to meet diverse learner needs, the topic of the modules to follow. The foundations on which the rest of this text will be built include:

Time management and classroom management routines

These are essential for three purposes:

- To maximize the instructional time available to the teacher for use with individual and small groups of learners

- To establish the expectations for routines, the flow of activities, and behaviours in the classroom that each member of the class can expect to apply

- To set out an understanding of the expectations that the members of the class community can use to develop a sense of self-direction and independence in managing their own learning time, to assist other students, and to take responsibility for their accomplishments and those of their peers

Planning and presenting a lesson or a unit of study

These consist of six phases:

- Planning the lesson or unit, incorporating instructional tools for meeting diverse learner needs

- Introducing the lesson

- Presenting new material (the expository part of a lesson)

- Practice and application (the interactive activities and guided practice components of a lesson)

- Completing the lesson (reviewing the main concepts and accomplishments)

• Recording student achievement and monitoring progress

Essential to planning and presenting a lesson are clearly stated instructional objectives that are embedded in the overall learning goals of the lesson or unit. These are linked to the curriculum expectations and standards that are set by the school system and provincial/territorial governments. The anatomy of an instructional objective was analysed and good and poor examples were considered.

The rubric is a useful tool for designing instructional objectives, communicating them to students, and providing a framework for evaluating student achievement and monitoring progress that is open and transparent for the members of the class. This format identifies the accomplishments of the unit and how marks will be assigned, permitting students to engage in the process of learning.

Instructional tools for meeting diverse learner needs are also considered as part of developing objectives and planning one's lessons. These ideas begin an examination of adapting instruction to meet diverse learner needs, the subject of the next module.

Glossary

Conceptual framework   People hold mental sets of interconnected facts, concepts, and strategies that they have developed to organize and make sense of their experiences. Each framework is individually developed and therefore unique to each person. In order to retain new information each person must "make sense" of it by incorporating into the conceptual framework. (p. 135)

Conditional knowledge or **Information-handling skills**   The processes that learners use to link previously-acquired knowledge and skills to new information and newly acquired strategies. (p. 132)

Content knowledge or **Declarative knowledge**   The basic building blocks of knowledge including facts, naming systems, rotely learned material, and content. (p. 132)

Direct instruction   The technique in which a teacher aims to supply content, conditional knowledge, and skills in explicit, systematically-sequenced steps (p. 157)

Expository teaching   The portion of instruction in which the teacher describes or "expounds" the material to be learned. (p. 117)

Individual Education Plans or **Programs** (IEPs)   A working document is required in most provinces for students receiving special education. It describes the strengths and needs of the individual student, the special education program and services prescribed to meet the student's needs, and how the program and services will be delivered. It also describes the student's progress. (p. 131)

Instructional cycle   The teacher undertakes a series of steps, assessing student needs, designing programs and services to address the needs, assessing the outcomes of instruction, and planning next steps on the basis of the results. Since this is a cycle, it can be self-correcting. (p. 147)

Kinesthetic   The sense of touch or feel. (p. 153)

Metacognitive   Higher order thinking processes that reflects an understanding of how one learns or thinks. Deciding how to carry out a task, how to supplement one's immediate memory by note taking, checking for understanding, and assessing progress are all metacognitive processes (p. 155)

Metacognitive strategies or processes   Thinking skills that take account of the complexity of the task in relation to the parameters of human thinking and memory (p. 135)

Pathognomonic   The assumption that a disability or learning difficulty is a fixed, internal characteristic of the individual, rather than the result of external influences such as the opportunity to learn, or to access needed resources. (p. 153)

Procedural knowledge or Task-specific skills   Thinking and learning skills that take account of the structural characteristics of a task to be learned including the concepts, skills and strategies needed to undertake that task. (p. 132)

Self-talk, also "**Think alouds**" and **Self-questioning**   Teacher provides a verbal running commentary to describe his or her thinking processes and problem solving strategies while demonstrating to students how to work through a problem. (p. 140)

Strategy instruction   A technique aimed at explicitly teaching learning strategies, thinking and metacognitive skills (p. 157)

Think aloud *see* **Self-talk** (p. 140)

Transmissive   The type of instruction in which the teacher is primarily the source of knowledge and instruction flows in one direction from the teacher to the students (p. 117)

With-it-ness   A term coined by Kounin (1970) to denote the ability of the teacher to be aware of all the activities in the classroom and to be able to orchestrate the flow of the class with minimal cues, while simultaneously engaged in teaching. (p. 116)

Zone of responsibility   This is the proportion of the class for which the teacher takes instructional responsibility. This may be narrow, as when the teacher directs instruction only to the average learners or to those who excel, or it may be broad, as when the teacher adapts instruction so that learners at different levels of achievement are simultaneously engaged in learning. (p. 113)

References

Atwell, N. (1998). *In the middle: New understandings about reading, writing and learning.* (2nd ed.). Portsmouth, NH: Boynton/Cook Publ.

Ayers, R. & Cooley, E. J. (1986). Sequential versus simultaneous processing on the K-ABC: Validity in predicting learning success. *Journal of Psycho-educational Assessment, 4,* 211–220.

Baker, S. K., Kame'enui, E. J., & Simmons, D. C. (1998). Characteristics of students with diverse learning and curricular needs. In E. J. Kame'enui & D. W. Carnine (Eds.), *Effective teaching strategies that accommodate diverse learners* (pp.19–44). Upper Saddle River, N. J.: Prentice Hall.

Berdine, W. H. & Cegelka, P. T. (1995). *Effective instruction for students with learning difficulties.* Needham Heights, MA: Allyn and Bacon.

Bereiter, C. & Scardamalia, M. (1986). Educational relevance of the study of expertise. *Interchange, 17*(2), 10–24.

Bereiter, C. & Scardamalia, M. (1993). *Surpassing ourselves: An enquiry into the nature and implications of expertise.* Chicago: Open Court.

Berliner, D. C. (1994). Expertise. In J. N. Mangieri & C. C. Block (Eds.), *Creating powerful thinking in teachers and students* (pp.161–186). Fort Worth, TX: Harcourt Brace.

Berliner, D. C. (2001). Learning about and learning from expert teachers. *International Journal of Educational Research, 35*(5), 463–482.

Berliner D. C. (2004). Describing the behaviour and documenting the accomplishments of expert teachers. *Bulletin of Science, Technology and Society, 24*(3), 200–212.

Bickel, W. W. & Bickel, D. D. (1986). Effective schools, classrooms and instruction: implications for special education. *Exceptional Children, 52*, 489–500.

Bloom, B. S., Englehart, M. D., Furst, E. J., Hill, W. H., & Krathwohl, D. R. (1956). *A taxonomy of educational objectives: Handbook 1. The cognitive domain.* New York: McKay.

Briggs Myers, I., & McCaulley, M. (1985). *Manual: A guide to the development and use of the Myers-Briggs Type Indicator,* Mountain View, CA, Consulting Psychologist Press.

Brophy, J. (2004). Remarks. Looking in classrooms again. Symposium: Social constructivist teaching: Affordances and constraints. Paper presented at the AERA Convention, San Diego, CA, April 15, 2004.

Brophy, J. & Good T. L. (1986). Teacher behavior and student achievement. In M. C. Wittrock (Ed.), *Handbook of research on teaching,* (3rd ed, pp. 328–375). New York: Macmillan.

Brown, B. W. & Saks, D. H. (1986). Measuring the effects of instructional time in student learning: Evidence from the Beginning Teacher Evaluation Study. *American Journal of Education, 94*(4), 480–500.

Carter, K., Cushing, K., Sabers, D., Stein, P., & Berliner, D. C. (1988). Expert-novice differences in perceiving and processing visual information. *Journal of Teacher Education, 39*(3), 25–31.

Castner, K., Costella, L., & Hess, S. (1993). Moving from seat time to mastery: One district's system. *Educational Leadership, 51*(1), 45–47.

Clark, C. M., and Peterson, P. L. (1986). Teachers' thought processes. In M. C. Wittrock, (Ed.), *Handbook of research on teaching,* (3rd ed, pp. 255–296). New York: Macmillan.

Cobb, P. T. & Yackel, E. (1991). A constructivist approach to second grade mathematics. In E. vonGlasersfeld (Ed.), *Constructivism in Mathematics Education* (pp. 157–176). Boston: Kluwer.

Cook, B. G., Tankersley, M., Cook, L., & Landrum, T. J. (2000). Teachers' attitudes toward their included students with disabilities. *Exceptional Children, 76*(1), 115–135.

Copeland, W. D., Birmingham, C., DeMeuille, L., D'Emidio-Caston, M., & Natal, D. (1994). Making meaning in classrooms: An investigation of cognitive processes in aspiring teachers, experienced teachers and their peers. *American Educational Research Journal, 31*(1), 166–196.

Cronbach, L. J. (1957). The two disciplines of scientific psychology. *American Psychologist, 12,* 671–684.

Cronbach, L. J. (1975). Beyond the two disciplines of scientific psychology. *American Psychologist, 30,* 116–127.

Department of Education, Republic of South Africa. (2005). *Curriculum adaptation guidelines of The Revised National Curriculum Statement.*

Doyle, W. (1986). Classroom organization and management. In M. C. Wittrock (Ed.), *Handbook of research on teaching* (3rd ed, pp. 392–431). New York: Macmillan.

Englert, C. S., Tarrant, K. L., & Mariage, T. V. (1992). Defining and redefining instructional practice in special education: Perspectives on good teaching. *Teacher Education and Special Education, 15*(2), 62–86.

Fuchs, L. S. & Fuchs, D. (1986). Effects of systematic formative evaluation: A meta-analysis. *Exceptional Children, 53,* 199–208.

Fuchs, D., Fuchs, L. S., Mathes, P. G., & Simmons, D. (1997). Peer assisted learning strategies: Making classrooms more responsive to diversity. *American Educational Research Journal, 34,* 174–206.

Gardner, H. (1983). Frames of Mind. New York, NY: Basic Books.

Gerber, M. M. & Semmel, M. I. (1984). The microeconomics of referral and reintegration: A paradigm for evaluation of special education. *Studies in Educational Evaluation, 11*(1), 13–29.

Goodman, K. S. (1976). Reading: A psycholinguistic guessing game. In H. Singer & R. B. Ruddell (Eds.), *Theoretical models and processes of reading* (pp. 497–508). Newark, DE: International Reading Association.

Grossen, B. J., Carnine, D. W., Romance, N. R., & Vitale, M. R. (1998). Effective strategies for teaching science. In E. J. Kame'enui, & D. W. Carnine. (Eds.) *Effective teaching strategies that accommodate diverse learners.* (pp. 113–137). Upper Saddle River, N J: Prentice Hall.

Haager, D. & Klingner, J. K. (2005). *Differentiating instruction in inclusive classrooms: The special educator's guide.* Boston: Pearson.

Hammill, D. & Larsen, S. (1974). The effectiveness of psycholinguistic training. *Exceptional Children, 41,* 5–14.

Hammill, D. & Larsen, S. (1978). The effectiveness of psycholinguistic training: A re-affirmation of the position. *Exceptional Children, 44,* 402–414.

Heward, W. L. (2003). Ten faulty notions about teaching and learning that hinder the effectiveness of special education. *Journal of Special Education, 36*(4), 186–205.

Jordan, A., Lindsay, L., & Stanovich, P. (1997). Classroom teachers' interactions with students who are normally achieving, at-risk and exceptional. *Remedial and Special Education, 18*(2), 82–93.

Jordan, A & Stanovich, P. (2001). Patterns of teacher-student interaction in inclusive elementary classrooms and correlates with student self-concept. *International Journal of Disability, Development and Education. 48*(1), 43–62.

Kame'enui, E. J. & Carnine, D. (1998). *Effective teaching strategies that accommodate diverse learners.* Upper Saddle River, NJ: Merrill.

Kame'enui, E. J. & Simmons, D. C. (1999). Toward successful inclusion of students with disabilities: The architecture of inclusion. Reston, VA: Council for Exceptional Children.

Kavale, K. (1990). The effectiveness of special education. In T. B. Gutkin & C.R. Reynolds (Eds.), *The handbook of school psychology* (2nd ed, pp. 868-898). New York: Wiley.

King-Sears, M. E. (1997). Best academic practices for inclusive classrooms. *Focus on Exceptional Children, 29*(7), 1–22.

Kirk, S. A. & Kirk, W. D. (1978). Uses and abuses of the ITPA. *Journal of Speech and Hearing Disorders, 43*(1) 58–75.

Kounin, J. S. & Doyle, P. H. (1970). Degree of continuity of a lesson's signal system and the task involvement of children. *Journal of Educational Psychology, 67*(2), 159–164.

Lickona T. (1991). *Educating for character: How our schools can teach respect and responsibility.* New York: Bantam Books.

Montgomery, K. (2000). Classroom rubrics: Systematizing what teachers do naturally. *The Clearing House, 73*(6), 324–328.

Morrison, G. R., Ross, S. M., & Kemp, J. E. (2004). *Designing effective instruction.* (4th Ed.) Hoboken, NJ: Wiley/Jossey Bass.

National Research Council. (1993). National Committee on Science Education Standards and Assessment. *National science education standards: A sampler.* Washington, DC: Author.

Olson, D. R. & Katz, S. (2001). The fourth folk pedagogy. In B. Torff & R. Sternberg (Eds.), *Understanding and teaching the intuitive mind: Learner and teacher learning* (pp. 243–265). Mahwah, NJ: Lawrence Erlbaum Assoc.

Orland-Barak, L. & Yinon, H. (2005). Sometimes a novice and sometimes an expert: Mentors' professional expertise as revealed through their stories of critical incidents. *Oxford Review of Education, 31*(4), 557–578.

Palincsar, A. S., & Brown, A. L. (1988). Teaching and practicing thinking skills to promote comprehension in the context of group problem solving. *Remedial and Special Education, 9*(1), 53–59.

Palincsar, A. S. (1990). Providing the context for intentional learning. *Remedial and Special Education, 11*(8), 36–39.

Piaget, J. (1952). *The child's conception of number.* New York: Humanities Press.

Popham, W. J. (1999). *Classroom assessment: What teachers need to know.* (2nd ed). Needham Heights, N.J.; Allyn & Bacon.

Poulson, L. & Avramidis, E. (2003). Pathways and possibilities in professional development: Case studies of effective teachers of literacy. *British Educational Research Journal, 29*(4), 543–560.

Pressley, M., Rankin, J., & Yokoi, L. (1996). A survey of instructional practices of primary teachers nominated as effective in promoting literacy. *Elementary School Journal, 96*, 363–384.

Pressley, M. E., & Woloshyn, V. (1995). Cognitive strategy instruction that really improves children's academic performance. Cognitive Strategy Training Series. 2nd Edition. Cambridge, MA: Brookline Books.

Reschly, D. J. (1996). Functional assessment and special education decision making. In W. Stainback & S. Stainback (Eds.), *Controversial issues confronting special education: Divergent perspectives* (2nd ed.) (pp. 115–128). Boston: Allyn & Bacon.

Reynolds, M. C. & Lakin, K. C. (1987). Non-categorical special education for mildly handicapped students: A system for the future. In M. C. Wang & H. J. Walberg (Eds.), *The handbook of special education research and practice Vol. 1* (pp. 331–356). Oxford: Pergamon Press.

Rieth, H. & Evertson, C. (1988). Variables related to the effective instruction of difficult-to-teach children. *Focus on Exceptional Children, 20*(5), 1–8.

Rosenshine, B. (1997). Advances in research on instruction. In J. W. Lloyd, E. J. Kameanui, & D. Chard (Eds.), *Issues in Educating Students with Disabilities* (pp.197–221). Mahwah, NJ: Lawrence Earlbaum Associates.

Rosenshine, B. & Stevens, R. (1986). Teaching functions. In M.C. Wittrock, (Ed.), *Handbook of research on teaching* (3rd ed.) (pp. 376–391). New York: Macmillan.

Shulman, L. S. (1986). Those who understand: Knowledge growth in teaching. *Educational Researcher, 15*(2), 4–14.

Shulman, L. S. (1987). Knowledge and teaching: Foundations of the new reform. *Harvard Educational Review, 57*(1), 1–22.

Smith, F. (1978). *Understanding reading.* (2nd ed.) New York: Holt, Rinehart & Winston.

Sousa, D. A. (2006a). *How the brain learns.* (3rd ed). Thousand Oaks, CA: Corwin Press.

Sousa, D. A. (2006b). *How the brain learns to read.* Thousand Oaks, CA: Corwin Press.

Sousa, D. A. (2006c). *How the special needs brain learns.* Thousand Oaks, CA: Corwin Press.

Stanovich, P. & Jordan, A. (1999). Exemplary teaching in inclusive classrooms. *Thalamus, 17,*(1). 69–70.

Sternberg, R. J. & Horvath, J. A., (1995). A prototype of expert teaching. *Educational Researcher,* 9–17.

Swanson, H. L. (1999). Instructional components that predict treatment outcomes for students with disabilities: Support for a combined strategy and direct instruction model. *Learning Disabilities Research and Practice, 14*(3), 129–140.

Swanson, H. L., Hoskyn, M., & Lee, C. (1999). *Interventions for students with learning disabilities.* New York: Academic Press.

Torff, B. (1999). Tacit knowledge in teaching: Folk pedagogy and teacher education. In R. Sternberg & J. Horvath (Eds.), *Tacit knowledge in professional practice* (pp. 195–214). Mahwah, NJ: Erlbaum.

Torff, B. (2003). Developmental changes on teachers' use of higher order thinking ad content knowledge. *Journal of Educational Psychology, 95*(3), 563–569.

Torff, B. & Sternberg, R. (2001). Intuitive conceptions among learners and teachers. In B. Torff & R. Sternberg (Eds.), *Understanding and teaching the intuitive mind: Learner and teacher learning* (pp. 3–26). Mahwah, N.J.: Erlbaum.

Vygotsky, L. S. (1978). *Mind and society: Development of higher psychological processes.* Cambridge, MA: Harvard University Press.

Wiggins, G. (1992). Creating tests worth taking. *Educational Leadership, 49*(8), 26–33.

Creating Access to Learning

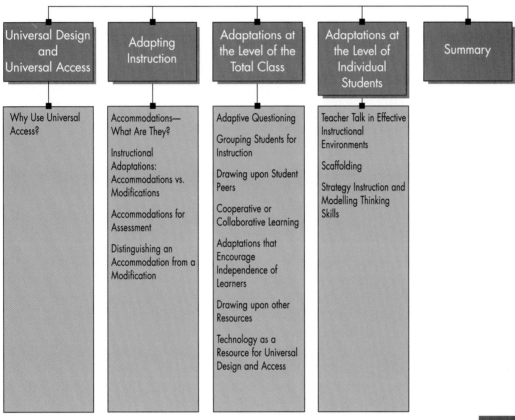

Universal Design and Universal Access	Adapting Instruction	Adaptations at the Level of the Total Class	Adaptations at the Level of Individual Students	Summary
Why Use Universal Access?	Accommodations— What Are They?	Adaptive Questioning	Teacher Talk in Effective Instructional Environments	
	Instructional Adaptations: Accommodations vs. Modifications	Grouping Students for Instruction	Scaffolding	
		Drawing upon Student Peers	Strategy Instruction and Modelling Thinking Skills	
	Accommodations for Assessment	Cooperative or Collaborative Learning		
	Distinguishing an Accommodation from a Modification	Adaptations that Encourage Independence of Learners		
		Drawing upon other Resources		
		Technology as a Resource for Universal Design and Access		

Complete the Module 3 pre-test on-line prior to commencing this module.

pre-test

3

Learning Objectives

In this module, teachers will learn:

1. the concepts of **universal design** and **universal access**, **educational adaptations** including **instructional accommodations**, and **curriculum modifications**;

2. to distinguish between an accommodation and a modification, including how to counter the "It's not fair!" complaint (i.e., that students who are given accommodations are at an advantage over those who are not);

3. how to adapt instruction to meet various learner characteristics at two levels:

   a) the total class level:
      adaptive questioning
      grouping
      adaptations of classroom management, time, and setting
      encouraging independence of learners
      working with colleagues and the educational assistant
      using technology for universal design and access

   b) the individual student level:
      teacher talk in effective instruction
      scaffolding
      strategy instruction and modelling thinking skills

Opening Vignette

View the video clip of Mr. Antonio Morra and his grade 12 Comparative Religion class. Mr. Morra reviews a previously-watched movie with his class about Siddhartha Gautama and the development of Buddhism. In this sequence, we see excerpts of today's lesson, understanding the Path to Enlightenment and the elements of the Eightfold Path which lead to ethical and moral development. The class is divided into eight groups, each to define one of elements of the Path, and to develop a dramatization of its meaning.

After viewing the video, consider the following questions:

1. In questioning the small groups during the seatwork portion of the lesson, Mr. Morra uses questioning techniques that extend students' thinking. Give an example of one of these techniques.

2. What instructional techniques does Mr. Morra use to encourage students to grasp the concepts of the lesson?

3. What is meant by "Right Livelihood"? What in the lesson assists you to understand this concept?

4. What are the various stages of the lesson presented in this video clip? Are there some stages not represented?

"Accommodating learner differences is often interpreted as 'watering down' the curriculum and as 'unfair' to other students who 'manage on their own.' When students with different abilities and skills have multiple ways to be engaged in the curriculum, it is possible for them to be comparably challenged by the same content." (V. Nolet and M. McLaughlin, 2000, p. 94.)

The previous module explored two major concepts: the effective conservation of instructional time, and lesson planning and presentation. Both of these are prerequisite for this module. Module 3 examines the many ways that teachers can expand their teaching repertoires to adapt to the needs of all students, including those with special needs at both ends of the achievement spectrum. It has been said that teachers often use the "shower model" of teaching: teachers deliver the curriculum to the students in the middle of the class in the hope that those on the fringes get a little damp. The purpose of this module is to help teachers turn away from the shower model of delivering curriculum and take charge of the water hose. Module 3 explores a variety of instructional techniques for working with students to ensure they all receive their share of instructional time in a way that is calibrated to their current levels of learning and their learning characteristics. But more than this, the module will help reaffirm and expand teachers' **personal theories** about the nature of ability and disability, and what this implies for planning and delivering instruction on a daily basis.

In order to do this, the module explores ways of thinking about instructional planning and delivery that vary from the traditional views of delivering curriculum as teaching content. Key concepts are "universal access" and "universal design," ways that a teacher can accommodate student differences in learning styles and needs by designing instruction that every member of the class can access. In other words, developing some accommodations for one or more individual students in the class can become part of a teacher's routine instructional repertoire from which all members of the class can benefit.

Universal Design and Universal Access

learning objective
3-1

Nolet and McLaughlin (2000) use a useful analogy to illustrate the principle of "universal design." They write that many people use Goodgrips© kitchen tools, designed by OXO International for people who have difficulty gripping the handles of conventional tools for opening cans, jars, etc. This product has had extraordinary success, not only because people who have limited manual ability due to arthritis or other motor problems have success using

them, but also because people without motor disabilities have bought them for their great design and ease of use. For most people, they are more "accessible" than conventional kitchen tools.

Go to the OXO website, www.oxo.com, to see what these tools look like. How do these products have universal design?

Universal design also allows for universal access; that is, allowing people with and without disabilities to have access to facilities. These facilities include the handicap washrooms and ramps installed in public buildings. Most of us without disabilities also use them from time to time because they are convenient and easy to use. They are also essential for mothers wheeling baby strollers and carriages through public buildings.

Glasses to correct vision are also a product of universal design. They allow people to access the telephone directory and texts, or they allow them to drive, watch movies on large screens, and much more. Glasses are so commonplace that we don't even think of them as specialized to people with a disability to give them access to services that require good vision.

Another example of universal access occurs at conferences where the speaker's words are simultaneously translated into print on a large screen for the benefit of those delegates with hearing impairments. The print version of the speech is accessed by the entire audience, as was indicated at a recent conference by the laughter of the audience when a spelling error came up on the screen that had an amusing double meaning. The simultaneous translation supplemented the speech by providing universal access which assisted the audience, both with and without hearing difficulties, to follow along.

Universal design and universal access can be applied in the classroom. What can a teacher plan and implement that will increase the access to learning for students with disabilities and learning difficulties, that will also be useful to all students? Can switching to such a technique increase the accessibility of the curriculum for everyone? If so, the teacher need only prepare one set of materials or activities to meet the learning needs of both groups of students. Further, the activities could be shared by everyone, permitting groups and pairs to work together with the same tasks and materials. Teachers in classrooms are designers; the more universal and accessible their designs for instruction, the wider the array of students they will impact.

Think of examples of universal design and universal access that are used in the classroom. For example:

- an overhead transparency that provides an ongoing record of the tasks for a group activity so the participants can keep referring to it as they work rather than having to keep returning to the directions if they forget the details

- an e-mail to students that sets out the requirements for an upcoming meeting to assist the members of a group to prepare for it without having to work from memory

Review Interactive Exercise 3–1 for some hints.

<table>
<tr><td>

interactive
exercise

3-1

</td><td>

Universal Access

</td></tr>
</table>

In this exercise, jot down as many examples as you can of universal design and universal access. When you finish the second section (classroom adaptations), compare your examples to the classroom adaptation list provided. Did you identify some examples that are not on the list provided?

1. Think of examples of universal access that you encounter in your **daily life**.
   Adaptations for people who...
   i. have limited vision:
   ii. have hearing loss:
   iii. have physical disabilities:
   iv. have developmental challenges:
   v. have trouble remembering:
   vi. have reading disabilities:
   vii. find mathematical computation a challenge:
   viii. are challenged by organizational demands such as timekeeping.

2. Think of examples of universal access that you can implement **in the classroom**.
   Adaptations for students who...
   i. have limited vision:
   ii. have hearing loss:
   iii. have physical disabilities:
   iv. have developmental challenges:
   v. have trouble remembering:
   vi. have reading disabilities:
   vii. find mathematical computation a challenge:
   viii. are challenged by organizational demands such as timekeeping.

After having devised your list, review the lists below. The following are some examples of adaptations that can be fairly easily put in place in a classroom or school. This is not a comprehensive list, so many more ideas can be added. Also, the specific needs of each student will determine which adaptations are beneficial. As suggested elsewhere, these should be selected as a result of a collaborative process between teachers, support workers, parents, and the student, where possible.

Students who...

i. have limited vision:
   • word processor with enlarged text
   • seating near blackboard
   • a reading buddy
   • verbal presentation of knowledge
   • larger font on printed material, blackboard, and computer screen

ii. have hearing loss:
   Mild hearing loss
   • provide seating near teacher
   • increase use of visuals and text handouts
   • provide visual fire alarms (flashing lights) and peers prepared to assist the student in emergencies and during complex transitions
   • teacher positions self to face student, keeps moustache, beard short to assist lip reading cues

   Moderate hearing loss
   • have teacher wear a frequency-modulated (FM) **hearing amplification system**
   • have teacher, classmates learn alternative communications system (**finger-spelling, signs**)
   • noise level of classroom is minimized by carpeting, room structure

iii. have physical disabilities:
   • provide pencils with adaptive grips
   • arrange classroom furniture to allow wheelchair access/ease of access to needed resources
   • provide peer support to assist with access
   • provide adaptive gymnastic equipment

- use computer for presenting work
- locate classes in ground floor accessible rooms

iv. have developmental challenges:
- form co-operative groups where student has a contributing role
- form heterogeneous groupings and pairs, a buddy system
- use computer for research, spelling, and grammar checks, and presenting information
- provide accommodated questioning
- assess current level of skills and knowledge to adapt curriculum
- modify curriculum
- model acceptance and inclusion
- implement programs for forming friendships (Tribes, Gibbs, 1995; Hughes et al., 1999)

v. have trouble remembering:
- use handouts and e-mails
- check daily agenda
- reinforce routines that check for completion
- involve parent support
- assess current level of skills and knowledge to adapt curriculum

vi. have reading disabilities:
- provide high interest reading at appropriate level of difficulty
- use the "3-finger test" to select reading
- use peer buddies and notetakers
- use word processing
- highlight key concepts in material to be learned
- preteach key vocabulary

vii. find mathematical computation a challenge:
- provide peer support
- form heterogeneous groupings and pairs
- accommodate by assigning every second problem in the text
- provide squared paper to assist organization
- assess current level of skills and knowledge to adapt curriculum

viii. are challenged by organizational demands such as timekeeping:
- use daily agenda reminders and e-mail
- provide printed instructions
- provide lined and squared paper
- use word processing to save work
- use peer buddies and groupings

Why Use Universal Access?

By using the principles of universal access, teachers demonstrate knowledge, concepts, and skills in multiple ways, and they design multiple ways in which students can demonstrate what they have learned. They also offer multiple means of engaging students in the lesson material, tapping their interests and motivation and providing them with appropriate challenges. Nolet and McLaughlin (2000) make the point that presenting materials in several media as several forms of representation makes the information available to most students. It also introduces information "redundancy" or the repetition of important information that assists students to learn and even over-learn the material, leading to better retention. Students too may benefit from responding to the material in multiple ways, allowing them to demonstrate what they know while circumventing the challenges brought by traditional means of demonstration. Nolet and McLaughlin (2000) suggest two ways of providing multiple means of communication in the classroom: multiple ways for the teacher to represent information, and multiple ways for students to express themselves. Together, these multiple means are intended to increase student engagement with the learning materials.

Multiple means for teachers and others to represent lesson materials

REDUNDANT REPRESENTATION FORMATS			
Say it	**Show it**	**Model it**	**Different media**
Lecture	Picture/graphics	Demonstrate	Video tape/disk
Discussion	Transparency	Think aloud	Audio tape/disk
Questioning	White/black Board	Act it out	Computer
Read aloud	Video	Build/construct	Television
Verbal description	Captions	Manipulatives	Manipulatives

Multiple means for students to express what they have learned

Students who are physically limited in their writing or who struggle with verbal expression or spelling may be able to demonstrate their learning and express their ideas by using:

1. Presentation and graphics software
   - Preparing electronic visuals, overhead transparencies
   - Using clip art and graphics
   - Using spelling and grammar checking

2. Oral presentation
   - Presenting in small groups or to a partner, as well as to the whole class
   - Presenting with the support of graphics, demonstrations
   - Presenting a play assisted by peers

3. Models and manipulatives
   - Using materials to create models, science exhibits, working demonstrations

Multiple means of engagement

Learners who struggle with text or who have difficulty remembering a string of details will often prefer to access the learning material through an alternative medium such as a television program or the computer. The challenge for the teacher is to provide more than the standard exposition of materials via expository lectures and textbooks, either for those students who need such alternatives (instructional accommodations) or for a group or class (universal access).

One common example of an instructional accommodation that is designed for universal access is the use of media to assign projects. Students are often given verbal instructions about the requirements for completing an assignment. If these are supplemented by allowing students to copy from the board or from an overhead transparency, or if they are given as a handout or e-mail, or posted on the classroom wall, students who are not skilled at retaining instructions in memory will have various ways to access the directions. Such alternative means help to ensure that their work, and not the students' memory of the task requirements, is reflected in their completed assignments. When this principle is applied in classrooms, the learning environment becomes more **inclusive** for all the students.

Acrey, Johnstone, and Milligan (2005) suggest the following underlying principles define universal design in the classroom by making learning more accessible:

- Inclusive classroom population: Design all classroom materials with the diversity of the student population in mind.

- Precisely defined constructs: Focus on the construct (i.e., instructional objective) you are trying to teach. Avoid construct-irrelevant materials that may be teaching or testing non-targeted skills.

- Accessible, non-biased materials: Select materials that are not offensive to a given group and that do not give an advantage to one group over another.

- Amenable to accommodations: Select materials and tasks that can be adapted by accommodations that increase accessibility to the curriculum.

- Simple, clear, and intuitive procedures: Make tests and materials clear and understandable.

- Maximum readability and comprehensibility: Use language that is clear, simple, and direct.

- Maximum legibility: Use font size that is large and familiar enough for students with visual difficulties (or those seated at a distance) to read.

These teaching methods can become part of the teacher's routine instructional style. Fuchs and Fuchs (1998) and others note that teachers are reluctant to create specialized adaptations for students with disabilities, but are generally willing to make accommodations that they consider to be a routine part of their teaching. The question becomes: Why do some teachers use accommodations routinely, often to the point of not seeing them as accommodations but rather as good teaching habits, while other teachers do not?

> The concept of universal design for learning is featured in a website: (http://www.cast.org). CAST is a non-profit organization that updates the website with electronic and technology-based learning opportunities especially for people with disabilities and for those who work with them. CAST (Pisha & Coyne, 2001) extended the concept of universal design in education (UDE) to include universal design for instruction (UDI) and for learning (UDL).

Review Research Box 3–1 for a summary of research studies that investigate teachers' willingness to make instructional adaptations. Consider the study questions as you read and then provide your answers.

research
box

3-1

research box 3-1

Teachers' Willingness to Adapt Instruction

Read the synopsis of studies below, and then answer the study questions.

Berliner (1994) distinguishes five levels of teaching expertise, from beginning and novice, through competent and proficient, to expert. He states that as teachers reach the competent level, they often feel more responsibility toward their students than at initial levels. A study involving student teachers examined the perceptions of general and special education teachers and their cooperating teachers regarding the use and importance of various instructional strategies in inclusive classrooms (Cole & Leyser, 1999). The vast majority of these beginning teachers would be at the stage that Berliner (1994) describes as novice, the stage at which beginning teachers follow a set of context-free rules until more experience is gained. The behaviour of teachers at the novice stage is often rational and rather inflexible as they conform to the rules and procedures they are told to follow. Beginning teachers are less likely to use cooperative learning and peer tutoring strategies, choosing instead to focus on a teacher-led instructional style that places fewer demands upon their classroom management techniques.

   As an introduction to their study, Cole and Leyser (1999) reviewed the literature and determined that teachers prefer to use adaptations that involve little change in their usual teaching practices. They are also more likely to employ adaptations that relate to the social adjustment of learning disabled students, such as providing support and encouragement.

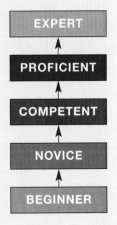

Adaptations identified as least desirable, and therefore less likely to be used, include changes to: instructional practices, assignments, and material; grading criteria; long-range plans; and the physical arrangement of the room.

Using strategies found to be effective in the empirical literature relating to effective interventions in inclusive classrooms, Cole and Leyser (1999) developed a teacher-rating questionnaire to measure beginning special education and experienced general education teachers' perceptions of the desirability of various instructional strategies. The results of their study showed a high degree of acceptance for about 10 items, including such strategies as modelling performance, providing examples, and being consistent in establishing consequences for inappropriate student behaviour. However, it is interesting to note that their results also showed that both beginning special education teachers and more experienced general education classroom teachers were reluctant to involve other professionals, including teacher colleagues, psychologists, counsellors, and social workers. The person identified as least likely to be consulted was the school principal (Cole & Leyser, 1999). This reluctance to consult others may explain why general education teachers often appear unwilling to collaborate with special education personnel on an on-going basis within the classroom.

Many general education teachers perceive adaptations as more desirable than feasible (Schumm, Vaughn, Gordon, & Rothlein, 1994). As a result, the majority of teachers become more concerned with the needs of the class as a group and with the flow of the group, than with the needs of the individual students. Middle school teachers and secondary school teachers, in particular, plan for the class as a whole and expect learning disabled and mainstream students to cover the same content and complete the same tasks as general education students. In Schumm et al.'s study, although teachers rated themselves highly in the areas of beliefs, skills, and practices, specific planning for individual students was observed infrequently during classroom observations. Participating teachers were less likely to use a variety of information sources, implement long-range planning, adapt course content, or adapt tests, since these strategies required more advance preparation. Teachers were more likely to implement adaptations that could be implemented "on their feet," rather than those which required advance planning (Schumm et al., 1994).

This finding is also supported by Fuchs, Fuchs, Hamlett, Phillips, & Karns (1995) who state, "The natural and persistent mindset of the general educator is on the needs of the class—not those of the individual" (p. 456). Teachers are "more committed to routine than to addressing individual differences" (Baker & Zigmond, 1990, p. 525). Practices implemented most often by teachers include adjusting the time and pace of assignments, providing peer support, and monitoring student understanding. Additional constraints such as class size, pressure to cover specific curriculum expectations, lack of planning time, and minimal teacher training at faculties of education may also prevent some general education teachers from making adaptations or providing the accommodations for individual student needs.

Many classroom teachers do not feel they have been properly trained to deal with individual differences and therefore lack confidence in their knowledge and skills (Schumm, Vaughn, Gordon, & Rothlein, 1994). Teacher training programs often include minimal special education training, and often do not address the need to plan for learning disabled and mainstreamed students within the framework of planning for the class as a whole. However, Berliner (1994) believes that teacher education programs will not produce competent teachers, but rather beginners primed to learn from experience, since many pedagogical skills are slowly acquired. Other researchers would agree, stating that experienced teachers have had many years to develop a well-filled toolbox by trying a variety of methods and strategies. It is this extensive background knowledge that allows them to integrate new knowledge with what they have learned in the past (Rankin-Erickson & Pressley, 2000).

Classroom teachers rarely alter the curriculum of students with special education needs by reducing the content of courses, and this is influenced strongly by state and local accountability requirements (Schumm et al., 1994). Teachers at the middle school and high school level may also be concerned about differentiating instruction for learning disabled students by "watering down" the curriculum and reducing expectations, since this only emphasizes inabilities and points out the differences between learning disabled (LD) and general education students (Schumm et al., 1994).

Study questions

1. Not all teachers demonstrate unwillingness to adapt instruction. What factors do you think contribute to their willingness? To their lack of willingness?

2. What kinds of adaptations are easier for teachers to make? Why do you think this is the case?

Adapting Instruction:

Accommodations—What Are They?

learning objective

3-2

Accommodations are changes to teaching, student responding, and the classroom environment that increase the students' access to the curriculum. They are not changes to the level of difficulty or expectation of the curriculum itself, but to the way the curriculum content is communicated between the teacher and the students, and among the students. There are three general kinds of accommodations.

Presentation or instructional accommodations (teacher to students):
- Changes in teaching strategies that allow students to access the curriculum (e.g., large print, calculators, Braille, and other communication techniques such as stick figure directions, learning guides, manipulative materials)

Response or assessment accommodations (student to teacher):
- Changes made to the way in which a student demonstrates learning (e.g., alternative presentation formats and alternative response formats, such as a tape-recorded essay, a dramatic demonstration); these changes do not compromise the achievement standard of the learning goal being assessed, but allow the student to demonstrate the standard of mastery in alternative ways

Environmental accommodations:
- Changes made to the classroom and/or school environment (e.g., wheelchair ramps, a quiet location, the time of day chosen to take a test)

In many texts, accommodations refer to provisions for the student which are different from those routinely provided to the class. Yet in many cases, many students would benefit if such accommodations were built into the routine instructional repertoire of the teacher. When considering accommodations as creating universal access, they become a characteristic of good teaching rather than an individualized form of instruction for a specific student. However, for many students, accommodations are specified in their Individual Educational Programs (IEPs). The onus is therefore on the teacher to look for ways in which accommodations that are prescribed for specific students can become more broadly used with other members of the class. In this context, the IEP becomes a working document; one which mobilizes staff and resources to support the teacher's efforts to meet the needs of each and every student.

Instructional Adaptations: Accommodations vs. Modifications

In the literature, particularly from some U.S. sources, the terms "accommodation," "modification," and "adaptation" are sometimes used interchangeably. In some Canadian provinces, there are specific meanings for the terms. These tend to differ slightly from one jurisdiction to another. In order to be clear about the use of these terms in this text, they are defined as follows.

TABLE 3-1: EDUCATIONAL ADAPTATIONS

A generic term encompassing both changes to the curriculum standards and to how the curriculum is presented

INSTRUCTIONAL ACCOMMODATIONS	CURRICULUM MODIFICATIONS
• changes to traditional ways of presenting and responding to material and to the learning environment	• changes to the level of difficulty or standard of performance for prescribed curriculum expectations and learning goals

DEFINITIONS OF TERMS USED IN THIS TEXT

One way to keep these distinctions clear is to think in terms of "*instructional* accommodations" and "*curriculum* modifications." Contrary to comments sometimes heard in school, accommodations are **not** simply mild forms of modifications. They are **not** reductions in the amount or difficulty level of work expected of a student. Accommodations address the "how" of learning, whereas modifications address the "what."

Accommodations do not affect the difficulty or grade level of the learning goals or curriculum expectations. Rather they are applied to the **communication** of learning material between teacher and students, among learners, between students and sources such as media, and to the environment in which the learning takes place; i.e., instructional accommodations. In contrast, modifications are changes to the curriculum expectations or learning goals for a given grade level, either reducing or raising the **level of difficulty** of the content, skills, or concepts required in the original curriculum standards or expectations. Modifications result from a reduction in or an enrichment of the amount and complexity of the content and skills in a subject area; i.e., curriculum modifications.

A student's program, as specified in an Individual Educational Program (IEP) for example, may contain accommodations and/or modifications. An example of a modified program in a grade 11 science class for a student working at a grade 5 level might be as follows:

> The student expresses in her own words the central ideas in the unit on health and safety in the chemistry laboratory, while the remainder of the class takes a quiz on health and safety procedures in the event of an emergency. This modification might be further supplemented by accommodations. For example, the student may have a scribe or translator to assist her to record her ideas, or a laptop computer to help her to write.

Another example of a modified program might be as follows:

> A student placed in a grade 4 mathematics class learns regrouping, a grade 2 level learning expectation. This modified program might also contain accommodations, such as using a calculator, or counting out each problem using manipulatives such as coloured blocks or counters.

Aren't most accommodations simply good teaching for all students?

There is a fine line between good teaching and preparing individually-tailored accommodations for a student. In many instances, instructional accommodations given to one student could also benefit others. This is the notion behind the concept of universal access. If the teacher takes the responsibility to include as many students in the instructional process as possible, it is likely that he or she will be using a variety of teaching techniques involving presenting concepts in several media (chalk or white board, handouts, overheads, etc.) and expecting students to demonstrate their understanding of the material in several ways (written, tape recorded, drama, illustration, etc.). In such cases, accommodation of student differences may be taking place as a part of the teacher's repertoire of teaching skills without being specified in individual IEPs. Working with students with special needs can therefore be good professional development for teachers, because it draws on their creativity to extend the instructional process over a wide variety of student characteristics. This in turn benefits all students.

Other accommodations may be more specialized and used exclusively by individual students. Examples include specialized communication systems such as computers and voice synthesizers, individual languages such as **ASL**, **Signed English**, or **Braille**, and using the specialized assistance of a paraprofessional such as a **teaching assistant** or **teacher's aide.** The teaching assistant's role will be examined in a later section of this module.

STUDENT POLL 3–1:

Instructional accommodations should be a standard part of good teaching and not just reserved for students with special needs.

Agree ☐   Disagree ☐   Undecided ☐

Examine Research Box 3–2. It contains a summary of a research article that makes the case that working with students with disabilities in inclusive classrooms is a good opportunity for professional learning.

research box 3-2

Inclusion as Professional Development

Modern classrooms are becoming increasingly more diverse. Policies for including students with diverse needs in regular classrooms are now standard in Canadian school systems, and are part of a much larger international recognition of the rights of students to be educated alongside their peers. Yet much of the research on inclusion has tended to focus on the impact of the location or placement of students with disabilities, and not on the effects of differences in teaching approaches and other characteristics of classrooms on students with disabilities.

We know that, within certain limits, the class size does not impact the achievement of students without disabilities. It seems that any benefits from reducing class size are inextricably related to a teacher's practices.

Teachers who are effective at sustaining high achievement with their regular students do so largely irrespective of class size. Further, the number of students with disabilities in a regular classroom also seems to have no effect on the achievement scores of non-disabled students, and might actually have a small positive effect on reading achievement scores (Demeris, Jordan, & Childs, in submission). This is contrary to the beliefs often expressed by educators that students with disabilities detract from the time available for instruction, and this has a negative impact on the other students in the class. It seems that teachers and how they practise are keys to achievement, for both students with and without disabilities.

The impact of teaching differences on the effectiveness of inclusion has been scarcely investigated. However, there is a growing body of evidence that effective teaching practices for students with disabilities are very similar to effective teaching practices for all students. It seems that high quality teaching impacts all students in regular classroom settings.

An in-depth examination of what is happening in the classrooms of effective teachers seems to support this.

Effective teachers:

1. focus on methods and techniques that work; they continuously experiment with different approaches to instruction and learning, and draw upon the experience they accumulate to recalibrate their instruction with individuals and groups

2. are adept at engaging students in learning

3. use a combination of teacher-directed (direct) and student-directed (guided) learning

4. individualize curriculum, materials, instructional methods, and instructional goals

5. continuously assess and evaluate their teaching and their students' learning, making adjustments to how they teach on a moment by moment basis

6. nudge students along an implicit track in the learning material toward the objectives that both students and teacher understand

7. know their students in considerable depth, and allow for their differences; however, they focus on each child as a whole person and not on their difficulties and differences

8. preserve the dignity of each individual and model respectful interaction

9. hold as their primary goal that all students should become independent as learners

It is with these findings in mind that researchers have started to examine what effects the presence of students with disabilities in a classroom might have on the development of teaching skills. In a passionate account by Giangreco and colleagues (1993), 19 teachers who were receiving their first student with a significant disability into their classes at the start of the school year were tracked over time. At first, the teachers worried about the newcomer and about their ability to meet his or her needs. By the end of the year, 17 of the 19 teachers described what Giangreco termed a transformation in their perspective about disability and in their confidence as teachers. One teacher expressed it this way. "At the beginning of the year, if I was making copies of something I might forget to count Jon: I just didn't deal with him.... When I count the kids in my class now, I've counted Jon. It just took me a while". (p.359).

Canadian researchers have observed elementary classroom teachers who begin their teaching careers with relatively traditional, teacher-directed, whole-class lesson formats and little teaching interaction with individual students (Stanovich & Jordan, 2004). Over several years, and sometimes almost immediately, they begin to develop more flexible lesson formats, experiment with groupings and peer partnerships, and find ways to engage in lengthy interactions with individuals and small groups. They attribute much of this to reflecting about their responsibility for underachieving students and students with disabilities and learning difficulties. They seek ways to increase the participation of these students and to create additional opportunities for these students to learn. They are active researchers, experimenting with different techniques and evaluating the outcome (Robinson, in preparation).

One might therefore conclude that the experience of accommodating students with disabilities in one's class can itself be a form of professional growth. Of course, as we learn from the two remaining teachers in Giangreco's study, this cannot happen unless teachers are willing to take up the challenge. It is also helpful, if not vital, that supports be in place in schools to provide teachers with job-embedded training and resources, as the need for them arises. Best practice inclusive schools share an ethic of inclusion. Staff contribute to a shared philosophy and the leadership in the school makes inclusive practice a priority. As a result, all members of the school staff are available to provide resources for each other (Ainscow, West & Nicolaidou, 2004). Stanovich & Jordan (1998) show that the positive perspective of a school principal toward inclusion is one of the strongest predictors of how well teachers will teach in that school—not just how they will teach students with disabilities, but students overall.

Accommodations for Assessment

Assessment accommodations are used in two differing situations. The first is in the classroom, where students are encouraged to demonstrate their grasp of curriculum concepts through a variety of means. In this situation, the teacher seeks feedback which demonstrates how successful students have been in responding to instruction and to the instructional accommodations used by the teacher. It is part of the teacher's **instructional cycle** initially described in Module 1:

1. assessing student needs,

2. intervening with, monitoring the effectiveness of, and adjusting instructional programs and services, and

3. assessing student outcomes.

An example of a response or assessment accommodation used in the classroom is a test assigned to the class on which some students who take more time than average to read or to respond need to answer only every second question. Students who process information slowly, but who have mastered the concepts and skills which the test measures, have an opportunity to display their knowledge without being penalized for their speed of responding.

There are some qualifications to this example, however, that are associated with how the test is designed and how it reflects the learning goals of the unit taught. If the test is measuring a skill for which speed is a criteria, such as testing whether students have learned facts or formulae to a level of automaticity so they can retrieve them quickly, then answering fewer items on this test will not be an appropriate accommodation. The test will simply provide an accurate indication of whether the students have attained the skill of automatic retrieval.

Popham (1999) notes that tests are designed to sample the skills and concepts which reflect the curriculum expectations and achievement standards.

Consider the structure of this test:

Question 1: Testing criterion skill 1

Question 2: Testing criterion skill 1

Question 3: Testing criterion skill 2

Question 4: Testing criterion skill 2

Question 5: Testing criterion skill 3

Etc.

A test that is constructed so that several items sample students' mastery of each skill, as in this example, can be accommodated to differences in students' response speeds by allowing slower students to answer only every second question. For example, if there are four skills to be demonstrated on a math test and there are two items for each skill, then some students could attempt one item only for each skill. The teacher would still be able to judge whether these students had mastered the range of skills sampled by the test. But if the test contains only one item for each of the skills to be assessed, then reducing the items to which students respond will make the test less reliable as a sampling of students' mastery of all the skills in the math unit. Such a shortened test no longer assesses the range of the skills that the teacher wants to measure, and therefore does not provide an accurate assessment.

Another way to design a test to allow for accommodation of differences in students' response times would be to ensure the criteria skills are reflected in a sequence. For example, the test could be designed to start with the earlier and therefore easier prerequisite skills and concepts. The test would include increasingly more difficult test items, for example by measuring more recently acquired skills that build on the earlier ones. The test questions start with simple skills and progress to the most complex, so that every second question provides a reasonable sampling of the skills taught in the overall teaching unit (provided, of course, that they are not time-dependent).

The adaptations of tests to measure learning goals and curriculum expectations will depend on how the test is designed, and how the learning goals and curriculum expectations that the teacher wants to assess are represented in the test. If these "accommodations" are beneficial for most if not all students in the class, the teacher can use them with everyone, and does not have to implement specialized adaptations for individual learners. They are designed to be "universal" and to permit universal access. They distinguish between the criteria learning goals (knowledge, skill, or concept) of the curriculum, and the means by which these are communicated, either by the teacher as he or she instructs or by the students as they respond to instruction.

The second situation in which assessment accommodations are used is during high-stakes (province- or state-wide) assessments. In Ontario, the regulating body for the provincial assessments, The Education Quality and Accountability Office (EQAO) (1997), prescribes a limited set of accommodations that can be used when students take the provincial tests in grades 3, 6, 9, and 10, provided their use is documented. These include accommodations of setting (a quiet place, prompting for students with attention difficulties who are seriously off task), different presentation formats (Braille, large print, coloured paper, **assistive devices**, and **technological resources**), and different response formats (scribing, word processing, assistive and technological devices). This information is available in the Administration Guide for the EQAO tests (page 18), which can be downloaded in PDF format at: http://www.eqao.com.

An important point, however, is that there should be consistency between accommodations for educational assessments in the two situations; in the classroom and in high-stakes assessments. The provincial assessment accommodations should not occur "out of the blue" for students. Students should have experienced similar accommodations routinely in their classroom learning, and be familiar with how to use them. The ultimate goal is, of course, for the student to progress to the point of independence when the accommodations may be needed only intermittently or not at all.

Distinguishing an Accommodation from a Modification: The "It's not fair" Complaint

From time to time, teachers will encounter a complaint from a student, a parent, or even a colleague, that an accommodation (such as extra time to complete an examination or a scribe to write for a student) gives an unfair advantage to that student compared to his or her peers without disabilities. This complaint is a challenge to distinguish between an instructional accommodation and a curriculum modification. As previously defined, a true accommodation supports the communication between the student and his/her teacher or examiner. It should not affect the level of difficulty set for the objective, and therefore should not alter the level of performance that the student must reach to demonstrate that he or she has reached the objective. If it does, it is likely to be a modification. In order to distinguish whether a proposed adaptation is an accommodation or a modification, take the following steps.

1. The teacher/examiner's objective (curriculum expectation) that is being assessed is:

2. In order for all students to demonstrate that they have met this objective, the teacher requires them to:

3. The accommodation in dispute is:

4. Think of one student who is strong in this subject area. If the teacher gave this accommodation to this student in order for him/her to meet the same expectation, would he/she do better as a result?

If yes—then the disputed adaptation is part of the curriculum expectation or learning goal and is a modification not an accommodation.

If no—then the disputed adaptation is an accommodation, and therefore should not give an unfair advantage to anyone else, but could "level the playing field" by allowing a student with a disability to show that he/she has met the curriculum expectation.

Work through Interactive Exercise 3–2. It uses the above steps to distinguish between an accommodation and a modification.

interactive
exercise

3-2

Distinguishing an Accommodation
from a Modification

In order to identify whether the teacher's adaptation of an assignment in science is an accommodation or a modification, apply the steps to counter the "It's not fair" argument.

A curriculum expectation of the grade 11 unit on Waste Management is for students to demonstrate an understanding of the types of industrial waste and their management in industry and in the community. One instructional objective is for students to explain the principles underlying management of gaseous waste and its consequences on global ozone depletion.

Michelle LePage, the science teacher for grade 11, has noted that there are several students in the class who struggle with producing written English. Some are still mastering English as their second language, while others have difficulty with English spelling, syntax, and punctuation. This tends to limit their written assignments to bare essential material, thus, she believes, under-representing their understanding of the science concepts. As a result, Ms. LePage has given the students a choice of two formats for the assignment to complete the unit on gaseous wastes.

Zara struggles with English and has difficulty expressing herself in writing. Zara has selected the option of producing a photo-essay for her assignment for the course. The photo-essay may contain material drawn from the Internet or photocopied texts, and photographs taken by Zara. The photo-essay will illustrate and support Zara's explanation of how gaseous wastes are generated, are or could be managed, and their impact on the ozone layer. Ms. LePage expects that, during a final assessment interview in which Zara explains how each photograph or illustration relates to the course objectives, she will be able to fairly accurately judge Zara's understanding of the course concepts.

The head of the school's science department, Ian Jong, has received a complaint from Leon's father about the "special treatment" that Zara and other students in the class are being given. Mr. Jong confronts Ms. LePage in the staff room. "This is an advanced level science course. It's the expectation that everyone who receives a credit in the course is able to express their scientific knowledge in English, that the technical and scientific terms are fully understood and applied in the context of all assignments. How can this happen in a picture book? I think your assignment is reducing the standard set for this course and making it into an arts credit!"

Ms LePage explains her reasoning to Mr. Jong.

Exercise:
Remember that there are four components in discriminating an accommodation from a modification, as set out in the response to the "It's not Fair" complaint:

1. What is the learning expectation, goal, or objective?

2. What are the criteria for demonstrating that the expectation, goal, or objective has been met?

3. What is the accommodation that is in dispute?

4. Thinking of one student who is strong in the area (and therefore will not need an adaptation); if this student was given this accommodation in order for him/her to meet the same expectation, would he/she do better as a result?

5. If the answer is "yes, the student would do better," then the proposed adaptation is a modification. If the answer is "no, the student is unlikely to do better," then the adaptation is an accommodation. Furthermore, it will be fair to all involved; that is, the proposed treatment meets the differing needs of each student without creating any undue advantage of one over another.

Put a ✓ beside the statements Ms. LePage should use to support her claim that the assignment is an accommodation and does not reduce the standard set for the science unit. Put an ✗ beside those statements that do not support the claim.

1. "This assignment would not qualify for an arts credit since the marks are assigned for content, not for production format."

2. "Zara is an excellent artist. This assignment builds on her strengths, not on her difficulties."

3. "Students have the choice of submitting their assignments as a photo-essay or as a written assignment."

4. "The curriculum objectives for this segment of the course is to have students demonstrate their understanding of the principles underlying management of gaseous waste and its consequences on global ozone depletion."

5. "Leon is a very capable student who has no difficulty mastering the concepts of the course. He is unlikely to gain any more points for producing a photo-essay version as compared to a written version of this assignment, because he will be able to demonstrate his understanding by either means."

6. "It will be easier for Zara to produce a photo-essay than to write about the concepts."

7. "Students must demonstrate their understanding of how gaseous wastes are generated, are or could be managed, and their impact on the ozone layer. They may either write about each of these topics, or illustrate them in a photo-essay and defend their selections during an interview with me. Marks will be given for evidence that the key concepts have been included in the assignment, regardless of the presentation format."

8. "The presentation format that Zara has selected will assist her to communicate her understanding of the principles without the additional burden of producing her thinking in written English."

9. "Therefore, the photo-essay assignment is an accommodation that maintains the curriculum standard set for the unit."

Solutions to this exercise are available on-line.

Discussion Questions:

1. What are the elements of universal design in Ms. LePage's assignment?

2. Are there other ways that Ms. LePage could have accommodated students' difficulties within the constraints of a written assignment?

3. What is your opinion about this type of accommodation? Under what circumstances might it work? Under what circumstances might it not work? For example, are there curriculum goals that depend on an accurately written English exposition?

learning
objective

3-3

Adaptations at the Level of the Total Class

In the next two sections, a variety of educational adaptations are discussed, mainly instructional accommodations that teachers can use in their everyday teaching with whole classes and with groups of students. Individual student accommodations will then be discussed in the following section.

The teacher using class-level strategies has the goal of preserving the dignity of students and creating a classroom environment in which students can risk tackling new learning without fear of humiliation. Many students avoid tackling new learning, especially if they already have difficulty learning. Teachers in effective inclusive classrooms design conditions to maximize their time to instruct, train the students to manage the classroom activities fairly independently of the teacher, and establish a social climate of mutual respect, support, and help in the classroom community.

research
box

3-3

Some students, particularly if they are struggling with learning, believe that intelligence is an internal, fixed characteristic or trait, and that they have the misfortune of not having much of it. Since they believe that effort and hard work cannot alter it, they try to avoid all situations where others will recognize their "handicap." Review this research and the implications for students' motivation to learn in Research Box 3–3 below.

research
box

3-3

Students' Theories About their Own Intelligence and their Impact on Motivation

"The whole idea of worrying about intelligence...implies that you think of it as a fixed, concrete thing. You only have a certain amount of it, so you'd better show that it's enough and you'd better hide it if it isn't" (Dweck, 2000, p. 20).

Carol Dweck and colleague Mary Bandura identified differing ways in which students thought about their own intelligence. Each student's self-theory results in predictable sets of behaviour during learning, and is linked to the motivation of each student to engage in learning. The first, the personal belief that intelligence is a *fixed entity*, makes students focus on whether or not to reveal the extent of their intelligence to peers. If they think that their intelligence is limited, that they are "dull," then they will engage in a variety of behaviours to conceal their limited intelligence to peers. Better to cause a distraction, leave the scene, or otherwise not complete one's work than to be thought of by one's classmates as dull. The alternative *incremental* theory, that intelligence is changeable and malleable and grows by increments as one learns, results in different patterns of behaviour. Students who hold this theory about themselves are more likely to be motivated to learn, and more willing risk being wrong in order to build their intellectual storehouse.

Dweck's research, conducted over several decades, contributes to our understanding of differences in students' motivation to work in school. Dweck points out that we hold common myths about both intelligence and motivation: that students with high ability are more likely to be mastery-oriented and to be more challenged than students with lower ability; that success contributes to greater effort; that praise, particularly ascribing success to students' intelligence, will encourage their motivation to learn. In fact, Dweck and colleagues show that students fall into two groups of approximately equal size. Regardless of the level of achievement that students reach, about half of them will be part of the "helpless pattern" group. These students hold the entity view of their intelligence, making them highly vulnerable when they face any kind of failure, and lacking in confidence when facing an intellectual or learning challenge. The other half belong in the "mastery-oriented pattern" group. They believe that their own effort is central to the development of their ability. In this group, even those who are not high achievers tend to relish challenges to learn. When they encounter difficult problems or failure, they do not view these as reflecting the limitations of their ability, but as problems and difficulties in the world that challenge their learning. In effect, the "helpless pattern" group, with entity beliefs, easily give up trying in the face of setbacks, while the "mastery-oriented pattern" group, with their beliefs in the malleability and incremental accumulation of intelligence, are more resilient.

Dweck points out that there are significant risks for high-achieving, very skilled students with entity beliefs. They see themselves as smart and are generally able to succeed until faced with a challenging situation or failure. Failure undermines their confidence, and as a result they succumb to defeat and ascribe blame for their difficulties on their own personal attributes. As Dweck notes, contrary to popular belief, one's personal theory of intelligence and ability is more likely to determine one's course in life than is one's achievement potential. In the same vein, students with an increment view of their intelligence and who belong in the "mastery-oriented pattern" group are likely to persist in solving difficult problems, regardless of their current and previous achievements. The net result is that their resilient perspective is more likely to result in success than that of their "helpless pattern" peers.

Study Questions

1. Think of a classroom situation in which you have noticed a student spending a considerable part of a lesson period daydreaming or doodling, thus delaying the start of his or her work. What attributions were made about this student's behaviour by the student? By those around him/her? Could this student's behaviour be explained by the possibility that the student views him- or herself as not very intelligent, and holds a "helpless" view of his or her ability? Might this student be attempting to hide from his/her peers evidence that supports his/her understanding that he/she is a hopelessly dull individual?

2. What other behaviours might be associated with students with:
   - an entity view of ability and a history of underachievement?
   - an entity view of ability and a desire to please?
   - an incremental view of ability and a history of underachievement?
   - an incremental view of ability and a high level of confidence?

3. What role do teachers have in changing maladaptive views of ability and motivation?

The principles of class-level adaptations are to:

1. maximize student engagement with academic materials, thereby increasing the time that students with special needs are attending and learning

2. conserve teacher time that can be used with individual students and small groups

Types of adaptations at the whole class level include:

- adaptive questioning

- grouping students for instruction—group size, pairs, and cross-age groupings

- using peers as tutors

- drawing on the resources of other adults

- using technology as an instructional tool

Adaptive Questioning: Techniques to Involve all Students

Consider the following scenario:

Joanne surveyed her grade 11 biology class. Matt and Steve were sitting in the back row whispering to each other across the aisle as usual. Mimi had yet to arrive. Joanne started her review. "Okay class. Hands up if you remember which gases are produced during photosynthesis." As Mimi wandered into the room arriving late for class, four students in the front row raised their hands. Matt and Steve continued their conversation in a loud whisper across the back row.

What could Joanne do differently?

She might start the class with a "bell work" problem on the board or as a handout that required the students to review the principle of photosynthesis. She could draw a diagram of the cross section of a leaf and ask students to label the components that are related to photosynthesis, and then draw and label the flow of gases. While they were doing this, she could walk to the back of the room where Matt and Steve are chatting. If they did not stop when she approached, she could quietly remind them to tackle the bell work problem. When they started working, she would get an idea of what they remembered and use this as the basis for a targeted question to one of them when she started her large group lesson. On the way back to the front of the room, she could make sure that Mimi has settled into her work.

Students with learning difficulties seldom volunteer to provide a response that might be wrong, so they drift into the far corner of the group and try either to become invisible to the teacher, or to create a distraction that gives them attention for off-task reasons. One solution to this is to establish a no-hands-up mode of large group questioning, and instead select students to respond. If students are aware that they are as likely to be called on as their neighbours, they will pay greater attention and become actively involved in formulating their responses. As seen in Research Box 3–3, it is also important for teachers to be sensitive to putting students in the possibly humiliating position of not knowing the answer or of being wrong in front of their peers.

Jacobsen, Eggen, and Kauchak (1999) summarize their research and that of Good and Brophy (1997) on effective questioning techniques. Teachers can do much to create a positive learning environment with a wide range of participation by modelling acceptance, participation, and belonging as part of large group questioning.

Rather than selecting who responds to questions on the basis of who raises their hands, the teacher selects students who will respond. This removes from the student the choice about whether or not to respond, since he or she can no longer choose whether to volunteer a response. It also raises the possibility that the student will be required to participate. Therefore the student is more likely to pay attention to the questions. The following techniques can also be successfully used to select students to respond in inclusive classrooms:

- drawing names or numbers randomly from a bag, jar of popsicle sticks, or a deck of cards

- calling on students by name

- informing one or more students that they will be asked next (to allow time to prepare), and even letting the students know what question they will be asked

- allowing a student to be assisted by a neighbour or buddy when answering a question

- using secret codes for students who lack self confidence but know the answer

The following scenario provides an example:

At a parent-teacher interview, Juan told his grade 8 French teacher that he felt embarrassed to answer in the large group brainstorming sessions. In fact he was terrified of not knowing the answer. "Juan," she replied, "Let's have a secret code, just between us. When I ask a question, if you think you know the answer, give me a sign. (She demonstrated by placing her index finger against her nose). If I see you doing that I'll know that you have the answer and then I can call on you."

There are also principles to increase confidence and participation during large group questioning. These include:

- adapting the difficulty of the question; gearing question difficulty and complexity to individual learning thresholds

- building in substantial amounts of small group work; questions and problems can then be tackled collectively, and any member of the group can volunteer to present them (The different types of groupings and their possibilities for increasing student participation are the topic of the next section.)

- increasing **wait time** to reduce the panic caused by time-limited responses

- using prompts and probes for incorrect first answers and non-responses, rather than moving to the next responder; for example:

Teacher: *Aldo, can you remind us of the relationship that we learned yesterday between density and weight?*

Aldo: (No response)

Teacher: *Aldo, when we placed the cork on the water, it did something different from the metal. Can you tell us what that was?*

Aldo: *It floated.*

Teacher: *That's right. It floated. What about the wood? What did it do?*

Aldo: *It floated too, but it didn't, like, bounce around like the cork did.*

Teacher: *Good observation. Now can you recall what made the cork and the wood behave differently from the metal?*

Aldo: *The air in them I think. Yea, they weren't as dense as the metal.*

Teacher: *Great, you remembered the term "dense." And you are totally correct! Jenny, what about the oil? It floated too but it didn't have air in it...*

An important part of questioning, probing, and prompting a student's understanding is that it allows the teacher to assess the learning threshold for that student, to identify gaps in skills and concepts to calibrate the instructional interaction to the student's threshold level of understanding, and then to "nudge" him or her toward the objectives. Unfortunately, questioning in some classrooms is a publicly intimidating and daunting process, especially for low-achieving students and students with curriculum-related disabilities.

Wait time is also an important element in teacher questioning. A student who does not know the answer feels intimidated in a group in which you get one shot to be right or you have failed. Good teaching involves staying with a student, supplying prompts to help the student retrieve the answer, accepting alternate answers, and modelling appreciation for effort as well as accuracy.

In the scenario above, Aldo's teacher both reformulates the question and prompts Aldo to recall. Deciding just where to prompt and at what level of difficulty is informed by a teacher's deeper knowledge of the student and belief in his or her capabilities. However, in a public forum such as a large group lesson, students with learning difficulties rarely feel confident and accepted, a problem that teachers can address by small group work and by establishing an accepting class climate in which mutual dignity and respect are modelled.

Adaptive questioning benefits all students by raising their level of engagement and attentiveness, and by preserving their self-esteem as a participant in the learning community. Without deliberate strategies on the part of the teacher to include all students, those with learning difficulties will withdraw, act out, and generally experience lower self-esteem and acceptance.

Video sequences of teachers using various questioning routines are available on-line. View them and note how the teachers engage the students in the lesson concepts and materials. A video summary and discussion questions are also available on-line.

Grouping Students for Instruction

Group size, pairs, and same- and cross-age groupings

Prior to the 1990s, the commonly accepted way of grouping students was by ability. Reading groups in elementary classrooms were designated as high, medium, and low ability, and sometimes even labelled accordingly: the eagles, jays, and sparrows! Changes in the North American legislation provided rights to students with disabilities and their parents: United States PL94–142, The Education of All Handicapped Children Act (1975), followed by similar legislation in Canadian provinces, such as Ontario's Act to Amend the Education Act (Bill 82) in 1980. The raising of awareness of the rights of students with disabilities resulted in changes to the way students were taught. One result was the recognition that same-age ability groupings tended to result in less instruction for students in lower groups. Such instruction tended to focus on low level recall and isolated skills, and to have fewer opportunities for practice than was the case for students in higher groups. Consequently the achievement gap between groups widened as the academic standing and self esteem of struggling learners decreased.

The changes in legislation were followed by U.S. federal funding to find ways to improve the academic achievement of underachieving students, such as students with disabilities and those from disadvantaged backgrounds. Projects such as television's Sesame Street were among the initiatives supported. Research studies examined such variables as size of instructional group, effects of cooperative groupings, peer tutors, and mixed ability groups on the achievement gains of low achieving students. The main findings of these studies on grouping were:

Size of groups for instruction

- Small groups of three to four students are more effective than groups of eight to 10 students (Lou, Abrami, Spence, Poulsen, Chambers, & d'Apollonia, 1996).

- Students of low ability benefit more from small groups than students of higher ability, provided groups are trained in group work procedures (Lou et al., 1996).

- Effective teachers in early elementary grades use small group instruction in reading nearly twice as often as less effective teachers (Taylor, Pearson, Clark, & Walpole, 1999).

Student pairs

- In reading, student pairs are the most successful form of grouping for raising achievement when

  - students who need the most practice have ample opportunities to serve in the role of teacher/mentor

  - peers are trained in their roles as tutors

  - student progress is carefully monitored and adjustments made to group composition, task, and feedback

Review Case Study 3–1 on the following page to see how Ann uses groups in her grade 2/3 mathematics program.

case study

3-1

case study
3-1

Ann's System for Grouping Students

As a split-grade 2/3 teacher, Ann revolves her class around small group activities. Over the years, Ann has created tasks that are stored in plastic bags and food containers, and on laminated cards. Around the room, clusters of two to four students huddle over math tasks, prompting and encouraging each other to complete the task.

The class has several students with significant difficulties. Alan, diagnosed with **PDD/Autism**, works with an educational assistant (EA). The two of them sit in a group with two other students, tackling a block-building exercise designed to provide a hands-on understanding of place value. When Alan shouts, his EA quietly leads him to a corner where Alan can defuse his frustration before returning to the group.

Winnie and Kate sit together at another desk, working with a large set of scales and task cards that direct them to find equivalent weights using bolts and screws. As Ann slides into the seat near them, Kate says to Winnie, "No. You aren't doing it right!" Ann quietly comments, "Kate, is there a question you can ask Winnie to get her to think about why that isn't the best way to weigh the bolts?"

Later, Ann announces to the class, "Time to start packing up now. Leave your work books in the red tray and put your materials in their places. The bell will ring in three minutes." Three minutes later, the tasks are neatly arranged on shelves beside their numbers. Recess starts.

When asked how she put the groupings in place, Ann describes the process she follows. A chart on the wall lists the numbered tasks. Each child's name is inscribed on a Velcro-backed card. These have been arranged beside the tasks. "I change the groups every two weeks. At first I decided who would work with whom, with struggling students paired with stronger students. I also worked with the class in September and October to help them understand that their role was to teach each other, not to beat out the competition. We talked about how we each learn, how each person has something unique to give. I've designed the tasks so that there are various ways for students to work with them. By the end of the first term, I didn't need to allocate students to groups any more; the students were able to choose each other and no-one was left out, including Alan, who is a wonderful design artist."

Ann then describes her reaction to the fairly noisy actively-moving class. "Some people would walk in here and see a three-ring circus! But I love it. I know exactly what everyone is doing, and now that I have set up the curriculum, I have loads of time to circulate among the groups, assisting the students on an individual or small group basis. I keep track of each of them individually on a chart that I carry around with me. I sometimes find that a number of them are struggling over a certain concept, and when I do, I'll bring them together and invite any one else in the class to join us, and we will review the concept. And I will also do a whole class lesson when I introduce a new kit. I find teaching this way almost leisurely—and I'm always thinking up new units to make that help them to understand the math concepts better. So my stash of materials is growing. Last year I took on this split grade arrangement and expanded the materials. I have enough for both grades, but I love how students will move backward and forward between the grade levels as they need to review something or as they gain the confidence to try something more difficult. I also have the time to lead the less secure ones to new tasks and stay with them till they are comfortable."

Drawing upon Student Peers

A commonly used whole-class technique for adapting instruction for the range of understandings is to use peers in the roles of tutor or mentor, and tutee or pupil. From the point of view of student achievement, it is generally the case that in peer-supported learning "two heads are better than one" (Elbaum, Vaughn, Hughes, & Moody, 1999). In principle, encouraging students to work together has many advantages. It should:

- increase the amount of task engagement of individual students with the lesson materials

- provide assistance on an "as-needed" basis between the members of the pair

- allow for multiple levels of curriculum and different instructional procedures to be available at the same time

- free the teacher to move among the dyads to assist, question, evaluate, and record progress for individuals and pairs, "nudging along" the learning process, and monitoring individual progress

In recent years there has been considerable use of peer tutoring, particularly in elementary classrooms. Peer tutoring has the advantage of allowing the teacher to plan different levels of instructional activities that take place simultaneously in the classroom. The students are grouped together in pairs or small groups, either by similarity of learning threshold (homogeneous pairs), or with more skilled students working with less skilled peers (heterogeneous pairs). Two of the most developed programs to design, implement, and evaluate the impact of peer tutoring are PALS (Peer Assisted Learning Strategies: Fuchs & Fuchs, 1998; Fuchs, Fuchs, Mathes, & Simmons, 1997) and CWPT (The Juniper Gardens Children's Project for Classwide Peer Tutoring: Greenwood, Delquadri, & Hall, 1989; Maheady, Harper, Mallette, & Karnes, 2004).

These techniques can increase the achievement of learners both with and without disabilities. They also assist the teacher to maintain a high level of student task engagement, in part because they place some of the responsibility for learning with the students, thus reducing the need for the teacher to take time to manage behaviours and organize tasks. These techniques also use peers to increase the overall instructional resources and support available to members of the class.

> The Division for Learning Disabilities of the **Council for Exceptional Children** (CEC) runs a website for teachers who are members of this division of CEC: http://www.TeachingLD.org
>
> There are many interesting papers on this site, with a context based in U.S. legislation. For example, a paper for teachers on Class-Wide Peer Tutoring (CWPT) appears in *Current Practice Alerts*, 8, Spring 2003.

There are, however, some limitations to using peers as tutors. Three factors seem to affect the efficacy of peer tutoring: the sophistication of students in acting as tutors, the composition of the student pairs, and the difficulty of the task they undertake (Maheady 1997; Greenwood, Maheady, & Delquadri, 2002). There are some students who fail to make adequate growth in a peer-assisted instructional format. Fuchs, Fuchs, Mathes, and Simmons (1997), for example, note that 20% of students designated as having learning disabilities failed to respond under a carefully implemented PALS program. They note the importance of ongoing monitoring and adjustment to instructional pro-visions for all students, no matter what program they are undertaking.

Second, the nature of the dyads and the complexity of the task on which they work appear to affect the learning outcomes, particularly of low-achieving students. There is evidence that homogeneous pairings, particu-larly among high achievers, are more successful than heterogeneous pairings (i.e., when a high- and a low-achieving student are paired) (Fuchs, Fuchs, Hamlett, & Karns, 1998). Homogeneous pairings of high-achieving students tend to treat each other as equal collaborators, or at least as equal turn-takers in the task. They are more likely to cooperate, to tackle more complex problems, and to provide each other with challenges in undertak-ing the task and with opportunities to apply constructive explanations to the task solution. As a result, they achieve higher scores on learning out-comes than pairings of heterogeneous students. When high achievers are paired with low achievers, the low achievers are sometimes excluded from involvement in decision-making and problem solving. Those students with learning disabilities in particular tend to be excluded from both peer and cooperative learning activities (O'Connor & Jenkins, 1996).

It is not yet known how the complexity of tasks is related to peer tutor-ing, although there is some evidence that low-achieving students work bet-ter with high- and medium- achieving students than with low-achieving peers, provided that the tasks are relatively simple. Given more complex tasks, low-achieving students, such as those with learning disabilities, are often excluded or given periph-eral tasks by their high-achieving partners (O'Connor & Jenkins, 1996).

Peer tutoring is potentially an important instructional adap-tation. It requires the teacher's skill and time to design the activ-ities and to train the students to tutor effectively. But like activity groupings, it can reward the effort by increasing the instruc-tional time available both for the teacher in the class and to indi-viduals and small groups.

Pairing skills that students need to learn

Students do not spontaneously apply behaviours that facilitate the learning of others, but need to acquire skills as tutors and to understand the nature of the role of tutor rather than learner (Webb & Farivar, 1994). Such skills include learning how to:

- construct explanations and elaborate concepts while allowing others to arrive at their own solutions; not simply telling answers

- resolve conflicts when the partner member of the pair offers different explanations and solutions

- interact so as to maximize the participation of the partner

Teachers also seem to benefit from training and ongoing support in how to use peer tutoring effectively (Fuchs, Fuchs, & Burish, 2000). Fuchs et al. (2000) note that teachers benefit from **"just-in-time" delivery** of resources and suggestions from coaches, such as knowledgeable colleagues and resource teachers, who assist them to implement the program and to adjust it as it is being implemented.

Well-developed peer support systems are also an integral part of a supportive classroom community, a characteristic of highly effective instructional environments, as will be seen later.

Cooperative or Collaborative Learning

A popular and effective classroom organizational strategy involves students working in collaborative learning groups with each other. Cooperative learning is an instructional format with many of the attributes of universal design and universal access. It can be designed so that all students, including those with both curriculum-related and complex disabilities, can participate with their peers.

The four principles of collaborative or cooperative learning (Johnson & Johnson, 1986; Slavin, 1991) are:

- interdependence—the requirement that all members of the group participate and learn; rewards are based in part on group performance

- individual accountability—rewards are also based on the individual contribution of each member, sometimes as rated by the teacher but often as assessed by the members of the group

- collaborative skills—materials and tasks needed to complete the assigned work are distributed across all members of the group; often roles are assigned (e.g., researcher, coordinator, designer, builder, etc.)

- group process—the opportunity for students to discuss how well they achieved their goals and how well they worked together

Peer techniques take advantage of the desire of students, and of secondary students in particular, to work with peers. There are other benefits to this approach, many of which address important learning goals of students with disabilities:

- increasing social and communications skills among members of the class

- developing friendships

- recognizing the contributions of peers with different backgrounds and learning experiences

Cooperative learning strategies include the *jigsaw format* in which each student in the group is assigned a task that contributes to the overall success of the project. Group project requires that members of groups pool their expertise to complete the assignment (Bennett, Rolheiser-Bennett, & Stevahn, 1991; Johnson & Johnson, 1986). Students with curriculum-related disabilities benefit from working alongside students with superior academic

and social skills, and may be able to take the lead on a variety of roles such as researcher (e.g., using the Internet to conduct research), team captain, or group convenor (e.g., monitoring and/or evaluating group process). Students with complex disabilities can often participate in cooperative groups when given roles such as the group co-ordinator, illustrator, or social convenor.

Like peer pairings, however, collaborative learning groups need training in how to work together. Cegelka and Berdine (1995) suggest 10 steps to implementing cooperative learning groups. Review this list in Research Box 3–4 below.

STUDENT POLL 3–2:

It isn't fair to non-disabled students to make them responsible for acting as tutors for students with learning difficulties.

Agree ☐   Disagree ☐   Undecided ☐

---

research box

3-4

Steps to Implement Cooperative Learning

Co-operative or collaborative learning is an important strategy for instruction in heterogeneous classrooms. Collaborative groups that contain students of mixed abilities can:

- increase the time that all students are engaged in learning by providing a small, and therefore safe, environment for attempting new learning skills and strategies, with feedback from other students to guide the learning process.

- assist students to acquire social skills and form friendships with peers.

- free the teacher to engage in extended instructional dialogues with individuals and small groups while the rest of the class is engaged in the lesson objectives.

However, co-operative or collaborative learning can only be successful if all students are trained in group process, and if all members of the group value the contribution which each member is making. This takes time to learn, especially when students have not previously experienced collaborative group work.

Modelling by the teacher of the kinds of acceptance and support that class members should provide is one important component. It can assist in establishing community acceptance and support. How the teacher addresses individual students will be reflected by students' interactions with each other.

Cegelka and Berdine (1995) suggest 10 steps for planning a co-operative learning program:

- Decide whether cooperative learning is appropriate for the instructional goals of the lesson or unit. Ask which goals can be reached by students working in groups.

- Assess students' prerequisite skills. Do students have the prior knowledge and the collaborative skills to attempt the assignment?

- Provide an **advance organizer** that states the instructional goals and performance expectations of the group and of the individuals in the group, as well as expectations for group process and for peer cooperation.

- Explain the nature of the peer-assisted groups, and the materials and procedures that they will be using.

- Demonstrate appropriate peer-assisted interactions by modelling the first steps of the assigned task. Remind students of cooperative effort and the need to support each other's work.

- Circulate among groups to monitor peer assistance and to provide appropriate feedback if needed about the peer-assisted assignment procedures.

- At the end of the activity, debrief about the co-operative process. Survey the students in regards to their perceptions of both the task and the peer-assisted process.

- After the lesson, evaluate both the learning (individual and group achievements) and the peer-assisted process (individual and group).

- Provide feedback to each group on the overall performance of the group and on group process. Set goals for improving group performance. Individual performance and contribution to the group may or may not be provided in the group setting.

- As group co-operation increases, continue to provide evaluative feedback.

Adapted from: Cegelka, P. T. and Berdine, W. H. (1995). *Effective instruction for students with learning difficulties*. Needham Heights, MA: Allyn and Bacon.

Adaptations that Encourage Independence of Learners

I had Mr. Clark [teacher] in grades seven and eight. And there again, I was given some independence, and that to me was...that was something that shaped what I do. You know again, given responsibility and, and given the expectation that, yes, you can do it. And he was, you know, full of enthusiasm and cared for the kids and willing to go, you know, willing to take kids on tournaments, doing those kinds of things out of school too, which I think is really important.

—(Teacher interview)

Consider the following scenario:

Kevin spends large amounts of time with students who are having difficulties. He places them around a table at which he is also seated. Other students bring their work to the table for him to check. Every so often he leaves this table to hold conferences with students who have not come up to his "Command Centre." He describes himself as monitoring at-risk students "out there on the periphery" while freeing up a lot of time to work one-to-one with the students with disabilities. Kevin is careful to emphasize, however, that his Command Centre is not to be associated with students' difficulties. He rotates students frequently, and deliberately selects students to join the table who are doing well, to assist them to further extend their thinking. "It's supposed to be a place for safety and help...it's a place to be encouraged and to be respected as opposed to a place to be told you mustn't do that."

For Kevin, an important component of accommodating the various students in his intermediate grade classroom is to ensure that none of them will feel singled out by the specialized attention he wants to provide. Although the class members are fully aware of the learning difficulties of each person, not to mention problems with their lives and friendships, Kevin models acceptance and recognition of their efforts. Establishing trust is raised here in the context of universal design. Teachers can start each school year by establishing the way in which students are expected to treat each other. The teacher's modelling of these expectations is a large part of establishing with the class the principles of respect for differences and non-judgemental support for peers.

The following scenario provides another example of how a teacher models acceptance. In this case, Sandi acts to preserve the dignity of a student who lapses from the progress recently made in behaving appropriately in the class. During large group discussion, Josh asks if he can ask "two silly questions."

Sandi: *Silly questions? Do you think they would help us to solve this?* [The mapping of animals onto their winter habitats.]

Josh: *No.*

Sandi: *So would you like to share those later?* (Josh nods) *Okay, good decision, Josh.*

After the lesson, Sandi discusses the situation with an observer:

Sandi: *Josh is one of the brightest boys, and again he was a behaviour problem when he came in...and he was very silly so he was always the class head clown. He was the smartest. He would push just to*

> *the limit yet know what line he couldn't cross over. So he was a real handful in the class...*

Observer: *How did you get him to the point where he would tell you he was going to ask a silly question?*

Sandi: *Um, I think just trial and error. He would say something and, you know, I would just sit there. I wouldn't laugh. I would just kind of look at him and let the others, you know, tee hee and everything, and then I would go to him after, I wouldn't do it in front of everyone. I would go to him after and I would say, "Now was that appropriate? What was the purpose in doing that? Was it to get attention? If you want attention, I'll give you a hug. You know, you don't have to do it by breaking up the class and what not." And also I said to him, "You're one of my brightest students. I need you to give me some really good answers that will make the others say, 'I wish I'd thought of that'."*

Observer: *You boosted his self esteem while you...*

Sandi: *Exactly. "Give me what I need and I'll not let you down." And now everyone wants him to be their partner. So it's not just me that he's gotten the positive feedback from, it's the other children, and I haven't said, "Josh is a great guy, he's the best student." They've just seen it in my responses to his answers.*

Observer: *Today did you get to hear his "silly questions"?*

Sandi: *After everyone had gone off the carpet to begin the activity he came up to me and said, "I'd like to tell you those two things now."*

Observer: *So he did actually tell you?*

Sandi: *You see, he knows that I will want to and that I will come and seek him out, and that I won't just brush him off.*

Observer: *You won't forget about it?*

Sandi: *That's right, and I think that that's important and that way he didn't blow my whole lesson by acting out. He let me know he wanted to say something, and...but then he knew that there was a time when he could say it.*

In order for a learner to reach this self-knowledge, the classroom has to be a safe environment in which to risk trying new skills. For students with a history of failure and labelled as exceptional, the need to feel safe and successful is enormous and difficult for teachers to satisfy. Teachers therefore emphasize the process of learning rather than the outcome. They model this behaviour and expect other members of the class to behave similarly. Abernathy and Cheney (2005) provide a self assessment tool, named Trek, for teachers to self evaluate their skills in encouraging students to be independent. Trek consists of three steps to review one's classroom practices and reflect upon the outcome.

A series of studies conducted in Canada by Nancy Perry at the University of British Columbia addresses how teachers can foster independence and self-regulated learning in heterogeneous classrooms (Perry, 1998; Perry, Phillips, & Dowler, 2004; Perry, Phillips, & Hutchinson, in press). A component of intrinsic motivation (see Research Box 3–3), self-regulated learning is the potential for students to apply their knowledge of their own learning strengths and weaknesses in choosing effective learning strategies and tactics for themselves. Perry identifies the characteristics of tasks that promote self-regulated learning and helps teachers to design such tasks and to interact with students to foster it. Tasks that are likely to promote self-regulated learning are complex and meaningful, allow students some degree of control over their learning process and production, and allow collaborative work with peers. Teachers who are effective in promoting self regulation carefully consider the choices they give to students, and make sure the students have the knowledge and skills to undertake the task, make good decisions, and be successful.

Authentic feedback such as praise is a component of teachers' effective interaction with their classes. It needs to be specific and authentic, rather than global and fatuous. Teachers are careful to praise effort and not to demean students' efforts. Good and Brophy (1997) studied the effects of teachers' use of praise. Briefly, students look for authentic praise that is specific to the individuals or groups, is given for deserved achievements, and is specific to the particular accomplishments. Global statements about the good work of individuals or groups are not reinforcing, as indicated in the following example:

Chantal: (colouring a picture to depict acid rain) *I'm sick of this.*

Teacher: *Okay, the brown tree, maybe the clouds. Can you put a little bit of blue in here?...even though you don't really see blue rain coming down but we show it this way.*

Chantal: *Okay.*

Teacher: *Yes, put some more colour, because you've got nice darks here. Take your seat. Come on. There's lots of time. What do you see in this? You're doing a super job.*

For the teachers who are attempting to encourage students to take risks and to assume ownership of their learning, the students with the most interfering behaviours present a special challenge.

In the following selection, Kevin discusses how he works with students with behaviour difficulties.

And the kids here, they'll know if they don't do something well but that they haven't labelled themselves and some of the labels that they felt they had in the past...C. has been one of the biggest problems in the whole school but you'd never know that. He's very rambunctious ...And S., he's very bright and he's had a horrible write up and report cards, personality, and I can't even go through it. In the class I had last year we had two kids that, these kids would pale in comparison, but it just depends on how you treat them and how you get along. For instance, I'll give you an example. They're so used to doing put downs and taking things very personally, that's why I'm always in a way...if I make a mistake...instead of just...if I were helping you instead of just saying, 'can you get a dictionary for me?', I'll make an announce- ment. 'Can somebody get me a dictionary please because I can't remember that word?' So now they know that when I do that with them they don't feel stupid. And I do it for show because the kids know when I do it for somebody else they don't...they'll all be picking on me. I'll make fun of myself because you should be able to laugh at yourself. And you can also make fun of others but they're so used to doing put downs that you can do it in a positive way and a firm way where a person knows that you're not challenging them.

Drawing upon the Resources of Other Adults to Maximize Teaching Time

The adults in a classroom can be a significant source of support for adapt- ing instruction. They can potentially free up the teacher's time to work with individuals and small groups.

View an example of staff members working together to devise a pro- gram that meets the needs of their students in an episode of *The National*. A video summary and discussion questions are also available on-line.

Co-teaching

This method of partnering two teachers has become popular in some school systems in the United States. Co-teachers might both be general education teachers working together in a combined grade, or a general education and a special education or resource teacher working together in an inclusive classroom. Partners need to plan their co-teaching activities: who will take responsibility for leading which unit, what the goals of each unit will be, and how the pair will work together to assist students to reach the goals. Without a clearly agreed-upon set of goals and instructional approaches, it seems from recent studies that co-teaching can deteriorate into a situation where one teacher conducts the class and the other serves as a "pair of hands" to undertake tasks that a non-qualified teacher such as an educational assistant or volunteer could perform (Marfo, Harris, & Dedrick, 2005). However, the role of a co-teacher, particularly one trained in special education, can have a significant effect on the range of instruction that can be planned and implemented in an inclusive class. The topic of collaborative consultation with fellow teachers is an important one and will be the subject of a later module in this series.

Working with a paraeducator (educational assistant, teacher aide):

Many teachers see their greatest resource as the educational assistant (EA) assigned to their class or to a student for part or all of a day. Like peer groupings, however, this resource needs to be planned, and considerable collaboration undertaken by both parties. EAs work under the direction of the teacher. It is the teacher who has responsibility for the curriculum and progress of all the students. The role of the EA and the expectations that the teacher has for the role need to be fully worked out, understood, and agreed upon by both parties. The following scenario demonstrates how that collaboration can work.

> Gil and Janette watch Sean as he puts yet another paper clip into his mouth. Gil, Sean's teacher, knows that she and Janette, the EA assigned to Sean, have a routine for handling the potential emotional storm that will follow when they have to remove the paper clip from Sean's mouth. Gil moves quietly over to Sean, opens his mouth, and extracts the paper clip before he has time to clamp down. He lets out a howl, the signal for Janette to move to him and distract him with a colouring pen that she

picks up on her way to his desk. Frequently, Gil and Janette work together to deliver the news that Sean must stop what he is doing, each knowing how he will respond to impending changes to his routine, to requests to stop mouthing objects, or to other requests. One will deliver the "bad news" to him that he must stop what he is doing, and then moves away from his outburst. The other follows with a quiet word, and assistance for him to move to the next activity.

If permitted by local policy, teachers often group together students with learning difficulties similar to those of the exceptional student to whom the EA is allocated, so that he or she works with a group. This makes the teacher's time available for the remainder of the class. Alternatively, an EA can monitor the larger class of students during seatwork and group activities, permitting the teacher to concentrate instruction with individuals or small groups.

Unfortunately, many educators think of classroom-based resources for inclusion as meaning they are allocated an EA or paraeducator to work with the students with disabilities. Once that person is installed in the classroom, there is a tendency for the teacher to rely on him or her to prepare and conduct the majority of instruction with the students with disabilities. Marks, Schrader, and Levine (1999) confirm the report of Giangreco, Edelman,

Luiselli and MacFarland (1997) that paraeducators often assume high levels of responsibility for meeting the academic and behavioural needs of special education students in inclusive classrooms. They often feel solely responsible for their students, and believe they have a role in ensuring that the student is not a "burden" to the teacher. This can lead to the EA assuming the role of expert, by being the liaison person between parents, other students, and the school. Consequently, EAs frequently make on-the-spot decisions about instructional and behaviour management and adaptations, in which teachers may not have been consulted.

Clearly, part of the role of the teacher is to orchestrate the learning and behavioural experiences of all the students. This requires skills in working collaboratively with others, as well as creative techniques to use the resources brought by other people to fulfil the teacher's objectives for all students. For example, in what ways can the EA, or volunteer, or student teacher, etc. be used to free the teacher to work with that small group?

Review Interactive Exercise 3–3 to examine the roles of the teacher and EA, and to apply these to the case study of John.

STUDENT POLL 3–3:

Giangreco et al. (1997) comments that paraeducators (EAs) are "the least trained, least qualified individuals assuming the primary responsibilities for students who have the most complex learning challenges" (p. 282).

Agree ☐   Disagree ☐   Undecided ☐

The Roles of the Teacher
and Educational Assistant
(EA or Paraeducator)

Giangreco and his colleagues (1997, 1999) and Wallace and colleagues (2001) suggest that a number of issues must be considered when deciding individual paraprofessional support for students with disabilities. Some of their points are listed below. Following that, the case study of John and his EA is then presented. Read the case and answer the questions.

Giangreco et al. raise several points, including:

Issue 1—Rely on collaborative teamwork.

- Effective decision making is facilitated when school personnel and family members function as a collaborative team.

- All team members should have sufficient knowledge about the student, his/her educational program, and the context for learning to be able to participate fully in decision making.

- Team members need to establish an agreed-upon set of values, beliefs, and principles designed to help decision making.

Issue 2—Build capacity in the school to support all students.

- The more knowledge, skills, and abilities the classroom personnel have to address diverse needs of all the students, the lower the need for paraprofessional support.

- In some cases, paraprofessionals are assigned to the class to support the teacher and all the students. This can reduce the competitive manner in which some have viewed the paraprofessional as "belonging" to the student. A balance is needed between meeting the rights and needs of the individual student and the needs of the classroom community.

- Resources such as system-level and school-level personnel, working collaboratively with the classroom teacher, cannot be replaced by the allocation of a paraprofessional.

Issue 3—Consider paraprofessional supports individually and judiciously.

- Be aware of unintended harmful effects (e.g., interference with peer interactions, overdependence, loss of personal control, invasion of privacy) (Giangreco, 1997).

Issue 4—Clarify the reasons why paraprofessional supports are being used.

- Having established the instructional goals for the student, consider why the student needs a paraprofessional's support, and clearly establish the challenges that he/she represents. The extent and type of support that will be needed will then be more evident.

- There are many reasons why a team member might suggest a paraprofessional's support: more instructional opportunities; adaptations to the curriculum; assistance between classes; personal care support; behaviour support; work site accommodations; communications support. Only some of these are appropriately provided by a paraprofessional. Consider who should be responsible for each outcome.

Issue 5—Seek a match between identified support needs and the skills of the person to provide the supports.

- Consider who should provide support and services (Issue 4). Involve individuals who might offer such supports in the team's planning and implementation (Issue 1).

- Ultimately, paraprofessional support should be temporary, and should be phased out as the students are able to assume self-advocacy and independence.

Issue 6—Explore opportunities for natural supports.

- The student and family should be involved in making decisions about natural supports, namely human supports (such as classmates, senior students, the librarian, school nurse, office staff, etc.). All supports should be chosen to ensure relevance, dignity, and privacy.

Issue 7—Consider school and classroom characteristics.

- The team should consider the physical characteristics of the school and classrooms: removing barriers to access, changing the location of material and equipment, ordering specialized equipment. The ultimate goal is to alter or reduce reliance on paraprofessional support.

The Case of John

John Hartley, a student in grade 9, has a profound binaural hearing loss that was acquired shortly after birth. John has learned to communicate in Cued Speech, a rarely used form of finger spelling in which words are spelled on John's wrist by a translator. John communicates similarly through the translator. John has very little residual hearing and has not been trained either in oral-aural communication or in a sign language (American Sign Language or Signed English). When John first entered kindergarten, the school board hired Jana Metcalf, a friend of John's parents, as a full-time educational assistant (EA), to be John's translator and to accompany him in his classes. Jana learned Cued Speech when John was an infant, and she has been his constant support since he entered school.

John has been placed in a special program in his new high school. A meeting between the special education resource teacher, Dan McIsaac, the vice principal, Jo Zafira, and John's mother, Mrs. Hartley, was recently held to review John's placement and progress.

Their conversation follows:

Mrs. Hartley: *I'm quite concerned that John has made very few friends over the years. In this new school, I'd really like him to form some friendships. Perhaps I can arrange his transportation so that he can stay after school once or twice a week. Then he could join an after-school group or club, or he could participate in team sports.*

Resource Teacher: *I agree with you. Not only would he benefit from more activities with students his own age, but I think he might be motivated to broaden his communication skills if he started to develop some friendships. That would in turn help him to participate more fully, especially when Jana cannot be right beside him, for example when he's playing volleyball.*

Vice Principal: *I agree that a priority for John this year should be to encourage him to choose some peer-related activities, and hopefully to reduce his dependence on Jana for all his communication, especially for non-academic activities. (Turning to the Resource Teacher) Dan, will you make a note of these in this term's revisions to his IEP? And also could you talk to Jana about the potential for John to participate more in peer activities with the goals of forming friendships and some independence in communication? We will need her advice and assistance in designing situations in which this could be tried and in monitoring the results.*

At a meeting between the resource teacher, Dan McIsaac, and the EA, Jana Metcalf, things did not go as well.

Jana: *I have looked after John since he was an infant and no-one, including his Mom, knows him as well as I do. To remove me is to cut him off from the world. He can't survive alone, and he can't tell you why he's suffering!! I think these are cruel and inhumane decisions. If John had been properly supported by this school system, there would have been programs for other people such as his classmates to learn to communicate with him. But the system just wants to keep costs down, and removing me is just another way of doing it!*

Discussion Questions:

1. What are the issues in this case? Refer to the points listed above.

2. If you were asked to participate in the team to consider what steps to take with John, what further information would you need about John?

3. What questions does this case raise that will need further exploration at the school level?

4. List one or more points that will be useful to keep in mind when working with an educational assistant in your classroom.

To review this topic further, you can complete a quiz on-line.

Technology as a Resource for Universal Design and Access

Technology is assuming an increasing prominence in today's classrooms, and since today's students are already sophisticated users of technological tools, this trend is likely to evolve at great speed. Prensky (2005) coins the term "digital natives" to describe students who are growing up with electronic technology. Educators need to take stock of the fact that students are generally fluent in the language of the computer, video games, and the Internet, and are comfortable with a variety of technologies. There are many roles that technology can play in a classroom to increase the involvement of students in learning and to broaden the teacher's instructional repertoire.

In this section, technology's role will be considered as a universal design resource for instruction. In a later module, assistive technology that has specialized uses for students who require communication, physical, and other assistive supports will be considered. Bowe (2000) makes the point that technology for universal design differs from assistive technology in that the former serves many students at once in adjusting and adapting instruction, and it can be renewed and reused. Assistive technology serves one individual at a time, is adapted for that user only, and is often designed to serve a specific accommodation function. An example of technology designed for universal access is the spell checking feature on a word processor, whereas an example of assistive technology is Braille reading materials.

There are four areas of universal design technology resources for educational uses: the computer, instructional software, multimedia and telecommunications, and the Internet.

The computer

The computer as a tool for learning

The tool software capabilities of computers make them ideally suited to meet a variety of learning needs. Tool software includes word processing and desktop publishing, database management, spreadsheets and graphic tools, and

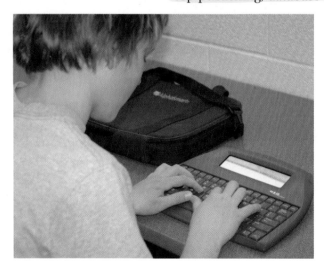

drawing and painting tools. Unlike educational software, which is designed for a specific learning objective, toolsoftware is applicable in many learning situations and can supplement most learning objectives. There are many word processing and publishing programs adapted for students, ranging from *Bank Street Writer* (Scholastic) and *Student Writing Center* (the Learning Company) for students beginning to read and write, to sophisticated integrated tool software such as *Microsoft Works* (Microsoft) and *Clarisworks* (Claris Corporation). Another group of tools includes encyclopedias, dictionaries, thesauruses, atlases, and reference materials. Tool software also assists students with keyboarding skills, including *Read Write and Type!* (The Learning Company) that integrates reading, writing, and typing. For students with diverse learning needs, teachers may need to select tool software that will be accessible and easily mastered by the students for whom it is selected.

The computer as a tutor

Computer assisted instruction (CAI) has been developing over the past 30 years. There is now a wide range of instructional software designed to teach skills ranging from keyboarding to complex scientific and medical procedures. Instructional software can be grouped into categories:

- drill and practice software that provides practice to supplement skills learned in the classroom (for example, *Mathblaster* (Davidson) for computation skills, and *Word Attack 3* (Davidson) for vocabulary)

- tutorial software that teaches a new skill, such as keyboarding

- problem solving programs that challenge students' imagination as well as thinking skills

- simulation programs that imitate situations or phenomena that students might meet in the non-virtual world

- exploratory software that allows students to explore concepts

View the CBC video sequence on-line and watch Jessica demonstrate her use of computer technology and of the adaptations that have been built into her computer hardware and software. A video summary and discussion questions are also available on-line.

Instructional software and e-books

Instructional software programs

In the last few years, some excellent learning software has been published. These range from reading and computation tasks for primary grades to sophisticated resources for research, language learning, and technical skills for young adult learners.

There are several websites and resources that review software to guide teachers and parents in the selection of appropriate applications:

- The on-line magazine *Technology and Learning* publishes sources for many educational applications, awards annual ratings to top-rated programs, and reviews new software publications. It can be found at http://www.techlearning.com.

- Children's Software Review at http://www.childrenssoftware.com reviews software applications for children aged birth to 15 years, including educational software, video games, smart toys, and websites.

- The High/Scope Buyer's Guide to Children's Software (High Scope Educational Research Foundation, Ypsilanti, Michigan) provides reviews of programs for children aged 3 to 7 years. It is available only in hard copy.

- Free downloads of educational applications from kindergarten to Grade 12 and beyond can be found at http://www.planetcdrom.com/educational-software.

There are a number of characteristics to be considered when selecting software for educational purposes. An obvious one is the compatibility of the available hardware with the software application. Many classroom computers are aging and do not have sufficient capacity or speed for recent software applications. The content of the software should also be examined for a clear statement of intended audience, purpose, and learning objectives, and whether it can track student progress. The application should be easily accessible by students without a great deal of learning how to use it. Students should be led through the material in a logical sequence, with prompts and feedback, and with a clear end point. Good software allows for adaptations that either the teacher or student can manage, such as rate of presentation, screen characteristics, level of difficulty, and easily accessible menus, and should be usable by individual students and by pairs and small groups.

E-books

Cavanaugh (2002) asks whether e-books may be the future of print accommodations. E-books are software recordings of books that are delivered through a hardware device or e-book reader (usually a personal computer, laptop, or hand-held device). There are sources of e-book files that can be accessed, often free of charge, such as Blackmask, an on-line library (http://www.blackmask.com).

The accommodation features of this format are many. Students can highlight, bookmark, and cut and paste sections, they can check words in a thesaurus or interactive dictionary, and students with visual impairments or reading problems can vary the point size of the text. Additional features can be added with further software, such as text-to-speech synthesis to create talking books that make the text accessible to students who are unable to read or who have disparate backgrounds, language skills, interests, and levels of expertise (Leong, 1995).

Some sites that feature e-books include:

- Adobe Acrobat Reader http://www.adobe.com—provides an e-book reader that allows users to scan, highlight, and hear the text and pronunciation of individual words; it preserves the characteristics of the original page in e-format through its .pdf files

- ReaderWorks http://www.overdrive.com—the user can upload a document file (e.g., .doc, .rtf, .txt, .wpf, and .wpd file) to be converted and made available as an e-book (.lit) file; EbookExpress is an on-line version of ReaderWorks with many downloadable ebook texts

- Microsoft Corporation's Reader—includes an interactive dictionary and text-to-speech engine; available from the download section at http://www.microsoft.com/reader

Multimedia

The term "multimedia" has come to represent a computer-based environment in which graphics, videos, text, and sound deliver instruction (Poole, 1997). However, there are other forms of technology that are useful and relatively simple to incorporate into instruction. The audio-tape recorder, for example, has many roles in recording and playing back lecture material, conferences between teacher and student, assignment requirements, deadlines, and other directions. It is especially useful as a playback machine for students who may forget detail, which of course applies to all learners at one time or another. For students who struggle with communicating their thoughts in writing, the tape recorder, used as a dictation machine, allows writers to listen to the fluency and structure of their written work, either as they generate it, or as an editing assistant after they have completed drafting. The tape recorder is especially useful in providing an intermediate stage between teacher and student that allows the student to re-listen to previous conversations such as tutorials and conferences, as well as assisting the teacher to decode the student's written work.

E-mail is also beginning to feature as a universal accommodation in schools. It allows students to send outlines and drafts to the teacher and to

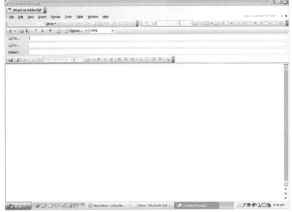

each other for review, to interface with a word processor, and to store directions, details of assignments, and so forth for retrieval at any time.

There are now software applications dedicated to conferencing and to on-line discussion groups and "bulletin boards." Web pages and "blogs" are potential classroom tools that expand the accessibility of learning material to a wide and diverse student group. The project IKIT (Institute for Knowledge Innovation and Technology) is a Canadian example of using electronic media to create a knowledge-building pedagogy for an on-line community that allows participants to collaborate, generate, share, and exchange knowledge (http://www.ikit.org/).

The use of both low and high-tech technology provides clear advantages for those who wish to provide flexible, supportive, and adjustable learning and productivity experiences to all learners. The principle of universal access is most compelling when a teacher can direct classes to computer-based resources that will allow each student to access learning materials that meet his or her language and reading needs, speed of working and level of expertise, and to contribute at his or her own level of interest and skill.

Telecommunications and the Internet

The World Wide Web is a primary resource for universal design education (UDE) and is increasingly used by teachers who seek tools for teaching and for students to conduct research. Wissick and Gardiner (2000) provide lists of software and Web resources grouped both by instructional principles and by intervention and accommodation uses. Two notable websites are:

- TrackStar:(http://trackstar.4teachers.org/trackstar/index.jsp) that assists teachers to create on-line lessons, and

- WebQuest: (http://edweb.sdsu.edu/people/bdodge/ttu1.html),a collection of software resources for teachers, sorted by subject and grade level.

Within the curriculum, the solutions to accessibility are typically dealt with by using a combination of hardware and software. In some cases, these can act directly upon the core content and activities of the general educational curriculum without undue accommodation or modification. In other cases, time and resources must be devoted to improving access, participation, and progress by means of extensively adapted materials.

The use of technology in the classroom is in its infancy. There are currently incompatibilities between different hardware and operating systems. It is hard to find guides to software products that a teacher can access quickly when searching for a specific topic or skills to provide to students. There is uncertainty about how to maintain and repair equipment. These problems are likely to diminish, however, as resources proliferate and as school systems, teachers, and students become more familiar with the possibilities of technology-based learning. Teachers who are most likely to successfully integrate technology into the curriculum in their classrooms see the computer as a tool for accomplishing a predetermined end, and are willing to explore alternatives to current practice (Labbo & Reinking, 1999).

Adaptations at the Level of Individual Students

The essence of good teaching lies in the nature of the dialogue between a teacher and students. Yet it is well known that teachers in regular classrooms spend very little time in extended dialogue with their students. An extended dialogue that fosters the cognitive development of a student includes teacher questioning to discover the student's current knowledge and understandings, followed by teacher responding to the results. In one study where teaching was observed for a half day in 45 classrooms, only four teachers had organized their classes and their instructional time so as to be able to linger long enough for a dialogue with students with learning difficulties (Roach, 1998). They used this time to hold an extended conversation with the student to ensure the student was on the right track for learning. The remaining 41 teachers tended to check work, make a remark about what to correct or what was completed, and then moved on to the next student. Teaching is a complex, high-energy profession, but somehow, the inability of the majority of teachers to reach a level of interactive dialogue with individual students may be the most significant barrier to learning.

Up to this point, this module has discussed whole class ways in which the amount and quality of dialogue can be increased—help from peers, other adults, and how good teachers conserve instructional time to enable them to linger with needy students. In this section, the nature of the instructional dialogue will be explored to see what characteristics of teaching can be optimally provided when that precious instructional time is made available for individuals and small groups.

Teacher Talk in Effective Instructional Environments

Effective teachers have the skill to follow the lead of a student when holding a dialogue about the topic at hand, dialogues which we term "cognitive extension." In these exchanges, the teacher does not supply answers or comment on the correctness or incorrectness of a student response, although the student's responses might be guided through several opportunities to reformulate it. The focus is on engaging the student in the process of learning rather than on arriving at an end point. There is a high proportion of questions in the teacher's talk and a willingness to follow the student's lead in searching for answers. Teachers see the students' answers as vehicles for teaching rather than as evidence of products or outcomes. This permits a wider set of acceptable responses from the diverse students in the classroom, since each response can signal not only mastery, but also an index of where to calibrate subsequent questions in the "nudging" process.

The following section describes the effective interactions a teacher, Sandi has in her classroom. Sandi has organized her seatwork to enable her to have long interactive conversations with pairs of students. Those interactions have a number of characteristics that are repeated in many situations in her classroom:

- linking current concepts to previously learned material and other lesson topics

- designing multiple questions to prompt students' thinking about their thinking strategies

- using descriptors about their own experiences

- accepting and encouraging students' speculations

- using spontaneous student comments as a springboard for linking concepts

Read a transcript of one of Sandi's lessons with two students in grade 3 in Interactive Exercise 3–4.

In order to structure their lessons yet maintain the flexibility needed to follow the lead of the students, teachers need to be clear about their instructional objectives, a topic that was examined in Module 2. To do this, teachers transcribe the curriculum expectations into learning goals and instructional objectives that require one or more of:

- content or declarative knowledge (the facts, vocabulary, and data—the freezing temperature of water, the properties of salt on the freezing point of water, the insulation effects of ice)

- procedural knowledge largely demonstrated through task-related strategic skills (since this is a science lesson, scientific thinking is asking questions, looking at anomalies, creating hypotheses)

- conditional knowledge or **metacognitive** strategies in which mastery of a topic, concept, or skill is applied beyond the framework in which it was learned (abstracting the nature of the problem, testing hypotheses about potential clues to the solution, linking previous data to create new inferences)

These objectives are associated with thinking processes that range from recall to application, synthesis, and interpretation. In the example provided above, Sandi has a good grasp of her instructional objectives for this lesson and how they fit with curriculum expectations and her learning goals. Without this clarity, she would be unable to accept the detour in her students' thinking and know how to guide them back to her objectives. But by following the spontaneous contributions of students to the lesson, Sandi is also able to create links between the concepts that the students have already mastered. This is highly personalized, since the students lead it; it can occur at any level of learning threshold that Sandi encounters as she circulates among her students.

---

interactive
exercise

3-4

Effective Teacher Interactions

Sandi Battista's grade 3 students are matching animals to their winter habitats in a large picture of a winter woodland scene. She stops at the desk of two students, Alicia and Tom, who are working together, discussing which of the numbered habitats belongs to the beaver. Alicia is struggling with the grade 3 curriculum. She has been referred for a psycho-educational assessment to see if she needs extra support in learning.

Alicia: *Does the beaver live in the water?*

Sandi Battista: *Oh, excellent question. Do beavers live in water? Well, if they live in water in spring and summer, what's wrong with living in water in the winter?*

Alicia: *It's frozen up.*

Sandi Battista: *Yeah it freezes. So it could be a problem, right?*

Alicia: *Does the beaver live in the water?*

Sandi Battista: *Oh, excellent question. Do beavers live in water? Well, if they live in water in spring and summer, what's wrong with living in water in the winter?*

Alicia: *It's frozen up.*

Sandi Battista: *Yeah it freezes. So it could be a problem, right?*

Tom: *They might go right down to the bottom.*

Sandi Battista: *Why would they go way down to the bottom?*

Tom: *'Cos it's warmer there; not frozen.*

Sandi Battista: *It's warmer at the bottom. Why do you say it's warmer?*

Tom: *I dunno, 'cos it isn't salty or anything.*

Sandi Battista: *Trout Lake and Lake Nipissing are clear. They're not salt lakes, and you're right, because we talked about that. We said that the Atlantic and Pacific oceans don't freeze because they're salty, but the lakes we have here do freeze because they are fresh water. So why is it warmer near the bottom?*

Alicia: *The heat gets trapped down there.*

Sandi Battista: *Okay, why is that?*

Alicia: *The cold air is outside.*

Sandi Battista: *That's right. What's keeping it warm underneath?*

Tom: *The cold air makes it freeze.*

Sandi Battista: *It freezes. So it could be a problem, right?*

Tom: *It's the ice.*

Sandi Battista: *The ice on the top. You're right Tom.*

Alicia: *It's just like an igloo.*

Sandi Battista: *It's just like an igloo. How's it just like an igloo?*

Alicia: *The igloo is warm in there.*

Tom: *(Mumbles under his breath and disrupts Alicia)*

Sandi Battista: *(Sh! Tom. I think Alicia is saying something really important here) Why's that?*

Alicia: *Because all the heat is trapped inside.*

Sandi Battista: *Heat is trapped inside. Very good Alicia. And what is trapping the heat?*

The lesson continues in this manner.

To review this topic further, you can complete a quiz on-line.

Scaffolding

Scaffolding is when a teacher provides the assistance necessary for a student to achieve success. The teacher supports or bridges a student's or group's thinking initially by direct instruction of strategies that are missed. The support is reduced to prompting and cues, and is gradually withdrawn as the students increase in competence and are finally able to be successful unassisted. During the scaffolding process, the strategic procedures such as questioning, thinking aloud, and modelling for and tutoring others, are transferred to the students.

At base is a skill that is neither unfamiliar nor inaccessible, and it has been around for a long time. Wood, Bruner, and Ross (1976) (cited in Stone, 1998) first noted how parents interact with their young children, picking up on their child's use of words as cues to the child's ideas, then elaborating those ideas to assist the child to form more complex ideas and concepts, and to relate and generalize those concepts to new situations. As the child masters these concepts, the parent relinquishes control of the interaction, allowing the child to take the lead. This fundamental act of teaching is termed "scaffolding" in the current literature (Butler, 1998; Stone, 1998), for it implies that, like a newly constructed building, the child's emerging concepts need to be supported by the judicious verbal guidance of others, until the ideas and concepts reach a stage of completion and connectedness with other concepts that makes them robust and deeply understood. Central to the notion is that teachers actively participate in the learning dialogue by modelling and describing the needed strategies, then relinquishing control as the student becomes able to use the strategies independently.

Scaffolding consists of a series of steps that usually begin when a new concept or learning strategy or skill is introduced. Harris and Graham (1996) propose that there are six stages. These begin with activating students' prior knowledge related to the new concept, skill, or strategy, and proceed until the student is able to "stand alone" in demonstrating achievement in the learning goal.

1. The teacher activates the students' relevant background knowledge, such as key vocabulary associated with the strategy, and prior knowledge of the topic.

2. The teacher and students discuss the concept, strategy, or skill to establish a purpose for using it and to identify expected outcomes. A guiding framework for the new concept may be presented. The purpose is to activate students' prior knowledge and experiences so they

can participate in constructing their own conceptual framework for the new material.

3. The teacher models the strategies and learning skills to be mastered, using a running commentary known as **"think alouds"** to describe how to think about the new concept or learning strategy or skill. In this stage, the instruction is teacher-led. This type of instruction has been termed "transmissive" because the teacher talk dominates the instruction. However, this transmissive component is used as an introduction only, and is supported by modelling and demonstrating the learning strategies to be mastered.

4. The students practise the new strategy or skill, using the strategies and thinking skills demonstrated by the teacher. Initial practice is overt, modelled to a partner or to the teacher. The purpose is to help the students memorize the steps in the strategy, often using **mnemonic devices**.

5. The students receive corrective feedback in the form of cues and verbal prompting from the teacher or partner, allowing them to adjust further attempts to model the concept, strategy, or skill.

6. Gradually the teacher withdraws his or her verbal prompting as the students' skills develop. The students internalize the concepts, skills, and strategies to being successful. The teacher monitors this process. The teacher then provides new opportunities to practice, which extend the skill and generalize the strategies and concepts to other problems. The student, like the completed building construction, becomes self-supporting.

In a classroom, the excellent teacher "scaffolds" students' learning in large and small groups and for individual students, "time-sharing" his or her instructional time among the students to keep them all on track. The teacher nudges them along by elaborating each student's responses, probing with questions to find out where they have reached in their various tracks, and setting tasks to enable them to consolidate and generalize their learning to broader contexts. The teacher is orchestrating the development of task-specific skills, pausing to deal with personal, social, and communication roadblocks, taking advantage of "teachable moments" to make connections with previously learned material. In this way, the teacher calibrates his or her nudging to each student's learning threshold, and makes mental notes of the skills and progress being made.

Two video sequences that demonstrate scaffolding techniques are available on-line. Mrs. Calderoni demonstrates with her grade 1 class and Ms. Frysztacki with the students in her grade 9 English class. A video summary and discussion questions are also available on-line.

Strategy Instruction and Modelling Thinking Skills

A study was conducted with teachers who were highly successful in raising the reading levels of their students (high-gaining teachers) compared to those who were less successful (low-gaining teachers). Mariage (1995) gives an example of the difference in the teachers' interaction patterns. In this example, both groups of teachers are discussing the same story about snakes and their habitats. Both teachers have been provided with training to assist them to develop students' thinking and with cue cards to prompt their questioning.

To see this example in a synthesis of the studies of the characteristics of teachers whose students make high achievement gains compared to low gains, read Research Box 3–5.

research
box

3-5

research box	Characteristics of Teachers
3-5	**Whose Students Make High Compared to Low Achievement Gains**

A case study conducted by Phillips, Fuchs, Fuchs, & Hamlett (1996) compared the instructional methods of two teachers whose students showed different achievement outcomes. Phillips et al. attempted to identify the instructional variables that distinguished the students of one teacher who performed at a level that showed little change from their prior learning histories, and those of another teacher whose students achieved well despite their prior learning histories. Four target students, a low-achieving, an average-achieving, a high-achieving student, and a student designated as learning disabled, were selected for observation and interview in each teacher's classroom. Their teachers were also interviewed. To measure student progress, the teachers employed curriculum-based measurement (CBM) by giving weekly parallel assessments to every student in the class using a standardized measure. The researchers compared the achievement of the four target students in the two classrooms.

Five variables distinguished the more effective from the less effective teacher:

- instructional format and pacing of lessons

- degree of student involvement

- completion of all planned activities

- motivational strategies

- judgement of student learning

The more effective teacher used concrete examples and a greater range of instructional experiences to motivate her students. Lessons were fast-paced and smooth, with the entire class cognitively engaged in hands-on learning activities for the majority of the time. Students did not spend very long sitting and listening passively; rather, they participated actively by writing, discussing, or problem solving. Students completed all planned activities, giving a sense of closure and accomplishment.

It is also interesting to note that the more effective teacher consistently praised effort and achievement, rewarding students for their accomplishments. This did not lessen the enthusiasm for learning among any of the less capable students. Rather, high levels of motivation promoted learning among all students, including those with learning disabilities (Phillips, Fuchs, Fuchs, & Hamlett 1996). One should note that this study compared only two teachers who differed widely in teaching experience. It is possible that many years of experience accounted for the well-filled toolbox of instructional strategies of the more experienced teacher.

Greenwood, Arreaga-Mayer, and Carta (1994) described a multi-step method for identifying effective instructional procedures based on classroom engagement and achievement gain, suggesting that these results be used to train and evaluate other teachers. Participants in the study were 59 grade 4 and grade 5 students with learning disabilities and their special education and general education classroom teachers. Students in the sample were identified as learning disabled, had an IEP, and were mainstreamed, but received a large proportion of their instruction in special education pullout programs. Student achievement was measured using the Metropolitan Achievement Test Battery language and mathematics scores. Classroom observations were conducted for each student, estimating task participation: the percentage of time engaged in reading, writing, academic talk, and asking and answering questions.

Instruction was analysed using five categories: method of instruction, orchestration of activities, pace of instruction, monitoring of students, and feedback. Results of the study indicated that students in the low-gaining group received more lecture and discussion format instruction, while the high-gaining groups received direct instruction. High-gaining teachers delivered lessons that were described as fast paced, as opposed to the low-gaining teachers who experienced delays in getting started. Feedback to the students in the high-gaining group was immediate and highly structured, using points or stickers. In contrast, the low-gaining teachers used only verbal praise. During instruction, low-gaining group students were given fewer opportunities to respond during instruction than high-gaining students, allowing for less active participation. Finally, during a typical school day, the high-gaining group spent more time cognitively engaged in activities such as academic talk. The authors concluded that pacing, instructional method, and feedback resulted in the different achievement outcomes between the high-gaining and the low-gaining students.

How teachers verbally model or "make visible" their thought processes and strategies is an important component in strategy instruction techniques. Mariage (1995) demonstrates scaffolding in a description of teachers whose students have made above-average gains in early reading achievement.

In Mariage's lesson transcripts, these "high-gaining" teachers do much of the talking, at least in the initial stages of introducing a new concept or skill. They engage in "think-alouds," verbalizing their thinking processes as they read a story with their students. They link their reading to the objective of the lesson; for example, the concept of the main idea of a paragraph. They ask questions of their students which require strategic awareness, such as predicting, justifying, and linking to previous material. They elaborate the ideas in the text, wondering aloud what might be happening in a story, indicating possibilities and ironies. They interpolate their own experiences with those of the text, and invite the children to do the same. They predict upcoming events and examine their plausibility. They ask students to supply other possible explanations and make predictions.

SAMPLES OF TEACHER STATEMENTS DURING READING	
Low-gaining teachers	High-gaining teachers
Okay. Wait a minute. Let's stop right there after that paragraph. Let's take out those cards.	While I'm reading I need to search for the main idea the author is talking about. In that paragraph, I think the main idea is that—it talks about snakes and their feet and how they are hatched from eggs. Anyhow, they take care of themselves from birth. I am going to say that snakes are very special animals. That's what I'm going to write for my main idea. Can any of you guys tell me why snakes are very special animals?
Go ahead Paul. Take it over.	
Snakes! Where would you like me to put that Cathy? In the middle, right? Right here?	
Alright, what about them? What's in the first paragraph Jeff?	
That's our main idea, right?	
Great! Snakes are very special animals.	Okay. Did any of you see where I got the main idea for that paragraph? I picked it right out; I picked out the very first sentence where it said "snakes are very special animals." Okay, so we said that they could take care of themselves; they can swim, crawl, and climb. But there is one more thing that is important in that paragraph that we didn't get. Jerry, do you know what that is?
That's our main idea. Go to the next card.	
Why can snakes take care of themselves right away?	
Snakes are very special animals. Why are they so ugly?	
Think about a teacher question about the main idea.	

In contrast, the teachers in "low-gaining" classrooms ask more open-ended questions that are indirectly related to the lesson objectives, such as asking students to relate the text to their experiences. Much of their talk is directed at evaluating students' responses and initiating conversations, and relatively little is spent on shaping student responses toward a desired strategic outcome. For example, they wondered about a detail in the text, but they may not make explicit the link between the process of wondering about it and being actively engaged in the process of making predictions and foretelling further information. These strategies are important components of reading comprehension and are useful when the students are asked to identify the main ideas and themes in the story. Mariage concludes that an instructional strategy or framework on its own cannot account for student gains, but rather student success, or failure, depends on how each teacher implements such a framework.

One limitation of study of Mariage's (1995) study is that it was conducted with 15 college seniors participating in a practicum experience in teaching literacy in special education. Teachers were ranked according to the average net gain in total ideas recalled from pre-test to post-test. None of the participants was a certified teacher, nor did anyone have prior formal teaching experience. It is therefore difficult to relate the findings to the repertoire of skills established through teaching experience.

There is a controversy underlying these differences in style. Some educators and researchers claim that learning proceeds through the students' construction of knowledge, and that construction is based in discovery. They do not agree with the teacher telling students what to find and where to find it. Yet research indicates that structured, direct instruction that focuses on making the strategies for learning explicit and that breaks down learning tasks into small chunks is more powerful and much more efficient for learners with special education needs than discovering the strategies for themselves (Swanson, 1999; Swanson, Hoskyn, & Lee, 1999).

In the example above, the low-gaining teachers also maintained control of much of the discourse, rather than transferring control of the reading process to the students, an element of the process of scaffolding which is sometimes termed "reciprocal teaching" (Palincsar & Brown, 1984). The notion of transferring the balance of control in instructional interactions from teacher to student emerges in other research with effective teachers (Jordan, Lindsay, & Stanovich, 1997; Jordan & Stanovich, 2001).

Teachers intent on elaborating students' strategic awareness tend to relegate their own opinions about a task to second place, unveiling them only when the student gets stuck or discovers during the interaction that his or her own strategy won't quite work. Englert et al. (1994) talk about fostering equality of power between teacher and students during instructional dialogues.

Mariage's work originated in a larger set of studies with struggling readers conducted at Michigan State University by the team of Carol Sue Englert and colleagues. Over several years, they have examined a multi-component strategy program that embeds instructional strategies of teacher modelling, scaffolded assistance to students, procedural facilitation, peer collaboration, and the development of inner language and vocabulary in students for engaging in self-talk about their own learning processes (Englert & Palincsar, 1991; Englert, Raphael, Anderson, Anthony, & Stevens, 1991; Englert, Roszendal, & Mariage, 1994). The teacher from the previous section, Sandi, spontaneously uses many of these in her teaching.

In the field of literacy instruction in struggling young readers, such instructional strategies include:

- procedural facilitation—assisting students to focus on procedural matters (e.g., in reading a passage, students are involved in predicting, questioning, summarizing, self-monitoring for meaning)

- strategy instruction—by directly teaching and requiring demonstration of mastery of strategies (predicting, searching for main ideas, finding synonyms and antonyms of concepts, and backtracking when the text seems not to make sense)

There are other important elements in reading instruction for students who face reading difficulties, such as phonemic awareness, letter-sound correspondence, and comprehension strategies, which will be taken up in detail in a later module. However, the strategy instruction described here illustrates the importance of teachers being aware of their instructional goal in terms of the thinking skills, strategies, and concepts which students need to acquire, and of how to monitor and provide effective feedback as learners move toward acquiring them.

Research indicates that teachers who are less successful in developing student achievement demonstrate characteristics reminiscent of the Mariage's low-gaining teachers (Jordan, Lindsay & Stanovich, 1997). The following scenario provides an example:

Josh is reading an assigned novel when the teacher arrives at his desk.

Teacher: *How's it going Josh?*

Josh: *Good.*

Teacher: *Have the vampires got them yet?*

Josh: *I dunno. I haven't got that far.*

Teacher: *What do you think will happen?*

Josh: *They're going to the White House to see the mayor?*

Teacher: *The White House?*

Josh: *Uhhuh. I think they're gonna get the people.*

Teacher: *Okay. You continue reading. You're making good progress.*

In this example, the dialogue is characterized by a teacher-led agenda in which the balance of power in the dialogue is maintained by the teacher. There is little evidence of a negotiated exchange based on the current level of student understanding, and the teacher is more keen to correct a factual error (Mayor or President) than to pursue the student's train of thought.

STUDENT POLL 3–4:

Regular classroom teachers should not be expected to undertake curriculum modifications for students with severe disabilities.

Agree ☐   Disagree ☐   Undecided ☐

Reading disabilities are often attributed to the learners rather than to the nature of the instruction that they are receiving. If reading disability was indeed a neurologically-based disability, it is unlikely that intensive intervention during the years between kindergarten and grade 2 would be able to change this. It would seem that one important and foundational set of skills, the acquisition of fluent reading, depends at least in part on the nature of the instruction received.

In this module, the case is presented that teaching is a fluid and responsive process that draws upon the current understandings—and misunderstandings—of students as a source for calibrating curriculum and instruction to learner needs. Effective teachers have a "kit-bag" of tools that enables them to identify the current learning strategies and needs of students, and then deliver instruction geared to each student's **zone of instructional readiness**.

Teaching individual students and small groups is, like lesson and unit planning, a series of steps:

- finding each student's entry point to the strategies, skills, and concepts that form the instructional objectives

- designing and delivering instruction and questioning to that level

- evaluating the student's responses for understanding, then moving forward or reviewing missed objectives

In working in a classroom where students are typically diverse in their skills, language, knowledge, and experiences, this can best be done when the teacher has time to work with individuals and small groups. In Module 2, some techniques for maximizing and conserving instructional time were presented. In this module, techniques for the effective use of the instructional time were examined, including:

- multiple means of presentation and response that can accommodate the learning needs of diverse students, with and without disabilities

- whole class techniques for diversifying the instruction available to the class

- further techniques to increase the available instructional time

- groupings, using peers and co-operative groups

- deploying the resources of colleagues and assistants

- the nature of the teacher's interaction with individual students and small groups

When one's personal teaching philosophy is that the most important goal of teaching is to assist students to become independent learners, teaching is focussed on individual progress in acquiring thinking skills and strategies and in gaining confidence to apply them.

Summary

In this module, the following concepts were explored.

Universal design and universal access

- multiple means of **representation** of learning materials to give learners various ways to acquire information, knowledge, and skills

- multiple means of **expression** to provide learners with alternative ways to demonstrate what they know

- multiple means of **engagement** to tap learners' interests and to create appropriate challenges

Educational adaptations

- Instructional accommodations are changes to the teaching and assessment environment that increase students' access to curriculum and learning.

- Accommodations can take the form of

  - presenting or instruction

- responding or assessment

- changes to the setting or environment

• Curriculum **modifications** are changes to the level of difficulty or standard of performance for prescribed curriculum expectations and learning goals. Modifications vary the amount and/or complexity of the content or skill to be mastered from that prescribed by the curriculum standards for a given grade.

Accommodations and modifications

• How to distinguish between accommodations and modifications

• How to handle the "It's not fair!" complaint

Adapting instruction at the classroom level

• Adapting questioning—"Hands up!" is an ineffective way to engage students who have learning difficulties; improvements include routines for selecting students (random, teacher-controlled), coupled with adapting the difficulty level and maximizing correct responding, wait time, and prompts

• Grouping students—optimal group size is three to four students; limitations to consider with heterogeneous (mixed ability) groups are:

- difficulty engaging students with learning disabilities

- training peers to act as group leaders and participants

- ways to ensure groupings are flexible, temporary

• Peers, learning pairs, and cooperative learning groups—skills needed by students to work in pairs and in cooperative groups

• Authentic feedback and praise

• Encouraging independent learning

- Ultimately teachers hope to assist all students to be "free standing"—to be self-regulated learners who are able to advocate for themselves and to take advantage of learning opportunities unassisted.

• Drawing upon the resources of adults

- co-teaching

- working with educational assistants (paraprofessionals)

- Technology as a resource for universal design and access—the role of the computer and other technological devices as potential supports for universal access in the classroom, including:

  - the computer—tool for learning and tutor

  - instructional software and e-books

  - multimedia

  - telecommunications and the Internet

Adapting instruction at the level of individual students

- Teacher talk as effective instruction

  - "staying with" students—nudging, prompting, and elaborating concepts and skills

  - scaffolding instruction—steps that lead students from the introduction of a new learning goal to mastery

  - strategy instruction and modelling thinking skills—explicit teaching of instructional strategies and thinking skills is related to effective teaching for students with learning difficulties

Complete the Module 3 post-test on-line to review topics covered in the module.

post-test

3

Glossary

3-finger test   A method used by students to select a book or story at an appropriate level of difficulty. The student reads through a single page or passage and lifts a finger for each word that he or she cannot read. At the end of the passage, if one finger is held up, the reading material is appropriate; if two fingers are held up, the reading material is challenging but appropriate; and if three fingers are held up, the reading material is too hard and an easier piece should be selected. (p. 185)

Accommodations   Services or supports that enable students to fully access the subject matter of instruction, as well as to demonstrate what they know and have learned. Accommodations include changes in how material is presented and learning is assessed, alternative means for students to respond, and changes to the learning environment that increase the students' opportunities to learn. Accommodations should not markedly change the content of instruction or the performance expectations.

Advance organizer   Summaries of the content and strategies to come, or of changes in the daily schedule, that prepare students in advance for what is to follow. (p. 217)

ASL (American Sign Language)   A visual-spatial language used by individuals who are deaf or who have profound hearing impairments. ASL focuses on communicating thoughts or concepts instead of signing the individual words of a spoken language. ASL has its own set of grammatical rules and is considered to be an independent language. It has dialects that vary from country to country and sometimes from region to region within a country. (p. 194)

Assistive devices   Tools or equipment that are used to allow individuals with exceptionalities to become involved in, and contribute to, classroom activities. (p. 198)

Autism Spectrum Disorders   Also known as **Pervasive Development Disorders (PDD)**, a group of disorders that may result in limited communication and social interactions and mild to severe delays in intellectual, emotional, and behavioural developmental.

Braille   A method for reading and writing used by people who are blind or who have severe visual impairments. Braille consists of embossed arrangements of dots on a page that are identified through touch. (p. 194)

Council for Exceptional Children (CEC)   An international professional organization for educators and parents that is committed to improving the educational experiences of individuals with exceptionalities. The CEC sets professional standards, provides professional development, and advocates for government policies that support individuals with exceptionalities. (p. 212)

Curriculum modifications Changes made to the content of instruction and/or to the performance level expected of the student that markedly differ from the standard expectations for the student's age. Curriculum modifications differ from accommodations, but both may occur in a student's IEP (p. 179).

Educational adaptations A broad term that includes both accommodations (changes to how learning material is presented or assessed and to the learning environment) and curriculum modifications (changes to the level of difficulty or expected level of performance for curriculum expectations). (p. 179)

Environmental accommodations Changes made to the classroom and/or school environment (e.g., wheelchair ramps, a quiet location). (p. 191)

Finger-spelling A type of sign language in which each letter of the alphabet is represented by a sign using the hands. Words are created by signing each letter in the word. (p. 184)

Hearing amplification system A device used to amplify the teacher's voice and broadcast it to the whole class or to one or more students with hearing impairments. While these devices are most often used with students with hearing impairments, they can benefit other students by permitting everyone to hear the teacher clearly, regardless of their location in the classroom. (p. 184)

Inclusive (inclusion) The perspective that individuals with disabilities are entitled to an education that includes full participation with their peers and an educational process that allows access to the same resources as other students. (p. 188)

Instructional accommodations Changes in teaching strategies that allow students to access the curriculum (e.g., large print, calculators, Braille, and other communication techniques). This term is also used for accommodations to distinguish them from curriculum modifications. (p. 179)

Instructional cycle A continuous process used by teachers to assess student needs, tailor an instructional program, and evaluate student progress and achievement. The instructional cycle should be self-correcting by using student achievement data to extend or adapt the program. (p. 196)

"Just-in-time" delivery   Materials, information, resources, or tools are provided to teachers at the time when teachers need to use them. For example, a student with a complex disability has just been enrolled in a school. Information about the student's disability, his/her needs, and the materials and resources that will be useful to assist teachers to work with the student are delivered to the staff in the school at a meeting prior to the student's appearance. (p. 214)

Metacognitive   Higher-order thinking processes that reflect an understanding of how one learns or thinks. Deciding how to carry out a task, supplementing immediate memory by note taking, checking for understanding, and assessing progress are all metacognitive processes. (p. 235)

Mnemonic devices   Strategies and techniques that assist students to retain information in memory. Mnemonic devices such as rhymes, images, or similes are often used to help students memorize the steps in a new strategy or skill. (p. 238)

Oral-aural communication   A method of communication used by individuals with a hearing impairment which focuses on the use of lip-reading and residual hearing (often enhanced through the use of assistive devices) to facilitate spoken language. (p. 226)

Personal Theories   An individual's set of beliefs or opinion regarding a concept that may influence thought, judgment, or understanding, and that ultimately guides that person's behaviour. (p. 181)

Response or assessment accommodations   Changes made to the way in which a student demonstrates learning (e.g., alternative presentation format or alternative response format) which do not compromise the standard of the test. (p. 191)

Signed English   A manual representation of the English language in which signs are used for words in a sentence. It also uses markers that reflect English grammar and syntax, such as plurals, tense, and 'ing' endings. Signed English is the form of sign language most commonly used in schools. (p. 194)

Teaching assistant (or teacher's aide)   An adult resource person trained to work with students with disabilities in an educational setting. Teaching assistants are not qualified to teach. They work under the supervision of and collaboratively with a qualified teacher. (p. 194)

Technological resources   Devices, equipment, or items that are used to support or help individuals with exceptionalities to learn and progress. (p. 198)

"Think alouds"   A transmissive form of instruction in which the teacher provides an oral commentary describing the thought processes involved while demonstrating a new concept, learning strategy, or skill. (p. 238)

Universal access   Good instructional practice includes built-in flexibility that reduces or removes barriers to learning for all students. This includes adapting teaching for students at various levels of understanding, and ensuring all students have opportunities to demonstrate their learning. (p. 179)

Universal design   Products or materials with 'designed-in' flexibility that allow people with a wide range of abilities to use them successfully. Their design ensures that the products or materials can by as many people as possible without the need for adaptations. (p. 179)

Wait time   A teaching strategy in which students are given ample time to formulate a response after a question has been posed. Wait time reduces anxiety in students as they do not feel pressured to provide a response immediately. (p. 207)

Zone of instructional readiness   Vygotsky (1978) used the term "zone of proximal development (ZPD)" to describe the level of learning which a student is on the verge of attaining or of making his or her own. Alternatively, the student may already partly understand the concepts or skills. This might also be thought of as the student's readiness to progress to a new level if given further instruction. (p. 244)

Additional Resources

Adobe Acrobat
Adobe Acrobat Reader provides an e-book reader that allows users to scan, highlight, and hear the text and pronunciation of individual words. It preserves the characteristics of the original page in e-format through its .pdf files.
http://www.adobe.com/

CAST: Universal Design for Learning
This website by CAST contains electronic and media-based resources that represent the principle of Universal Design in Learning.
http://www.cast.org

Children's Technology Review
A site that reviews software applications for students aged birth to 15 years, including educational software, video games, smart toys, and websites.
http://www.childrenssoftware.com

Curry School of Education
Resources for teachers on the World Wide Web from Wissick & Gardiner (2000):
http://curry.edschool.virginia.edu/go/frog/

Education Quality and Accountability Office
EQAO provides parents, teachers, and the public with reliable information about student achievement.
http://www.eqao.com

Microsoft Reader
An interactive dictionary and text-to-speech engine are available in the download section of this site.
http://www.microsoft.com/reader

Planet CD-ROM
Free downloads of educational applications from kindergarten to Grade 12 and beyond are available on this site.
http://www.planetcdrom.com/educational-software/

ReaderWorks
Review this site for information on how to upload a document file
(e.g. .doc, .rtf, .txt, .wpf, and .wpd file) to be converted and made
available as an ebook (.lit) file.
http://www.overdrive.com

TeachingLD
This website is a resource for teachers of students with learning disabilities.
http://www.TeachingLD.org

TrackStar
TrackStar is a free on-line resource that assists teachers to collect website
addresses and to annotate them for use by students in order to create on-
line lessons.
http://trackstar.4teachers.org/trackstar/index.jsp

Webquest
This site provides an inquiry-oriented activity in which most or all of the
information used by learners is drawn from the internet. This site consists
of a collection of software resources for teachers, sorted by subject and
grade level.
http://edweb.sdsu.edu/webquest/matrix.html

References

Abernathy, T. V. & Cheney, C. O. (2005). TREK to student independence.
Teaching Exceptional Children, 37(3), 52–57.

Acrey, C., Johnstone, C., & Milligan, C. (2005). Using universal design to
unlock the potential for academic achievement of at-risk learners.
Teaching Exceptional Children, 38(2), 22–31.

Ainscow, M., West, M., & Nicolaidou, M. (2004). Putting our heads together:
A study of headteacher collaboration as a strategy for school improve-
ment. In C. Clark (ed.), *Improving schools in difficult circumstances.*
London: Continuum.

Baker, J. M. & Zigmond, N. (1990). Are regular education classes equipped to accommodate students with learning disabilities? *Exceptional Children, 56,* 515–526.

Bennett, B., Rolheiser-Bennett, C., & Stevahn, L. (1991). *Cooperative learning: Where heart meets mind.* Toronto: Educational Connections.

Berliner, D. C. (1994). Expertise: The wonder of exemplary performances. In J.N. Mangieri & C.C. Cook (Eds.), *Creating powerful thinking in teachers and students* (pp. 161–186). Fort Worth, TX: Harcourt Brace.

Bowe, F. (2000). *Universal design in education.* Westport, CT: Greenwood Publishing.

Butler, D. B. (1998). In search of the architect of learning: A commentary on scaffolding as a metaphor for instructional interactions. *Journal of Learning Disabilities, 31*(4), 374–386.

Cavanaugh, T. (2002). Ebooks and accommodations. *Teaching Exceptional Children, 35*(2), 56–61.

Cegelka, P. T. & Berdine, W. H. (1995). *Effective instruction for students with learning difficulties.* Needham Heights, MA: Allyn and Bacon.

Cole, K. B. & Leyser, Y. (1999). Curricular and instructional adaptations: Views of special and general education student teachers and their cooperating teachers. *Teacher Educator, 34*(3), 157–172.

Demeris, H., Jordan, A., & Childs, R. (in submission). The impact of students with disabilities included in third grade classrooms on the large scale achievement scores of their non-exceptional peers.

Dweck, C. S. (2000). *Self-theories: Their role in motivation, personality, and depression.* Philadelphia: Psychology Press (Taylor & Francis).

Education Quality and Accountability Office. (1998). *Inventions, investigations, and discoveries: Administration guide for teachers and school administrators.* Toronto: Queen's Printer of Ontario.

Elbaum, B., Vaughn, S., Hughes, M., & Moody, S. W. (1999). Grouping practices and reading outcomes for students with disabilities. *Exceptional Children, 65*(3), 399–415.

Englert, C. S. & Palincsar, A. S. (1991). Reconsidering instructional research in literacy from a sociocultural perspective. *Learning Disabilities Research and Practice, 6*(4), 225–229.

Englert, C. S., Raphael, T. E., Anderson, L. M., Anthony, H. M., & Stevens, D. D. (1991). Making strategies and self-talk visible: Writing instruction in regular and special education classrooms. *American Educational Research Journal, 23,* 337–372.

Englert, C. S., Tarrant, K. L., & Mariage, T. V. (1992). Defining and redefining instructional practices in special education: Perspectives on good teaching. *Teacher Education and Special Education, 15,* 62–86.

Englert, C. S., Roszendal, M. S., & Mariage, T. V. (1994). Fostering the search for understanding: A teacher's strategies for leading cognitive development in "zones of proximal development." *Learning Disabilities Quarterly, 17,* 187–204.

Fuchs, L. S. & Fuchs, D. (1998). General educators' instructional adaptations for students with learning disabilities. *Learning Disability Quarterly, 21,* 23–33.

Fuchs, L. S., Fuchs, D., Hamlett, C. L., Phillips, N. B., & Karns, K. (1995). General educators' specialized adaptations for students with learning disabilities. *Exceptional Children, 61,* 440–459.

Fuchs, D., Fuchs, L. S., Mathes, P. G., & Simmons, D. (1997). Peer assisted learning strategies: Making classrooms more responsive to diversity. *American Educational Research Journal, 34,* 174–206.

Fuchs, D., Fuchs, L. S., & Burish, P. (2000). Peer assisted learning strategies: An evidence-based practice to promote reading achievement. *Learning Disabilities Research and Practice, 15,* 85–91.

Fuchs, L. S., Fuchs, D., Hamlett, C. L., & Karns, K. (1998). High-achieving students' interactions on complex mathematical tasks as a function of homogeneous and heterogeneous pairings. *American Educational Research Journal, 35,* 227–267.

Fuchs, L. S., Fuchs, D., Hamlett, C. L., Phillips, N. B., & Karns, K. (1995). General educators' specialized adaptations for students with learning disabilities. *Exceptional Children, 61,* 440–459.

Giangreco, M. F., Broer, S. M., & Edelman, S. W. (1999). The tip of the iceberg: Determining whether paraprofessional support is needed for students with disabilities in general education settings. *Journal of the Association for Persons with Severe Handicaps, 24,* 281–291.

Giangreco, M. F., Edelman, S. W., Luiselli, T. E., & MacFarland, S. (1997). Helping or hovering? Effects of instructional assistant proximity on students with disabilities. *Exceptional Children, 64,* 7–18.

Gibbs, J. (1995). *Tribes: A new way of learning and being together.* Sausalito, CA: Center Resource Systems.

Good, T. L. & Brophy, J. E. (1997). *Looking in Classrooms.* New York: HarperCollins.

Greenwood, C. R., Arreaga-Mayer, C., & Carta, J. (1994). Identification and translation of effective teacher-developed instructional procedures for general practice. *Remedial and Special Education, 15,* 140–151.

Greenwood, C. R., Delquadri, J. C., & Hall, R. V. (1989). Longitudinal effects of classwide peer tutoring. *Journal of Educational Psychology, 81,* 371–383.

Greenwood, C. R., Maheady, L., & Delquadri, J. C. (2002). Class-wide peer tutoring. In G. Stoner, M. R. Shinn, & H. Walker (Eds.), *Intervention for achievement and behavior problems* (2nd ed.). (pp. 611–649). Washington, D.C.: National Association of School Psychologists.

Harris, K. & Graham, S. (1996). *Making the writing process work: Strategies for composition and self-regulation.* Cambridge, MA.: Broadline Books.

Hughes, A., Guth, C., Hall, S., Presley, J., Dye, M., & Byers, C. (1999). "They are my best friends" Peer buddies promote inclusion in high school. *Teaching Exceptional Children, 31*(5), 32–37.

Jacobsen, D. A., Eggen, P., & Kauchak, D. (1999). *Methods for teaching: Promoting student learning* (5th ed.). Upper Saddle River, NJ: Merrill.

Johnson, D. W. & Johnson, R. T. (1986). Mainstreaming and co-operative learning strategies. *Exceptional Children, 52*(6), 553–561.

Jordan, A., Lindsay, L., & Stanovich, P. J. (1997). Classroom teachers' instructional interactions with students who are exceptional, at-risk and typically achieving. *Remedial and Special Education, 18,* 82–93.

Jordan, A. & Stanovich, P. J. (2001). Patterns of teacher-student interaction in inclusive elementary classrooms and correlates with student self-concept. *International Journal of Disability, Development and Education, 48*(1), 43–62.

Labbo, L. & Reinking, D. (1999). Negotiating the multiple realities of technology in literacy research instruction. *Reading Research Quarterly, 34*(4), 478–492.

Leong, C. K. (1995). Effects of on-line reading and simultaneous DEC talk auditing in helping below-average and poor readers comprehend and summarize text. *Learning Disabilities Quarterly, 18*(2), 101–116.

Lou, Y., Abrami, P. C., Spence, J. C., Poulsen, J. C., Chambers, B., & d'Apollonia, S. (1996). Within-class grouping: A meta-analysis. R*eview of Educational Research, 66*(4), 423–458.

Maheady, L. (1997). Preparing teachers for instructing multiple ability groups. *Teacher Education and Special Education, 20*, 322–339.

Maheady, L., Harper, G. F., Mallette, B., & Karnes, M. (2004). Preparing pre-service teachers to implement class wide peer tutoring. *Teacher Education and Special Education, 27*(4), 408–418.

Mariage T. V. (1995). Why students learn: The nature of teacher talk during reading. *Learning Disability Quarterly, 18*, 214–234.

Marfo, K., Harris, D., & Dedrick, R. F. (2005). Role sharing of co-teachers in inclusive classrooms. Paper presented at the Annual Meeting of the American Educational Research Association, Montreal, April.

Marks, S. U., Schrader, C., & Levine, M. (1999). Paraeducator experiences in inclusive settings: Helping, hovering or holding their own? *Exceptional Children, 65*(3), 315–328.

Nolet, V. & McLaughlin, M. J. (2000). *Accessing the general curriculum: Including students with disabilities in standards-based reform.* Thousand Oaks, CA: Corwin Press.

O'Connor, R. E., & Jenkins, J. R. (1996). Cooperative learning as an inclusion strategy: A closer look. *Exceptionality, 6*, 29–52.

Palincsar, A. S., & Brown, A. L. (1984). Reciprocal teaching of comprehension fostering and comprehension monitoring activities. *Cognition and Instruction, 1*(2), 117–175.

Perry, N. E. (1998). Young children's self regulated learning and contexts that support it. *Journal of Educational Psychology, 90*, 715–729.

Perry, N. E., Phillips, L., & Dowler, J. (2004). Examining features of tasks and their potential to promote self-regulated learning. *Teachers College Record, 106*(9), 1854–1878.

Perry, N. E., Phillips, L., & Hutchinson, L. (In press). A comparison of experienced and beginning teachers' support for self-regulated learning. *Elementary School Journal* (2005).

Phillips, N. B., Fuchs, L., Fuchs, D., & Hamlett, C. L. (1996). Instructional variables affecting student achievement: Case studies of two contrasting teachers. *Learning Disabilities Research and Practice, 11,* 24–33.

Pisha, B., & Coyne, P. (2001). Smart form the start: The promise of universal design for learning. *Remedial and Special Education, 22*(4), 197–203.

Poole, B. J. (1997). *Education for an information age: Teaching in the computerized classroom* (2nd ed.). Boston: WCB/McGraw Hill.

Popham, W. J. (1999). *Classroom assessment: What teachers need to know* (2nd ed.). Needham Heights, N.J.: Allyn & Bacon.

Prensky, M. (2005). Listen to the natives. *Educational Leadership, 63*(4), 8–13.

Rankin-Erickson, J. L. & Pressley, M. (2000). A survey of instructional practices of special education teachers nominated as effective teachers of literacy. *Learning Disabilities Research and Practice, 14,* 206–225.

Roach, D. (1998). Factors that affect the instructional interactions of teachers with exceptional, at-risk and typically achieving students. Unpublished Ph.D. thesis. OISE/University of Toronto.

Robinson, P. (in preparation). *The characteristics of teacher expertise in inclusive elementary classrooms.* Unpublished Ed.D dissertation, University of Toronto.

Rolheiser, C., Fullan, M., & Edge, K. (2003). Dynamic duo. *Journal of Staff Development, 24*(2), 38–41.

Schumm, J. S., Vaughn, S., Gordon, J., & Rothlein, L. (1994). General education teachers' beliefs, skills, and practices in planning for mainstreamed students with learning disabilities. *Teacher Education and Special Education, 17*(1), 22–37.

Slavin, R. E. (1991). Synthesis of research on cooperative learning. *Educational Leadership, 48*(5), 71–82.

Stanovich, P. J. & Jordan, A. (1998). Canadian teachers' and principals' beliefs about inclusive education as predictors of effective teaching in heterogeneous classrooms. *The Elementary School Journal, 98*(3), 221–238.

Stanovich, P.J. & Jordan, A. (2000) Effective teaching as effective intervention. *Learning Disabilities: A Multi-disciplinary Journal 10*(4), 235–238.

Stanovich, P. & Jordan, A. (2004). Inclusion as professional development. *Exceptionality Education Canada, 14*(2–3), 169–188.

Stone, C. A. (1998). The metaphor of scaffolding: Its utility for the field of learning disabilities. *Journal of Learning Disabilities, 31*(4), 344–64.

Swanson, H. L. (1999). Instructional components that predict treatment outcomes for students with learning disabilities. *Learning Disabilities Research and Practice, 14*(3), 129–140.

Swanson, H. L., Hoskyn, M., & Lee, C. (1999). *Intervention for students with learning disabilities.* New York: Guilford Press.

Swing, S. R. & Peterson, P. L. (1982). The relationship of student ability and small group interaction to student achievement. *American Educational Research Journal, 19*, 259–274.

Taylor, B., Pearson, P. D., Clark, K. F., & Walpole, S. (1999). Effective schools/Accomplished teachers. *Reading Teacher, 53*(2), 156–159.

Wallace, T., Shinn, J., Bartholomay, T., & Stahl, B. J. (2001). Knowledge and skills for teachers supervising the work of paraprofessionals. *Exceptional Children, 67*(4), 520–533.

Webb, N. M. & Farivar, S. (1994). Promoting helping behaviour in cooperative small groups in middle school mathematics. *American Educational Research Journal, 31*, 369–395.

Wissick, C. A. (1996). Multimedia: Enhancing instruction for students with learning disabilities. *Journal of Learning Disabilities, 29*, 494–503.

Wissick, C. A. & Gardiner, J. E. (2000). Multimedia or not to multimedia? That is the question for students with learning disabilities. *Teaching Exceptional Children, 32*(4), 34–43.

Photo Credits

All images are copyright © Photodisc, Inc./Getty Images unless otherwise noted.

Module 1

4: FrontRow for Active Learning; 6: Rebecca Emery/Getty Images; 12: Everett Collection/CP Images; 18: Gabe Palmer/Corbis; 22: Everett Collection/CP Images; 27: Getty Images; 29: Corbis Digital Stock; 36: Corbis; 39: The Doctor's Dilemma, directed by Christopher Newton, Shaw Festival, 1999; 49: Bob Rowan, Progressive Image/Corbis; 52: CP Images; 53: CP Images; 60: Lauren Shear/Photo Researchers, Inc.; 64: Gabe Palmer/Corbis; 68: Will & Deni McIntyre/Photo Researchers; 70: Press Association/CP Image; 76: Richard Lam/CP Images; 77: Everett Collection/RobRich/CP Images

Module 2

127: Corbis; 156: Image 100 Ltd.; 158: George Doyle/Getty Images

Module 3

182: GoodGrips/OXO Product, Getty Images; 213: Purestock

Index

Notes

Notes

Notes

Notes